When Religious and Secular Interests Collide

When Religious and Secular Interests Collide

Faith, Law, and the Religious Exemption Debate

Scott A. Merriman

BLOOMSBURY ACADEMIC
NEW YORK • LONDON • OXFORD • NEW DELHI • SYDNEY

BLOOMSBURY ACADEMIC
Bloomsbury Publishing Inc
1385 Broadway, New York, NY 10018, USA
50 Bedford Square, London, WC1B 3DP, UK
29 Earlsfort Terrace, Dublin 2, Ireland

BLOOMSBURY, BLOOMSBURY ACADEMIC and the Diana logo
are trademarks of Bloomsbury Publishing Plc

First published in the United States of America by ABC-CLIO 2017
Paperback edition published by Bloomsbury Academic 2025

Cover photo: Lady Justice statue in Frankfurt, Germany. (Anastazzo/Thinkstock)
Jacket design by Silverander Communications

Library of Congress Cataloging-in-Publication Data
Names: Merriman, Scott A., 1968–author.
Title: When religious and secular interests collide : faith, law, and the
religious exemption debate / Scott A. Merriman.
Description: 1st edition. | Santa Barbara : Praeger, 2017. |
Includes bibliographical references and index.
Identifiers: LCCN 2017018256 (print) | LCCN 2017031363 (ebook) |
ISBN 9781440847080 (Ebook) | ISBN 9781440847073 (print)
Subjects: LCSH: Freedom of religion—United States.
Classification: LCC KF4783 (ebook) | LCC KF4783 .M47 2017 (print) |
DDC 342.7308/52—dc23
LC record available at https://lccn.loc.gov/2017018256

ISBN: HB: 978-1-4408-4707-3
PB: 979-8-7651-3665-2
ePDF: 978-1-4408-4708-0
eBook: 979-8-2161-6456-2

To find out more about our authors and books visit www.bloomsbury.com
and sign up for our newsletters.

To my dad,
who showed me the values of compassion and hard work.
And to my mom,
who gave me strength of character and a solid foundation.

Contents

Acknowledgments

As this project winds to a close, I am indebted to many different groups and individuals. I'd like to thank first ABC-CLIO for their help on my previous books, which this effort is based on. Elana Palace, who was my editorial coordinator, and James Ciment, acquisitions editor for popular culture, were strong supporters of this project at Praeger and helped it all the way along.

Troy University, my academic home for the last nine years, kept me fully engaged in teaching, for which I am grateful. My chairs and deans have been supportive of my efforts. Dan Puckett, my colleague, has provided me a model of scholarship.

Along the way, many librarians, fellow academics, and others have answered questions and offered their support. They are too many to mention here. I greatly appreciate their help.

I'd like to thank the places that I have presented my scholarship in the past, including the Faulkner University Law Review Symposium. I enjoyed discussing the topic with them and appreciate their allowing me to reprint some of the article I contributed to their 2016 *Law Review.*

My wider family has always celebrated my scholarship, and I thank them for it.

I would be remiss if I did not thank my two children, Caroline and Sam, who often wondered why my book took so long (and wrote their own to show me the value of brevity). They did, though, tolerate having an absent father often.

My wife, Jessie Bishop Powell, is an accomplished writer in her own right, but her editing skills are shown here in the good passages (and I ignored her advice in the bad ones).

My mom has been in my corner since she typed my first book (in first grade), and my dad has always asked (and cheered) what I was working on. To both of them, I dedicate this work.

Introduction

> We hold these truths to be self-evident, that all men are created equal, that they are endowed by their Creator with certain unalienable Rights, that among these are Life, Liberty and the pursuit of Happiness.—That to secure these rights, Governments are instituted among Men.[1]

Thus begins the Declaration of Independence. But this document has no legal standing. The rights it calls "inalienable" are not all enshrined in U.S. laws. The rights we *do* possess are named in the U.S. Constitution. In particular, the First Amendment says, "Congress shall make no law respecting an establishment of religion, or prohibiting the free exercise thereof; or abridging the freedom of speech, or of the press; or the right of the people peaceably to assemble, and to petition the Government for a redress of grievances."[2] But the very term "freedom" is a vague one, requiring definition. Repeatedly in the more than 225 years since the amendment was ratified, the Supreme Court has faced questions about what actions it protects. More and more—and thanks to the Fourteenth Amendment's language—"All persons born or naturalized in the United States, and subject to the jurisdiction thereof, are citizens of the United States and of the State wherein they reside. No State shall make or enforce any law which shall abridge the privileges or immunities of citizens of the United States; nor shall any State deprive any person of life, liberty, or property, without due process of law; nor deny to any person within its jurisdiction the equal protection of the law"—the nine justices have weighed freedom against equality in their decisions, in an effort to right the scales of justice for traditionally marginalized groups.[3]

Increasingly, in the last two decades, the U.S. Supreme Court has addressed cases in which those claims of equality contrasted with claims of religious liberty. Raging debates over whether religious liberty permits discrimination, particularly in recent decades with regard to women's reproductive rights and same-sex couples, have hinged on the Court's interpretation of the First and Fourteenth Amendments. These cases differ from any First Amendment cases that have previously come before the Court, and they have created a new sort of battleground for constitutional law.

Like "freedom," "equality" is a general term requiring analysis. America's first citizens sought to assure themselves fair treatment from the government and freedom from oppression. Historian J. R. Pole stated, "Those states who adopted declarations of rights as preambles to their constitutions used the occasion to affirm the egalitarian basis on which the authority of the new government was held to rest."[4] Many states' bills of rights echoed language in the Declaration of Independence. However, the nation has shown itself historically capable of making a group equal in name, though wholly unequal in practice, and of using legal loopholes to maintain the division, such as with African Americans after the Civil War. The Supreme Court has had to apply new interpretations to the Fourteenth Amendment to close those loopholes and specify what it means to be equal. J. R. Pole writes, "If people under American jurisdiction are equal in their rights, they cannot in the nature of things have unequal rights to other goods such as liberty or property."[5] Pole also notes that "undoubtedly the Civil War and its aftermath brought about a redefinition of equality."[6] The redefining process continued with the civil rights and women's rights movements, with the Supreme Court playing a pivotal role in expanding the ways in which, and the groups to whom, legal equality is guaranteed.

Finally, "liberty" is a term with a broad definition. The Declaration of Independence makes its meaning quite general, and the Fifth and Fourteenth Amendments, which seem to echo the words of the Declaration the most closely of any part of the Constitution (or its amendments), do not narrow its meaning. If this lack of a definition meant that American citizens weren't guaranteed any specific liberties, then the liberty Jefferson considered as important as life itself would have no meaning. Moreover, liberties overlap and compete, and boundaries limit situations in which one person's liberty interferes with that of another.

If liberty must have limits, then it seems equality must as well. However, some scholars have held that the nation was shaped by the concept's ideal more than any specific parameters. While the Founders recognized early on that liberty could not be unrestrained, they paid less legal attention to the idea of competing equalities. Pole notes: "The Declaration of Independence proclaimed a universalist egalitarian rhetoric as the standard of a highly differentiated social order. It could not determine the future of that order, and its language could never be translated into specific institutions. What it could do in the hands of social reformers was to serve as a kind of moral prompter, a reference text for self-evaluation."[7] This implies that the nation's legal institutions were founded with the knowledge that each generation needed to define what equality (and liberty) meant and that the definition would evolve.

In fact, before the Fourteenth Amendment, equality was nowhere guaranteed in American law. Before the Civil War, Pole describes America as having "two populations—those who were of the Republic and those who were merely in it."[8] By the twenty-first century, from a legal standpoint, all citizens are at least technically classified in the "of" category, with the "in" category having been shifted to include primarily noncitizens.

Until the Fourteenth Amendment, and really until it was effectively applied to the states in the 1920s, as we will see later, those with rights were part of a political family and that those without rights were just permanent denizens deserving of whatever they got and lacking redress for any grievances. Scrambling to join the class sitting at the table has prompted and continues to prompt a lot of American family feuds. In the twenty-first century, all American citizens deserve to be part of that family, regardless of age, race, sexual orientation, disability, religion, or any other difference. In order to ensure parity, the Supreme Court must seek to balance not only competing liberties but also liberty and equality.

When written, the First Amendment collected historical ideals from a variety of sources, including Enlightenment philosophers. While the Magna Carta proposed general ideas of liberty, the idea of religious freedom was refined during the Enlightenment. Many of the colonists who came to America from England did so in pursuit of this religious liberty, as they opposed the Church of England for political or moral reasons. As there was little religious freedom, neither the separation of government from religion (the ban on the establishment of religion in the First Amendment) nor the protection of an individual's freedom of religion (also in the First Amendment) existed in that era. And some English colonies, even ones established in search of religious liberty, echoed the behavior of the Anglican Church.

Massachusetts Bay, for instance, allowed only Puritans to be residents, driving out all dissidents. In 1650, Massachusetts went so far as to hang a Quaker for no greater a crime than practicing the wrong religion. Other colonies were more tolerant, with Rhode Island adopting a more modern freedom of religion and Pennsylvania generally doing the same. Where

Rhode Island's statutes stemmed from fears that the government would corrupt religion, Pennsylvania's stemmed from the Quaker belief that its practitioners should not seek to religiously influence others, even in their own meeting houses. Other colonies' populations were less geographically concentrated, limiting state control over inhabitants' religion. Thus, genuine diversity existed in the colonial era, with regard to the treatment of minority religions.

With the American Revolution and the change to a more uniform national government, the newly formed states agreed that they did not want a strong religious influence in the new federal government, though opinions varied regarding interactions between religion and state governments. However, neither the Articles of Confederation nor the main body of the Constitution considered freedom of religion. The new Bill of Rights, prompted by the states and created by Congress shortly after the Constitution went into effect, finally and formally prohibited Congress from either establishing a religion (what is now called the freedom from religion clause) or interfering with the free exercise of religion (the free exercise clause).

Increasingly, Supreme Court cases have addressed the free exercise clause, and academic studies of these cases typically concentrate on the current political and legal atmosphere. A more thorough historical examination of the matter, looking at the significant social and political movements and legal cases underlying the most recent decisions, will establish the reasons the Supreme Court must break new legal ground as it balances equality and the free exercise of religion.

That balance will need to take into account claims that freedom of religion can be used to justify the denial of services on moral grounds. For example, while there is no question that religious institutions that do not wish to perform marriage ceremonies between same-sex couples are not mandated to do so, individuals such as Kim Davis, a county clerk from Kentucky, have claimed this same constitutional freedom and refused to issue civil marriage licenses to same-sex couples, even though such documents are wholly governmental in nature and in no way affiliated with a religion. Similarly, opponents of marriage equality have denied the services of their private businesses to same-sex couples, claiming protection under the free exercise clause of the First Amendment.

Those who argue for equality point out that same-sex marriage is legal at the national level. Even though the Supreme Court determined that the Constitution in no way limited marriage to being between only one man and one woman, homosexual couples still find themselves marginalized by moral opposition to their marriages. Instead of encountering universal equality, they have only overcome one of the hurdles standing between themselves and truly parallel treatment with heterosexual couples. Religion here is being used to justify bigotry and discrimination, and this new level of clashing values will force the Court to further define true equality. However, where past clashes of a similar nature have involved the behavior of government institutions, today the Court will have to determine how to balance the competing constitutional claims of individuals against one another, even if the nature of the argument is such that the Court appears to be analyzing only one type of right.

In the past, the Court evaluated cases relating to the ways the federal Bill of Rights limited power. Generally, this meant it examined whether particular government practices were legal or not. The only federal cases where one individual might sue another typically related to libel and slander. In those cases, the Court was not proclaiming some right to commit libel or slander. Rather, it was examining whether libel or slander had taken place or whether the questionable words were actually protected by the First Amendment.

It makes sense that cases connected to specific government actions were the most common. The purpose of any Bill of Rights as a whole, whether at the state or federal level, was to ensure the government did not get too powerful. Legally speaking, these Bills of Rights existed to ensure the preservation of an individual's rights specifically against governmental power. Cases of one individual versus another, in the absence of a federal or state law, were generally ignored at the constitutional level.

Indeed, because it was initially inapplicable to state governments, the federal Bill of Rights was not used that much during its first century of existence. The federal government, while heavily influenced by religion in this era, took few actions that interfered with any one individual's rights. The most notable decision during that time period involved polygamy, and the Court put boundaries around federal (but not state) interference in certain areas.

Then, in the 1870s, a federal law prohibiting polygamy in the largely Mormon Utah territory clashed with the values of the Mormon Church, and the Church went to court against the government under the federal First Amendment's freedom of religion clause. The resulting case, *Reynolds v. United States* (1878), forced the Supreme Court to define "freedom of religion" and establish its boundaries, at least in a broad sense. The case questioned whether a law could ban certain religious practices and to what degree religion could be restricted without violating freedom of religion. In its decision, the Court differentiated between religious beliefs and religious practices, and held practices can be restricted while beliefs cannot, upholding the law in question. It did not evaluate the degree to which practices could be restricted, nor did it consider when such restrictions were appropriate. Thus, the case established that there were no constitutional bans on government regulations for behaviors violating generally applicable laws, even behaviors motivated by a religious belief. To put it another way, the Court held that religion did not exempt individuals or churches from being subject to laws that applied to all groups. In contrast, the Court held (as it has always held) that beliefs cannot be restricted.

However, it did not specify which potentially religiously motivated actions were affected, nor did it propose a system to legally address any widely distasteful generic actions that might be allowed (and even encouraged) by religious belief. These are the questions it has had to return to in the twentieth and twenty-first centuries. Recently, the debate has widened to ask what to do when conduct motivated or required by a religion but banned by society harms or burdens another person.

The twentieth century saw the rise of individualism, along with an application of the First Amendment to the states. The rise of individualism in some ways started first, as privacy started being considered right around the turn of the twentieth century, with an article published by Louis Brandeis and Samuel Warren.[9] They argued that people needed to be able to control their own lives and some things should be beyond state scrutiny. In other words, they suggested that people have a right to privacy.

The right to privacy has been championed by supporters and opponents of marriage equality. Those favoring equal marriage argue that homosexual couples deserve the same rights as heterosexual couples and that love is a private emotion, beyond state control. Those opposing marriage equality typically express religious reasons for their positions. They feel their privately held religious beliefs are being unreasonably burdened when they must work for the benefit of homosexual couples. More than that, they consider homosexuality to be morally subversive and fear that it has a corrupting influence on what they argue are the traditional values espoused in their churches.

The case that would end with the application of the First Amendment to the states began in 1925 and had no direct relationship to the freedom of religion. Benjamin Gitlow was convicted of subversive behavior for disseminating communist literature, and he sued to have his conviction overturned under the federal First Amendment. The justices upheld his sentence, but they set a precedent with an ongoing impact in our society. The decision stated directly that portions of the Bill of Rights, including the First Amendment, applied to state laws, because of their interaction with the Fourteenth Amendment, which promised liberty and guaranteed against state interference. Until this time, only federal laws were affected by most constitutional law cases. Initially, the decision's implications were tested in the areas of free speech and freedom of the press in the 1930s.

However, both the establishment and freedom of religion clauses now applied to state laws, and cases involving Jehovah's Witnesses in the 1940s would begin to show the changes such an application meant. The first state law struck down was in 1940 when, in *Cantwell v. Connecticut*, the state was held to have violated the free exercise of religion by requiring door-to-door proselytizers to obtain licenses and giving local officials the right to deny those licenses.

Throughout the 1940s and 1950s, the free exercise of religion was not the top topic in most people's minds, as World War II and then the Cold War raged. Those cases that did reach the federal court system generally involved minority religious groups. For instance, many of the early cases were brought by Jehovah's Witnesses, which still has a population of only 1 million adherents in the United States. That is only one-third of 1 percent of the population. The laws they challenged were aimed at preventing their door-to-door witnessing and limiting their exercise of religion.

Although the establishment clause is well covered elsewhere, a few noteworthy establishment clause cases also affected the freedom of and from religion in some way and bear discussion. The establishment clause was first used to strike down a state statute in 1947, halting a program allowing religious groups to operate in public schools, during the school day, as part of the curriculum. It remained a subject of frequent litigation in the 1960s. Additionally, all of the cases involving prayer at public school graduations and football games and relating to the placement of the Ten Commandments in schools and in government buildings connect to the establishment, rather than the free exercise, clause. That said, the recent hot debates center around the free exercise clause, and the Court, with the exception of one Ten Commandments display, tends to rule heavily against any appearance of the school or state establishment of a religion.

The freedom of religion is most significant when considered in terms of the good it has caused. Bette Evans writes: "Our history is replete with heroic acts of religiously inspired conscience that challenged governmental authority in the name of higher law. The Abolition movement derived much of its leadership from Christian activists, as did the civil rights movement."[10] On the flip side of that, those who defended slavery cited the Bible in their defense, as did many who opposed the civil rights movement. In fact, the District Court decision that ultimately led to the Supreme Court case *Loving v. Virginia* (1967) argued that segregation had been created by God, meaning segregated marriages were also the will of God.[11] Of course, this gets into the territory of the establishment clause, as the Court, by invoking God, seems to be establishing religion, suggesting that the freedom of religion is only useful for the purpose of reducing strife. However, the freedom to practice religion individually and privately inspired consistent peaceful protest against such logic, and the very fact that this is guaranteed by the Constitution ensured that religiously inspired civil rights protesters could use their devotion to fight against oppression.

But equality's supporters are not always the ones most strongly inspired by religion in a debate. In these cases, the courts must essentially choose between one group's or individual's definition of his or her right to the free exercise of religion and another group's right to equality, and sometimes their freedom of religion, as well. These cases require nuanced evaluation in an effort to balance the conflicting values and achieve some degree of legal parity.

Moreover, the First Amendment's protections are often claimed by disenfranchised or, at the very least, minority groups. Evans also writes: "Our survey of controversial religious practices confirms the common understanding that the Free Exercise clause is essentially a protection for religious minorities."[12] In the modern legal arena, in contrast, large corporations are claiming those same protections, using precedents that declared corporations could be people. Decisions such as the one reached in *Hobby Lobby v. Burwell* (2014) essentially favor corporate interests in the guise of the freedom of religion. Powerful religious groups are also using the First Amendment to advance their own agendas in the twenty-first century.

Some argue that the First Amendment creates a liberty in addition to the freedom of religion. This implication has been used to argue that the liberty inherent in religious freedom trumps the liberty necessitated by marriage equality cases. In these cases, the courts must evaluate the degree to which the freedom of religion is being used to hide bigotry and balance rights in a fair way.

Christopher Eisgruber and Lawrence Sager, for instance, argue for what they call an equal liberty policy toward the freedom of religion. They state, "What Equal Liberty Demands of the State is that it attend to the deep minority religious commitments of its citizens with the same regard that it brings to bear on other, more mainstream concerns."[13] One would wonder, though, if that would be fully applicable in the present, though, as many of those now trying to use the First Amendment to advance their agendas are not the powerless minorities that the First Amendment (and the Bill of Rights as a whole) was created to protect, nor are they the ones who have used it mostly in the past. Also, of course, even if the government were to treat the First Amendment equally with other concerns, would it not also have to balance off the liberty of religion versus the rights of those oppressed by the religion? This is not to say the government is incapable of oppressing a religion. The courts must be careful not to allow this to take place when balancing state goals against religious ones. However, in the two main areas today where religious liberty is being used, that liberty's activation results in the suppression of another's rights. The concept of equal liberty includes a balancing act, and the forces that need to be balanced now are quite different from those balanced in the past.

The increased rise of individualism and increased multiplicity of religions also complicate any balance the Court must strike. In particular, these changes affect arguments regarding the ways the cases facing the Court now might have been decided in previous eras. The balance between government and individual power has shifted in favor of the individual. Some argue that this rise of the power of the individual is the exact reason why religious liberty takes precedence. That might be true if all that was being considered was the right of the state to restrict religious liberty. Again, the theory of equal liberty argues that using religion to justify inequality is unreasonable.

In 1789, with women not being able to vote, and many without property denied a full place in government (to say nothing of state restrictions based on religion), there was not full equality. Today, the American legal system is closer to full equality, and that is especially true in the Constitution with the Fourteenth Amendment's requirement of equal treatment for all under the law. This means that true liberty, in order to avoid being exclusive, must consider claims to equality alongside the liberties granted by the freedom of religion. When a claim for religious exemption asks for the right to treat people unequally, the courts are doubly tasked with finding a balance between equalities and liberties and determining whether religion can be used to justify prejudicial behaviors. Thus, even if the spirit of the 1789 Constitution might allow for religious exemptions where those exceptions restricted the equality of another person, the courts must ask if an appropriate current interpretation of the Constitution would be the same.

The theory of original intent argues that the Constitution does not change, and interpretations should take into account the framers' intent.

Even if this is accurate, such a determination merely shifts the burden of analysis. Barring a reversal of the last few years of constitutional doctrine, same-sex marriages are given the same constitutional standing as opposite-sex marriages. If one argues that that constitutional development is unconstitutional and should be reversed, the question then becomes where the doctrine should be rolled back to, which increases the complexity. Throughout this book, it will be noted what the level of protections given to certain groups was at any time and how this level of protections, if factored into a balancing, would impact people's rights. One could also balance today's rights against the freedom given to religion at a certain point, but either would be problematic.

A lot of effort has been put into the whole "freedom of" part of the phrase "freedom of religion." However, in this debate, less emphasis has been put into the word "religion." Definitions of religion are problematic, and Evans notes that "we seem to be forced to conclude that no single definition of religion can do the job required of it."[14] She points out "a defining characteristic of a religion is that it entails a 'metaphysical as well as a moral aspect . . . [a]n understanding of oneself or one's purpose includes an understanding in some measure of some larger reality or whole in which self and others are distinguish and to which ones choice will make a difference . . . every religion . . . includes a metaphysical claim about the character of reality."[15] Religion also includes another element, in that "an adequate definition of religion must at least suggest why the actions that stem from beliefs warrant special protection."[16] Finally, a working definition of religion can be condensed as follows: "a system of faith and worship usually involving belief in a Supreme Being and usually containing a moral or ethical code."[17] Often, religion addresses the afterlife, in a variety of different meanings of that term and deals with at least some things that are not measureable in discrete units. How then can a company be religious? The courts can sidestep this question when they consider companies as individuals, but at a practical level, if religion is about the individual's relationship with a Supreme Being, often through a religious group of some kind, then the insertion of a corporate body with a nonreligious function becomes problematic.

Companies, for instance, are not religious in that at the end of the year, everything they do is measured in minute units. They deal with profits, losses, hiring, firing, and, typically, the sale of some kind of product. What is the difference between a group or individual operating a company according to religious precepts and the company claiming that religion? Legally, the difference is significant as without the company being treated as an individual, the company cannot be granted freedom of religion.

Moving in the other direction, it is important not to simply conflate religion with morality and moral behavior, even though these concepts are clearly related. Morality gives reasons for proper behavior due to short-term consequences. Religion gives reasons for proper behavior due to long-term (and perhaps eternal) consequences. Even long-established religions like Buddhism include concerns of being reborn into a better state.

Conversely, something with religious connotations is not solely concerned with the here and now. Religion is also not wholly of the here and now. One should then consider that as a corporation cannot die, its contemplation of the afterlife or state of the soul upon death is something of a Schrödinger's cat. The *Black's Law Dictionary* defines a corporation as "an entity (usually a business) having authority under law to act as a single person distinct from the shareholders who own it and having rights to issue stock and exist indefinitely."[18] Thus, a corporation cannot be religiously motivated. A corporation also cannot be involved in faith and worship, except in that its shareholders or executives do so. How could anything be motivated by, for itself, something it cannot attain? Also, a critical reason for a corporation is to provide limited liability, that is, that the corporate entity is separate as far as bankruptcy and liability go, so that the personal assets of the investors are not threatened by a corporate bankruptcy—so is the Hobby Lobby decision partly a matter of religiously inspired owners having the cake (limited liability) and eating it, too (their religious convictions being upheld)?

Perhaps corporate concerns for others' welfare can be used to justify the position. However, the *Burwell v. Hobby Lobby* case did not present religion as a collective right but something that the Hobby Lobby corporation was due as it was a person. That whole issue is something that America will have to resolve if it wishes to give corporations religious freedom, and perhaps another definition of religion will emerge, but that also has its own drawbacks. If religion is a personal right, then one must be interested in it for personal reasons.

Moving beyond the issue of whether corporations should have religious rights, the next question is how previous courts have treated competing claims of equality. During the civil rights era, the U.S. Supreme Court began to examine the relationship between equality and the freedom to discriminate, but, prior to the Civil Rights Act of 1964, those cases related to the state's ability to do so. Later, federal cases predominantly examined the constitutionality and boundaries of the various Civil Rights Acts. Thus, though the Court was examining the right to equality, it was not examining cases where one private individual's constitutionally established liberties conflicted with another individual's constitutionally mandated equality.

At a certain level, all federal cases are based in individual conflict. However, an increasing number of modern cases involves a complex relationship between two private entities and the state. Even though, at the surface, these cases involve an entity engaged in a lawsuit with the state, there is a silent third party whose needs are truly at the root of the case, whose rights are overlooked. For example, at its surface, the *Hobby Lobby* case pitted the Hobby Lobby's claims of religious liberty against the Affordable Care Act.

However, the particular issue in that case was whether the company, when treated as an individual, could exercise its religious liberty and refuse to fund insurance for certain kinds of birth control. The government's argument was concerned *only* with whether an entity could be excepted from certain portions of a federal act for religious reasons. But public debates looked at the questions of religious liberty *and* the larger underlying concerns relating to women's reproductive rights. The Court's decision ignored women's reproductive rights, concentrating entirely on the rights of a corporate entity to be excepted from an act objectionable to its religion. Thus, it failed to seek balance between equality and the freedom of religion, setting up a situation where a liberty could infringe on the principles of equality.

Finally, these cases considered today force the Court to determine when liberty can be restricted and how. While the First Amendment forbids laws restricting freedom of religion, that freedom has never been absolute and so not all restrictions on religion have been banned. After all, no one would defend a modern day Aztec who wanted to take slaves and practice human sacrifice, because that harms another person. Thomas Jefferson himself referenced the idea of harm, writing: "But it does me no injury for my neighbor to say there are twenty gods or no god. It neither picks my pocket nor breaks my leg."[19] The other side of this, of course, is the implication that when one's religious ideas or practices do cause injury, and a deprivation of equality is injury, they can be restricted. Jefferson also only mentioned ideas, not acting on those ideas. Throughout the history of America, the questions of whose religious liberty can be contained, and when (and, of course, why), have been answered in different ways.

In the end, the different tenor of today's cases requires a different approach. Jefferson was one of the few Founding Fathers whose viewpoints would have been in any way at home in the twenty-first century, and even his views are wedded to his era. If no Founding Fathers should be considered, the issue is an easier one, one of merely determining how to interpret the Constitution in terms of the present. Even if the Founding Fathers are considered, though, some of the leading ones, like Jefferson, suggest that limitations on freedom are sometimes allowed.

Most blockbuster Supreme Court cases have dealt with governmental laws trying to do something. *Roe*, *Brown*, and similar cases all dealt with governmental attempts to accomplish some goal. Even most First Amendment cases have dealt with governmental controls. Those include *The Pentagon Papers* case of 1971, *Gitlow v. New York*, and others. Merely applying the old rules does not produce the proper considerations at the constitutional level. One might protest that the *freedom of* and *from religion*, or however we want to conceptualize the First Amendment's religion parts, are different. It definitely has different issues, but most of the cases have still dealt with governmental controls. *Engel v. Vitale* (1962), the *Gobitis* (1940) case, and so forth all dealt with governmental restraints or commands (most often commands), and the whole freedom from religion clearly means that you are free from the government imposing a religion (whatever that is conceptualized to mean). Thus, that part of the First Amendment's religion clauses clearly deals with governmental controls (and has in the past).

The freedom of religion part of the First Amendment might be thought to be different, but most cases contained in studies on the subject still deal with governmental restraints. For instance, Peter Irons's first study of a variety of cases, *The Courage of Their Convictions*, dealt with only *Gobitis* as a freedom of religion case.[20] Surveys in works looking at a particular case often produce a similar result. Carolyn Long's list of cases, as part of her historical survey of the Supreme Court's past treatment, in her book on *Oregon v. Smith*, starts with *Cantwell v. Connecticut*, a classic case where freedom of a person's religion was pitted against a state regulation. Her list goes on to include other cases, but in her early treatment, she concludes that a person operating under the free exercise clause failed, sometimes "in his challenge to the government's regulation."[21] Thus, Long does not even consider that one might have freedom of religion in the absence of a government regulation, or, more to the point, does not suggest that any relevant court case considered the issue. Long goes on to list the most on-point cases for her to be *Sherbert v. Verner*, dealing with unemployment compensation, and *Wisconsin v. Yoder*, dealing with school attendance laws. None of the cases she lists is that of one individual versus another.

Even more comprehensive (and more recent) case lists do not include many which pit one individual (however constructed) against another.

One study, by John Witte and Joel Nichols, lists as of 2010 some 219 cases (since the Founding) and included quite a few freedom of religion cases. The first case on their list is *United States v. Reynolds*, dealing with a polygamy statute in 1879. The first case that they held to represent a successful use of the free exercise clause did not come until 1943, with two cases, one dealing with the distribution of literature (making it thus both a freedom of the press case and a freedom of religion case) and the *Barnette* case that same year, dealing with a flag salute. In all three of these cases, the aims of the government were being balanced off against the liberties of the individual. While one might argue in some cases that the liberties asserted were not liberties (as in the polygamy case), that was still the balancing that was going on. In the 1960s, the compilation notes that the number of free exercise cases was increasing. Quite a few of the cases in the 1960s and 1970s dealt with conscientious objectors, as might be expected with the Vietnam War going on, but that is clearly a case of the state versus the individual. Even some cases where there were other rights in consideration, such as the *Yoder* case, where the rights of the children to be educated might have been considered, the only rights considered by the courts were the government's and those of the person being arrested. The courts have also generally considered foundations and corporations in those eyes, not individuals, as in the case of *Tony and Susan Alamo Foundation v. Secretary of Labor* (1985).[22] None of the 219 cases dealt with, as best can be told, one individual battling another. It might be argued that high profile cases, like *Hobby Lobby* and those involving same-sex marriages, put the individual's rights in opposition to the government's. However, they really pit one individual (if you consider Hobby Lobby, the corporation, to be an individual) versus a class of others—its employees. In essence, they are a mix of employment law and equality laws and the First Amendment. The same-sex marriage cases of the bakers and the florists are a mix of equality and the First Amendment, as the question is, Does the florist or the baker have to treat all equally, even if (and/or even when) the baker or florist's religion tells him or her not to? It is an individual versus another individual. Some of these cases do involve a governmental law, thus making it a three-part balancing act—individual versus individual versus state—but others are the baker or florist arguing for a religious exemption even when the rules do not yet tell him that he is not forbidden to discriminate. In that case, it is just individual versus individual.

Those are entirely new classes of answers, but there have been answers given to other questions throughout history. This book looks at those answers.

Should corporations be treated as people for the purposes of religion? Cases in the past have considered religious groups but have dealt with them in terms of the impacts on the adherents, without granting any additional rights to the corporation itself. What does a member of a religion need to do in order to be part of that religion and can a corporation do that? Those are all complex questions that we must answer if we continue down the road of *Hobby Lobby* and grant personhood to corporations.

A final consideration is whether to treat some point in the past as the key time or to base our considerations in the present. If the Religious Freedom Restoration Act of 1993 is correct and, as the title suggests, religious freedom should be restored, then what year do we restore religious freedom to? What year should society move our current level of religious freedom back up to? Some might want to go back all of the way to the Constitutional Convention as a baseline. (This book will look at whether or not to have a baseline.) Two problems exist, though. First, most groups considered equal today were not considered equal back then. Thus, if we today believe in equality, as most of us do, to base our considerations on a time when people were not thought of as equals seems a bit misguided. Second, a lot of issues that are currently under serious consideration were not contemplated at the time of the Constitutional Convention (or at least were not written about). Questions of LGBT rights and contraception, among other things, were not often discussed. Some might argue that we need to base our considerations on the time when the RFRA test was passed (or when it was created), but things have still changed. If we cannot figure out a date to use for a baseline, then how do we tell which thinkers of the past to use as models for our reading of the First Amendment? If we cannot figure out what to balance from some point in the past, should we just balance things in the present? Of course, that might not produce outcomes preferred by some groups, but that seems the most sensible.

This book aims to tell the story of these questions and of some answers that have been reached and to suggest some ways to reconsider the answers in light of new developments on the eve of the 230th anniversary of the First Amendment.

CHAPTER ONE

The Founding Generation*

From our vantage in the twenty-first century, it is easy to imagine the Founding Fathers, with tricorne hats, parading to the Pennsylvania State House in 1787, with the solemn goal of enshrining their collective views of liberty into the American Constitution. However, the reality is much more disparate. Far from a group of like-minded individuals with a shared vision for our young nation, these were men seeking compromise between varied beliefs. They were primarily concerned with improving the federal government's weak structure without undermining the integrity of the states.

In fact, the group initially convened to revise the Articles of Confederation. When it became clear that an entirely new code was needed, compromise increased in importance. The resulting document, therefore, established the executive, legislative, and judicial branches and clarified the relationship between the three.

Only when some states hesitated to ratify the Constitution, noting its failure to address individual liberties, did James Madison draft the ten amendments that would, when ratified, become the basis of much of our beliefs about liberty, religious and otherwise, in the United States today. One of those amendments, defending the freedom of religion, has become a topic of hot debate, swirling with micro-analyses of word choices and questions of authorial intent.[1]

Influences

Looking back, James Madison's work had numerous influences, ranging from the Magna Carta to Great Britain's tumultuous political-religious

*I prefer this term for the people and the era as it is more inclusive and also reflects the longer period of time over which these ideas were formed.

history and from the French philosophers to the Virginia Bill of Rights, authored by George Mason. The First Amendment has two parts dealing with religion: a ban on an establishment of religion and a clause explicitly allowing all Americans the freedom of religion. In this way, Madison implemented the concept Thomas Jefferson termed "a solid wall" between church and state. He also specifically protected the rights of individuals to the freedom of religion, no matter where they lived in the United States.

However, this is but one portion of the larger body of ten amendments ultimately ratified, and the history of the American Bill of Rights should be examined more broadly. The basic idea of a Bill of Rights extends back to England's Magna Carta in 1215, signed by King John. Many take the literal Latin translation, "a great charter," and assume the document's significance on that basis alone. However, the name does not refer to significance but size. The Magna Carta is actually more about taxing (and, more importantly, limitations on the king's ability to tax) than people's rights. The Magna Carta did, however, provide a basis for the idea that limitations on government should be written down.

The Magna Carta was still the most relevant government document when the British entered the Age of Exploration and established colonies on the American continent in the 1600s. However, little cohesion existed between the laws within individual colonies. Indeed, some had royal charters and governors, while others were governed by companies, with drastic variance between legal practices, especially when it came to the topic of God.

Though more than a few colonists left England in pursuit of the freedom of religion, their concept of such freedom was usually quite narrow. Often, as can be seen in laws in the Massachusetts Colony, it meant the freedom for one former minority religion to impose its own structure upon everyone, an attitude that would carry into the Revolutionary Era and beyond.

Of course, in England, personal religion was expected to be dictated by the state religion, and the crown had enormous powers. Indeed, the next major written limitations on English government came only after two major revolutions. The first, the English Civil War, told the kings that their power would be limited by the people, violently if necessary.

The second, the Glorious Revolution, created a document limiting the monarchy's powers. Starting in the 16th century, England's (and later, when England, Ireland, and Scotland were merged, Great Britain's) political fate was tied to the monarchy's break from the Catholic Church. Thus, the status and even safety of any given family hinged upon whether the king or queen was continuing down Henry VIII's path away from Catholicism or attempting to reconcile with Rome.

Great Britain had been Anglican for over a century when the Catholic King James II came to the throne in 1685. His ouster in the Glorious Revolution a mere three years later led directly to the issuance of a decree limiting government powers. (It also laid the foundation for the Act of Settlement of 1701, which would bar Catholics from inheriting the throne.) There was—and is—no written constitution in England, and an idea of outlining people's rights was revolutionary. The document would become known, in time, as the English Bill of Rights (to differentiate it from the American Bill of Rights).

In the American colonies, the Glorious Revolution led to few immediate direct governmental changes. In the colonial days, unless a government was nonfunctional, it was seldom replaced. Even at the time of the American Revolution, some colonies existed under charters several decades old. Massachusetts's Charter, for instance, had been issued in 1692 and was only cancelled, effectively, by the American Revolution. However, the English Bill of Rights *did* demonstrate that government could be more specifically limited by written laws that aimed to protect the populace.

At the same time as the Glorious Revolution, French philosopher John Locke was developing theories that would influence all of America's Founding Fathers a century later. Indeed, two of Locke's fundamental notions found their way into some of the United States of America's most famous early documents. Thomas Jefferson, of course, captured the idea that the government's right to control should be based in reason and the consent of the governed, an idea put forth in Locke's "The Second Treatise on Civil Government" (1690). Additionally, Jefferson, like several other Founding Fathers, supported the idea of separating church and state. When drafting the first of the ten amendments that would provide personal rights under the Constitution, James Madison helped codify this separation, first presented in Locke's "A Letter Concerning Toleration" (1689).

Examining the colonies' early histories makes the need for such protection evident. Massachusetts, for example, had been particularly fanatical in its oppression of religious dissent and difference. The Salem Witch Trials are simply the best known of the colonial government's uses of power to enforce religious goals. Looking at the colony more broadly, Quakers could be hanged for their religious views, and many others were expelled for failing to toe the Puritan forefathers' religious line.

One such religious leader, Roger Williams, was forced out of Massachusetts, and he founded his own colony, Rhode Island, in 1636. The colony of Rhode Island was one of the first that held for religious liberty. It also upheld this idea much longer than some others. While Williams was not wholly modern in his views, which always had a religious basis (as one would expect of a minister), he did write, "no person in this colony shall be molested or questioned for the matters of his conscience to God."[2] Those who believe such a statement favors all religious exemptions from law would do well to also read the rest of that sentence in his tract, which was "so be he loyal and keep the civil peace."[3] This distinction between conscience and behavior indicates Williams's awareness both that law and religious belief were separate entities and that the freedom of religion could be abused if not extended carefully.

Williams was nonetheless deeply concerned about people being persecuted for their religious beliefs. He extended this freedom of conscience to many more groups than most did during his time period, including "Jews . . . Turks . . . Papists [Catholics] . . . [and] pagans."[4] A third colony, Maryland, extended similar protections, but only to any Christian.

Contrasting these three colonies' practices shows the dramatic impact a government's relationship with religion could have on the lives of its citizens. Early inhabitants of Massachusetts faced potential religious oppression and persecution, whether or not they violated the public peace in any way. Maryland's citizens were generally safe to practice their religions, so long as they were Christian, and Rhode Island admitted that Christianity was not the only religious option, going so far as to permit paganism within its borders. Such a range of potential outcomes makes overall conclusions about the general state of religious freedom in the early colonies difficult to develop. Because no colony's laws applied in another's, no one colonial leader can be effectively studied for an average example of early political attitudes toward the relationship between church and state.

Following the American Revolution, the Articles of Confederation created a weak central government, and the U.S. Constitution was drafted and adopted because of the Articles' fundamental failure. While the Articles had been useful to hold the fledgling country together during the Revolution, in the years following, their lack of cohesiveness caused both internal and international problems for the United States. They gave the federal government no power to leverage an army, no taxing power, and no power to regulate commerce, among other issues. When the Constitutional Convention was called in 1787, therefore, the focus was on what powers to give government, rather than on rights and liberties. Because of this, the resulting document mentions liberty directly only in the preamble and does not list specific liberties at any point.

The Constitution also barely says anything about religion and never in the context of religious liberty. The preamble does refer to the "blessings of liberty." Perhaps this phrase could be construed to include some element of religion, but that extension seems a stretch. In any case, the courts have consistently held that the preamble does not grant any rights or confer any powers in and of itself. Thus, even if the phrase "blessings of liberty" included religion, the concept did not specifically shape government.

In the body of the Constitution, religion is mentioned only once, in Article VI, which holds "but no religious test shall ever be required as a qualification to any office or public trust under the United States." When written, this instruction actually countered several states' practices. Religious test oaths were common in this time period, and the practice held on until the 19th century, and some of these oaths were continued well into the 20th century in some places. The point, however, is that the only Constitutional mention of religion is an attempt to insure it would never be an official bar to an individual's becoming a senator or representative.

There was some discussion of a bill of rights and liberties at the Constitutional Convention, but it was limited. Supporters like Virginia representative George Mason argued that individual and state rights needed to be protected. Opponents suggested that states already had the power to protect individual rights and would continue to do so. Mason, who disliked the amount of power being given to the federal government, maintained that if the Constitution was to be supreme, it would trump those rights. In the end, no bill of rights was written, and the issue was tabled, in large part due to a need for expediency, but also because more than a few representatives failed to believe it was needed. Even the man who would ultimately write the Bill of Rights, James Madison, did not address concerns like those Mason expresses, suggesting he was less certain of its necessity at that time than he would become later.[5]

It's possible to ask why religion did not play a larger role in such a foundational document. After the Constitution was announced, one person asked Alexander Hamilton why the authors left religion out. Hamilton allegedly answered "we forgot," but that answer seems to suggest that Hamilton was dodging the question rather than the best minds of the time forgetting to put something in that they had wanted to include. The better answer might lie in their goal and their concerns. Their goal was to create a stronger government to allow functional commerce, and religion played only a small role here, at best, and their concern was in passing the reforms and ratifying a Constitution, and mentioning religion (a topic that colonies had widely varying opinions about) only risked opposition and so the best mention was none at all, from a purely political standpoint.

Opposition to the Constitution remained strong after its publication. In addition to feeling the federal government was made too strong by the document, many opponents feared concentrations of power. Even then, some Constitutional supporters argued that individual liberties did not need to be listed, countering that the federal government had no right to interfere with them. They argued the Constitution's guarantee that "the citizens of each state shall [be] entitled to all privileges and immunities in the several states," and its writ of habeas corpus was a sufficient protection.[6] But this did not silence many critics of the document, like George Mason and Revolutionary War hero Patrick Henry. Mason was among those who pointed to the bills of rights in many state constitutions, arguing that the same should be included in the federal document.

Indeed, these state constitutions had provided a larger impact on citizens' daily lives under the Articles of Confederation, and those that included bills of rights often demonstrated an intention to protect individual liberties. Because Virginia's state bill of rights in particular was so influential on the religious protections ultimately placed in the First Amendment and because Virginia was most adamant about the need for a bill of rights in general, its relationship with religious freedom is relevant to any historical examination of the topic.

The state of Virginia initially had included public funds for ministers in its budget. The state bill of rights did include language related to the freedom of religion. However, the Presbyterian minority feared that the Anglican majority would have too much power setting up the funds' administration. They therefore spearheaded the defeat of the system. Ultimately, none less than Thomas Jefferson would write the Virginia Statute for Religious Freedom, designed to completely separate church and state, and the Virginia state legislature would adopt the document. Clearly, then, there was precedent in the United States for formalized freedom of religion.

Initially, James Madison did not believe that state bills of rights had been wholly successful. In fact, "at the national level of government, Madison believed, a bill of rights would prove redundant or pointless."[7] He also doubted the power of the Bill of Rights to stop people who were fully bent on harming the rights of others. This suggests that Madison's ultimate support and fight for the Bill of Rights was at least partly tied up in his overall battle to get the Constitution adopted and accepted by the American people.

It is impossible to know how many people were concerned by the lack of a federal bill of rights. There were no public opinion polls, and other opposition, like the fear of federal power, existed. Nonetheless, this absence *was* one that could be addressed effectively. It was one of the larger arguments against the Constitution, especially after the first wave of adoptions, and it was a breaking point for some delegates to the Constitutional Convention.

New York and Virginia were the two most important battlegrounds in the spring of 1788. While eight states had adopted the Constitution, these two remained key. New York was the most important commercial state, and Virginia was the most populated state in the union. In Virginia, prominent anti-Federalists, including Patrick Henry, argued against the Constitution. In New York, Madison worked with Alexander Hamilton and John Jay to write *The Federalist Papers*, a series of essays defending the Constitution and attempting to answer the various arguments set out against it. While they could not answer all of the arguments of the opponents, Madison realized that he *could* answer the argument over the lack of a bill of rights. He promised Virginians (and the nation by extension) that he would work for a bill of rights if the Constitution were adopted and if he was elected to the first Congress.

Keep in mind that at this stage the freedom of religion was not a key concern for Constitutional supporters. Many leading American thinkers had moved away from the draconian practices of Massachusetts, and the states allowed more freedom, especially in terms of picking one's religion. However, how such freedom would work in practice in terms what liberties one would have from state interference, both in general and based on religion and both on the federal and state level, still remained to be seen. These topics were not discussed by Madison, Hamilton, and Jay, though.

William Miller writes "the silence of The Federalists [i.e., *The Federalist Papers*] on religious matters is almost as striking as the silence of the Constitution. Nowhere in its eighty-five essays, covering the whole polity in defense of the Constitution, is there any discussion of religion as an element in the social order."[8] This seems to contradict those who glorify the Founding Fathers as holy men who wanted to run the nation according to their religious convictions. Certainly, many exhibited evidence that they felt God was important in their personal lives. However, they either did not see the Constitution as a threat to God or felt that religion was a private matter. The first idea, without any evidence, would be hard to prove.

The second would suggest they felt religious liberty should not be used as a reason to infringe on the rights of others.

In fact, *The Federalist Papers* shows an understanding of politics that is highly relevant to the 21st century. Miller notes that Madison "had begun to believe that the uniting of political and religious power . . . was a mistake [that] . . . 'tended to produce oppression.'"[9] While Madison, in this instance, was specifically opposing uniting church and state, his statement has further implications. One must wonder, for instance, what he would have thought about political power being united, ostensibly in defense of religious liberty but often in reality in defense of a few religions, as is happening currently. Madison believed more in and preached the value of pluralism, or the value of having multiple different sects.

In New York, *The Federalist Papers* proved successful, and by 1789 enough states had ratified the Constitution that it was formally adopted. Madison *was* elected to the First Congress, and he immediately went to work carrying out his promise to promote a bill of rights. To this end, he solicited suggestions from all of the states that were a member of the United States at that point. He received a wide range of suggestions and then had the difficult job of combining them into a workable set of amendments, while managing the competing interests of all of the other members of Congress. Some still opposed Constitutional amendments, feeling it was, instead, time to finishing setting up the country. Others thought that the bill of rights issue would be the best way to scuttle the Constitution they opposed and so called for a new Constitutional Convention with the goal of subverting the original document. Fortunately for history, Madison and others were able to stop this second group and work with the first. But deciding how to create these amendments and how to mesh competing ideas was not easy.

As Donald Drakeman notes, part of what Madison faced was a wall of unrelated interests. The First Congress was less concerned with settling things for the future and more interested in satisfying those people complaining in the here and now: in 1789. Drakeman writes, "What eventually drove the consideration of the religion clauses was a different task from laying a foundation for modern civil liberties or delicately balancing secular and religious interests; rather the Congress grudgingly took up the issue of a Bill of Rights simply to appease the states that required or requested them so as to avoid calling the entire constitutional enterprise into question."[10] Thus, even though the Bill of Rights was ultimately tweaked by Congress, the concepts on the page came from Madison's efforts to combine competing interests. Drakeman notes that the First Congress had a great deal to accomplish and so were not that interested in debating most of the points. Congress as a whole played a role, but Madison's work drove the document: quite a different picture from that of the wise Founding Fathers obsessed with the finer points of liberty that we sometimes get.

State governments of the era were largely silent about what the Bill of Rights meant to them. Of the first six states to approve the Bill of Rights, none discussed any specific amendment in detail. Massachusetts did debate the Bill of Rights in early 1789, but its only substantial concerns related to what has become the Tenth Amendment (reserving powers to the states). Madison's home state of Virginia held up the process by being contentious in a general way. Though George Mason was pleased with the amendments, Patrick Henry was among those hoping to overthrow the federal powers conferred by the Constitution. He couched his attitude as a belief that the amendments would be ineffective. In fact, in spite of being Madison's inspiration for actually drafting the amendments, Virginia did not adopt them until 1791.

On the topic of religious protection, Drakeman points out that most of the states that proposed anything on religion were concerned only with what we have come to call the establishment clause. For that matter, only 5 of the 11 states sent in amendments. (Rhode Island and North Carolina had not yet joined the country.)[11] It is therefore difficult to judge what level of interest each state thus had in the amendment process, and the overall lack of participation complicates any desire to look back to the Founders for guidance about the meaning behind the free exercise clause.

Certainly, the concept of religion's free exercise existed in this era, as is evident from Roger Williams's philosophies in the colonial era. However, such rights were not considered boundless. Jack Rakove summarized the situation this way: "nearly all the activities that constituted the realms of life, liberty, property and religion were subject to regulation by the state; no obvious landmarks marked the boundaries beyond which its authority could not intrude, if its actions met the requirements of law."[12]

Some modern scholars who argue that the establishment and free exercise clauses "should be 'read as one' then find the combination essentially defined by absolute separation—any violation of the strict separation of church and state is identical with a violation of the free exercise of religion, which is defined as an absolute split between the state and religion."[13] However, others hold a quite different view. Miller explains, "others—former Solicitor General and Harvard Law School professor Erwin Griswold, for example—read the two clauses 'as one' to an opposite result: Church-state separation is itself not a principle; it is an arrangement that may serve a principle and is mandatory only insofar as it is a servant of the only and governing fundamental principle, religious liberty—meaning that all human beings are free from coercion in religion. Governmental supports to religion do not fall under constitutional ban."[14]

Indeed, some cases do fall into the middle, as a particular statute in question is regulated by neither the free exercise clause nor the establishment clause. In general, however, the courts have treated the two clauses separately and the words' exact meaning is hard to discern. Some have thrown up their hands entirely. Eisgruber and Sager note that "we believe that the most honest assessment of the historical record requires a conclusion more or less like the one offered by Donald Drakeman in his study of the Establishment Clause—namely, that the record provides no answers to the normative raised by the plain text of the religion clauses."[15]

The founding generation also did not have as much foresight as what is sometimes attributed to them. J.R. Pole notes, "The extraordinary complexities that were to be experienced in the process of applying this language [of the First Amendment's religion clauses] to cases of specific—often severe—conflict between different religions and between the state and individuals, were wholly unanticipated both at the time of drafting and for a long time afterward."[16]

However, the Founders' viewpoints are frequently raised in discussions about the First Amendment. Historians typically hold that the only way to approach the Founding Fathers' thoughts on any topic is through their own writing. Though speaking exclusively of religious beliefs, Gregg L. Frazier's argument on the topic has broader validity. He writes, "It is tempting for some to go beyond what the Founders actually said about their religious beliefs by speculating more generally about those beliefs and about their spiritual lives—if only because we want to 'know them' and because there is so much more we would like to know that they did not speak to. And so—from sympathy or affection or curiosity—we fill in their silences and speak for them when they refuse to speak for themselves. But this is a mistake, one that is more likely to distort our understanding of the Founders than deepen it."[17] He further writes, in discussing churchman Samuel Clarke (whose views impacted the founding generation), "Clarke's work contains a statement concerning religion and morality that might have been made by almost any person in this study [of the Founders' views on religion], 'Moral Virtue is the Foundation and the Summ, the Essence and the Life of all true Religion.'"[18] However, these ideals come with no precise and applicable definitions, leading to modern debate about what exactly those beliefs and intentions were.

Philosophy

What then did the Founders write and think? Frazier explains that they leaned toward religious views that also incorporated individual reason. He describes them as "theistic rationalists." Even those formally affiliated with religions often picked and chose which areas of the Bible to apply in their daily lives. Frazier notes, "When reading these sermons carefully, one is struck by the frequency with which passages of Scripture are interpreted in a manner convenient to the argument being made but unrelated or opposed to their clear sense."[19]

The Founders often followed members of the intellectual elite who did not aim to stamp America as Christian. These include the religiously inclined John Witherspoon. In fact, Frazier quotes another scholar as saying, "In Witherspoon, the most self-consciously evangelical of the founding fathers, there is little of the effort which marked the work of earlier Christian thinkers to ground politics in specifically Christian propositions."[20] Here again, we can see the ways the Founders were influenced by the belief that reason should temper religious sentiment, along with the idea that religion might not be best expressed in the political arena.

One lesser known, but specifically relevant, voice was Virginia's George Mason. Mason was a reluctant representative to the Constitutional Convention, and he refused to sign the Constitution because he favored the power of the states and disliked the Constitution's broad power. Inspired by John Locke, he penned the religious protection included in the Virginia state bill of rights. "That religion or the duty which we owe to our CREATOR and the manner of discharging it, can be directed only by reason and conviction, not by force or violence, and therefore all men are equally entitled to the free exercise of religion."[21]

At the other end of the spectrum, Thomas Jefferson and James Madison are two highly influential and renowned Founding Fathers, in Virginia alone and the nation at large. Jefferson's views about the freedom of religion are well known and frequently quoted, and Madison ultimately drafted the Bill of Rights. When Madison ultimately scripted religious protection into the U.S. Constitution, he would include similar language that echoed Jefferson's sentiments, though the Bill of Rights' final wording seems murky upon close inspection.

When Jefferson drafted the Virginia Statute for Religious Freedom, "the issue [of religious freedom] had been effectively reduced to these two alternatives: a 'general assessment' for religion, under which citizens would pay their tax for the denomination of their choice, and a complete separation. Jefferson's bill was the expression of the second position."[22]

After Jefferson penned the bill, it was actually James Madison who championed it through to passage, as Jefferson was in Paris by that point.

Indeed, Jefferson, though contradictory in many ways, consistently demonstrated the theistic rationalism Frazier describes. One of Jefferson's (and the other Founders') influences was philosopher Joseph Priestly, who wrote, "If the interference [in religious liberty] would be for the good of the society upon the whole, it is wise and right; if it would do more harm than good, it is foolish and wrong."[23] Frazier continues quoting Priestly as saying, "fact and experience seem to be our only safe guides."[24]

Frazier explains that, additionally, "[Conyers] Middleton's Letter to Dr. Wonderland, then, reaffirmed for Jefferson the method of submitting religious questions to the test of reason and observation. It encouraged him to determine for himself the legitimacy of biblical revelation, and it emphasized the value of religion as a moralizing force in support of social order."[25]

Jefferson argued, in his notes and in general held forth in the Virginia Statute for Religious Freedom, for total separation and total religious freedom. Though he discussed only beliefs, not actions, his thoughts were unmistakable. His Notes on the State of Virginia hold: "But it does me no injury for my neighbour to say that there are twenty gods, or no god. It neither picks my pocket nor breaks my leg."[26] This clearly suggests that, for Jefferson, beliefs without actions do no harm. However, beliefs with actions, Jefferson seems to imply, would be not allowed if they do harm.

He also coined the phrase that most associate with the separation of church and state. In a letter to a group of Baptists in Connecticut, Jefferson argued for "a wall of separation between church and state." Historian Philip Hamburger notes, "Jefferson's phrase . . . provides the label with which vast numbers of Americans refer to their religious freedom. In the minds of many, his words have even displaced those of the U. S. Constitution, which, by contrast, seem neither so apt nor so clear."[27] In the context of the letter, Jefferson was largely discussing the interaction between a person's religion and the state, or the establishment clause.

In fact, Jefferson never formally attached himself to a specific religion, but his philosophies indicate a much more deist than Christian perspective. Certainly, he was interested in religion, and was, as in many areas, a mass of contradictions. In addition to opposing any connection between church and state, he produced a variety of Bibles, including one with only the words of Jesus in it. However, he generally seemed to believe that God set forth nature and then left it alone. That is evident in the Declaration of Independence when he refers to "nature's God."

Largely, he believed people should have their own freedom of conscience. He wanted to influence people to do good more than to promote any one faith. William Miller writes that, like many of the Founders, "[f]or Jefferson, morality could as well replace religion. For none [of the several Founding Fathers he listed] . . . did creed matter very much."[28] Jefferson's words, then, show him as a deistic man who, while involved with religious matters in his personal life, opposed any political union of church and state. While church and state are more in the establishment area, he also would have opposed allowing the state to favor one religion over equality, one might presume, as along as the result was moral.

Finally, though, Jefferson did not draft the national Bill of Rights; James Madison did, and Madison's religious views are much more enigmatic than Jefferson's, and the two did not share identical perspectives. Madison was educated in a Presbyterian college (The College of New Jersey, now Princeton University), but that experience seems to have led Madison more to free thought than any permanent religious attachment. One biographer went so far as to say, "There is no trace, no clue as to his personal religious convictions."[29] What can be determined here is that even during his education, he intended to keep his views private with a clear conviction that he did not want to influence other's views.

Where Jefferson resisted formal religion, finding very little of value in it, Madison was comfortable with religion in general principal, unmolested by state interference. Most of Madison's written words about religious freedom either predate or date from the time when he was drafting the first Constitutional amendments. In Federalist number 51, he said, "but what is government itself but the greatest of all reflections on human nature? If men were angels, no government would be necessary. If angels were to govern men, neither external nor internal controls on government would be necessary. In framing a government which is to be administered by men over men, the great difficulty lies in this: you must first enable the government to control the governed; and in the next place oblige it to control itself."[30] Thus, Madison showed concern for the ways in which people behaved, concentrating on the importance of government's ability to function. He did not suggest that religion should be the basis for evading generally applicable laws.

In addition to those amendments that were ultimately adopted, Madison penned others that were struck down. Among these was an amendment specifically written to prevent states from infringing upon personal liberties, including the freedom of religion, the freedom of the press, and the right to trial by jury. He also wanted religious conscientious objectors to have protection in their antiwar perspectives. From this, it seems safe to say that Madison wanted a wide area of religious freedom to be protected from state interference. He viewed the Bill of Rights, as adopted, as limiting the federal government.

After the Bill of Rights was adopted, Madison wrote less on religion and other domestic issues. As Congressman, secretary of state, and then president, he focused on national and foreign affairs. As he was considered more a statesman than a religious figure, and as religion was not a contentious political issue in the 19th century, this absence of a public religious stance seems logical.

He did issue a call for a national day of religious consideration when he was president, although he carefully couched it as voluntary and the word "God" when used is clearly included by Congress's express request.[31] When he issued the call, the War of 1812 was drawing to a close. He later noted that he was not comfortable with his own role in the proclamation's creation, so it seems that this seeming anomaly related more to a war that the United States wasn't certain of winning.

Typically, his perspective was quite different from that when he called for the day of prayer. Not long after he left the presidency, he wrote in opposition to the existence of army chaplains and House and Senate chaplains. He believed that the army men could find services on their own and that the United States having chaplains would produce political strife.[32]

In the end, both Madison and Jefferson clearly wanted to move religion beyond the area of possible regulation. "[A]t the heart of their support for disestablishment and free exercise lay the radical conviction that nearly the entire sphere of religious practice could be safely deregulated, placed beyond the cognizance of the state and thus defused as both a source of political strife and a danger to individual rights."[33]

Jefferson's words about personal liberty, while restrictive of the role of the state in the matter, give little guidance in the current battleground. The most one can say is that Jefferson suggested that the freedom of religion did not justify personal injury, implying the need for balance.

Miller observes, "The problems associated with telling the story of the original construction of the religion classes of the First Amendment are these: It is immensely complicated; the records are skimpy; disputants with entrenched polemical positions from later centuries swarm over every inch of the territory; and the provisions that came out of the legislative meat grinder at the end of the process included an usually opaque phrase: 'respecting an establishment of religion.' "[34] Thus, it is difficult to tell what the parameters of that religious freedom are and where the religious freedom ends.

Implications

Madison and Jefferson lived in an era when the country was smaller and most citizens seemed to think even a strong federal government should factor less significantly than the state government in their personal lives. Moreover, religion for some theistic rationalists (and, by implication, some of the Founding Fathers) was a defense of whatever portions of the Bible they found agreed with their own ideas. One early thinker, Conyers Middleton, was described as having "paved the way for a theistic rationalist with a pair of scissors to determine for himself which portions of the Bible were legitimately from God."[35]

Today, theistic rationalism is less an individual and more a denominational endeavor. Different religions (or denominations within those) choose which portions of which sacred texts to apply and pass this instruction down in services. However, few need to publicize the philosophy behind their choices. While many individuals are encouraged to explore their religious foundations, the Founders' focus on personal reason as a criterion for belief is less popular.

Even at a personal level, a theistic rationalist today might well "scissor" out those portions of the Bible that are read as condemning (and those few which specifically condemn) homosexual behavior, which would, in turn, mean that at least one morally based view, founded in the religious ideas of the times of the Founding Fathers, would prohibit discrimination against marriage equality. Thus, even if the Bible was held to be relevant to the debates on same-sex marriage, and even if one camp held that the Bible dictated discrimination based on it, the other, congruent with attitudes derived from those of preachers in the founding era, could interpret those same passages to mean just the opposite. Surely, such a result renders truly moot the issue of how the Bible should regulate public policy. Indeed, such an argument would, at a practical level, force the courts to choose between competing religious visions, which would, by its very nature, seem to create a government establishment of religion, moving the issue from one part of the First Amendment to another.

Looking more broadly at the concept of morality, the changes become more apparent. Increasingly, in the last 200 years, the concept of equality has been given a place at the legal table in issues where morals are concerned. This sets up an interesting clash. Some religious communities hold morality to include the equality of all, while others hold that discriminatory practices that prohibit immoral behavior are allowed. The first group includes those who hold that love is not immoral, and gender shouldn't be a bar to marriage. The second group often places same-sex marriage firmly on the "immoral" side of the line, suggesting that legalizing the practice is sure to lead to worse offences, ranging from the most repressive forms of polygamy to legalized pedophilia. If the court system prioritizes its decisions based on morality, it must then pick which morality is more moral.

Of course, this discussion begs the question of whether those with religion should be favored over those without any recognized religion. The courts have consistently held for some years that the freedom *of* religion includes the freedom *from* religion. Even setting this aside doesn't solve the issue. While some would want the First Amendment to favor those with religion over those without religion, from a policy standpoint changes little. It merely shifts the focus to a debate over what constitutes a religion.

In addition to changes in religious perspective, the United States has undergone a shift in legal philosophies in the last 200 years. In the modern era, with far more states in the union, people are more accepting, even welcoming, of national laws than the Founders. Thus, Madison's, Jefferson's, or any of the Founders' perspectives cannot be lined up point for point with the major issues facing the nation today, including laws governing the freedom of religion.

Miller argues that, for most people, the focus and understanding should not be on a treatment of these clauses as holy and perfect but an understanding of them as they were written. He writes, "If, on the other hand, you hold, with all due patriotic respect, that one of the deeper meanings of the national commitment those clauses is trying to express is that 'Almighty God hath created the mind free,' then you may be permitted to use your freedom of mind to observe not only that those religion clauses were composed by a committee—actually by many committees—but that they read like it. They are not a particularly lucid epitome of the great principle, or principles, of religious liberty."[36]

Nonetheless, some scholars argue that America has a Christian heritage, that the Founders were Christian men, and that Christian ideals should therefore play some role in the government, as religion shaped the moral behavior the Founders favored. The Constitution prohibits government interference with religion, this argument continues, but does not promote government indifference toward religion. Placing the argument into the context of Frazier's description of the Founders as theistic rationalists brings two important points to light. First, though the Founding Fathers *did* believe that religion and morality were closely tied to one another, they didn't hold a clearly unified vision of what that morality might look like. Thus, even a shared belief system would have allowed for a plurality of definitions about moral behavior. Second, America's Founders wanted the relationship between religion and morality to be subject to a personal test of reason. With limited lucidity as to what their religious morality might look like, and with the written evidence that many of them wanted religion subjected to a test of personal reason, it seems difficult to say whether they would or would not allow discrimination on the basis of religion, particularly in relationship to a law that would have been inconceivable in their era.

Examples of morality's changing definition will help illustrate the problems of applying the Founders' positions on morality to modern issues. In the 1780s and 1790s, it was generally legal for a man to physically abuse his wife, and most states allowed slavery. John Adams politely ignored Abigail's plea for him to "remember the ladies" when adding his contributions to the decisions that would shape the nation's. Jefferson and Madison both owned slaves. Plenty of the white men running the nation when the Constitution was written would have defended both practices on moral, reasonable, or religious grounds, or all three together. Few indeed would make such arguments today.

Whether the Founders' religion is considered or not, waves of religious sentiment periodically sweep the nation. The federal Religious Freedom Restoration Act (RFRA) of 1993 ostensibly reaffirmed the nation's commitment to religious freedom, though its primary argument was that legal religious neutrality can place an unfair burden on a religion. Though the Supreme Court struck down the act as unconstitutional in 1997 in terms of how it limited the states, many states had already created such mandates at the state level, adding a level of complexity to the scholar determining when religious freedom has been preserved and when the guise of religious freedom has been raised to allow one individual or corporation to infringe upon the rights of another.

Applying the Founders' religious perspectives to today's legal situations becomes even more tricky, then, in light of the passage and rejection of the RFRA. People in the 19th century would have held significantly different perspectives about morality than people living in the 21st. Indeed, the very Constitution has changed. This suggests that a different balance between one individual's rights and another's might have been found legal 100 or 200 years ago. It doesn't seem reasonable to apply the same balance as our forebears on the basis of the fact that they came first, given the number of changes since Jefferson and Madison's era.

Consider the range of issues that would have surely been balanced differently by moral men 200 years ago. Women were not allowed the right to vote or own property. Jefferson, Madison, and his contemporaries would not have been expected to take them into account in their philosophies. Recall that it was not only Southern men who ignored the rights of women; John Adams was from Massachusetts. Other rights, such as contraceptive rights, would have been unheard of, and any discussion of the topic might probably have resulted in an arrest for violating pornography laws. The LGBT population lived closeted lives until well into the 20th century. Thus, the founding generation either was silent about the current issues or would have arrived at results generally at odds with what most would want today.

A slightly longer examination of a modern Constitutional debate will help address the concerns created by the RFRA's ambiguities. The U.S. Supreme Court's June 2015 decision in favor of marriage equality for same-sex couples has been opposed by some groups on religious grounds in a revitalization of the old argument that homosexuality is immoral and therefore legally wrong.

Extrapolating from the definition of the Founding Fathers as theistic rationalists and attempting to apply such an extrapolation to the law and justify religious opposition to marriage equality is hazy at best. The resulting concept seems like a philosophy written in vapor trails. Indeed, if only morality matters under the law, and if all people (or even all religions) define morality slightly differently, it would seem the First Amendment has a tiny addendum similar to the invisible (and sometimes quite visible) one held back in the Colonial era. *Americans have the freedom of religion . . . so long as they adhere to my definition of morality.*

The vapors dissipate completely the more closely they are studied. The Founders expected individuals to place morality against a test of personal reason. The modern basis for the Biblical argument against homosexuality comes from a few verses in the Bible. The conclusions drawn from any one individual's or denomination's reasonable analysis of those lines will vary dramatically from one person or group to another. (Remember, theistic rationalism allows the individual to decide which portions of a religious text to follow.) If every person can legally discriminate based on these moral-religious determinations, it would seem that the very foundations of the Constitution with one rule applied to everyone could be undermined simply by applying the philosophies of author to text.

The objections to the 2015 Supreme Court decision have resulted in some very real discrimination against couples applying for same-sex marriage licenses. Rowan County, Kentucky, county clerk Kim Davis repeatedly refused to issue such licenses, citing that doing so would force her to violate her own religious beliefs, making the requirement a violation of the Constitutional separation of church and state. Essentially, her argument breaks down to an interpretation that her Constitutional freedom of religion trumps the right to be married of the same-sex couples whose certificates she refused to issue.

Looking to the Constitution itself is not helpful, as its wording leaves quite a bit of gray. And looking to the Founders' words outside the Constitution offers only limited guidance. For one thing, the aforementioned explanation of morality's changing nature certainly applies. For another, there are few parallels. About the closest that can be found is Madison's call for a national day of religious consideration. However, even this doesn't fit the bill. The question here is really whether one person's religion should be allowed to restrict another's freedom, and a proclamation calling for a national day of religious consideration in wartime does not have a clear peacetime parallel. Perhaps, if all religions held the same stance as Davis's, the situation would be closer, but this is hardly the case. Many Christian denominations will marry two husbands or two wives. On the other side, there is the question of when does one's liberty restrict another person's religion.

However, most discrimination arguments in the recent past have not been about Davis, a governmental official, but about when a private citizen, acting as a business or a corporation, restricts another person's equality. The test to be used there still needs to be determined. How government treated religious freedom (and equality) in the 19th century offers few clues but needs to be reviewed.

CHAPTER TWO

Freedom from Religion

Until the 1870s, the freedom of religion clause rarely came under fire in the federal courts. While cases regarding the state establishment of religion sometimes arose early in the period, they did not typically overlap with government infringement of the right to practice religion. However, as the century wore on, the issue of slavery, the moral questions raised by the Civil War and Reconstruction, and the implementation of the Thirteenth and Fourteenth Amendments would result in cases that would act indirectly to alter the free exercise clause's impact on the states. In a direct sense, following the end of the Civil War, a national engagement with morality drew attention to the Mormon Church's practice of polygamy and resulted in a Supreme Court ruling, *Reynolds v. United States* (1878), distinguishing between religious belief and religiously inspired action and permitting government to regulate the latter.

There are three primary reasons that religious freedom did not become a federal matter until late in the nineteenth century. First, as noted in Chapter 1, the Bill of Rights is the only place in the Constitution where religion is addressed in depth, and in 1833 the Supreme Court held, in *Barron v. Baltimore*, that the Bill of Rights applied only to the federal government. The *Barron v. Baltimore* decision essentially evaluated the purpose of the Bill of Rights, even though it did not use that terminology, and determined that it existed to limit the abuse of powers by the federal government.

Chief Justice John Marshall wrote, "Serious fears were extensively entertained that those powers which the patriot statesmen who then watched over the interests of our country deemed essential to union, and to the attainment of those invaluable objects for which union was sought, might be exercised in a manner dangerous to liberty. In almost every convention by which the Constitution was adopted, amendments to guard against the abuse of power were recommended. These amendments demanded security against the apprehended encroachments of the General Government—not against those of the local governments."[1] He focused exclusively on potential government interference with citizens' rights. He did not consider how the Bill of Rights might apply when the rights of one individual conflicted with those of another. Nor did he address how individuals might be required to behave in order to respect others' constitutional rights. Indeed, if he felt *any* part of the Bill of Rights protected one individual against encroachment by another, that perspective is not reflected in the language of *Barron v. Baltimore*. At a practical level, the decision would have squashed complaints against any state laws on religion, which were reasonably common, because it made the federal Bill of Rights largely inapplicable to state governments.

The second reason that few cases came up regarding the First Amendment's freedom of religion clause is that the federal government was focused elsewhere, particularly on westward expansion. Although religion and religious issues played a part in many personal conflicts, the federal government did not enact any legislation directly affecting freedom of religion, limiting federal laws until the end of the period. Indeed, both sides of moral conflicts often believed themselves to be in the right with God, and the free exercise of religion wasn't typically affected, so legal complaints typically centered on different issues.

In particular, religion motivated both those opposed to and in favor of slavery, but none of the most commonly considered federal laws on slavery limited the free exercise of religion. It might have been possible to treat the federal ban on petitions regarding slavery as an infringement. However, the ban did not actually prevent petitions from being submitted; it rather rendered them useless as Congress automatically tabled them. So anyone religiously motivated to file a petition regarding slavery could do so, though the court couldn't address the case.

The third reason for the lack of federal religion cases is that the federal government did not have any institutions likely to interact with, let alone restrict, religious liberty. For instance, the post office was the largest federal government department for much of the early history of the United States. Recently, much has been made regarding declarations of days of prayer and thanksgiving by early governments, but, in reality, these were few and far between. Federal money didn't bear the phrase "In God We Trust" until the Civil War, when it was added to address fears that the Union might look unloved by God if it lost. At a legal level, then, there was little federal attention given to religious ideas in a broad sense, let alone the narrow one of personal freedoms.

With that being said, there *were* still indirect interactions between the federal government and religion prior to the *Reynolds* decision, and one influential case directly connected to freedom of religion. When a case simply involved a church, but didn't delve into religious issues, the court typically took a religiously neutral stance. However, when federal courts did address freedom of religion, their stance often held heavy religious overtones that seem, to us in the twenty-first century, to overstep the church-state divide.

The cases with religiously neutral grounds typically concerned property issues. The property cases centered on three areas. Either a church would conflict with a state over land ownership or a church would schism, leaving questions of whose rules governed the distribution of property, or one individual would file a complaint against a religious entity, claiming the church body had infringed on some other, secular, constitutional right.

Once the issue entered the court system, decisions concentrated on whether and when the government could regulate the conduct of individuals or church organizations. The decisions had the practical *potential* to affect freedom of religion, but neither the courts nor the affected parties seemed to feel they actually did so. In fact, neither actual religious beliefs nor religiously motivated actions came into question.

Early decisions typically dealt with the control of church property, as might be expected. Following the Revolutionary War, state churches lost their government affiliation, and transitions to independent churches could be rocky. In 1815, the Supreme Court heard its first property ownership case, *Terrett v. Taylor*, which asked whether the state of Virginia owned the property it had allotted to the church before the Revolution, or whether that property now belonged to the church. The Supreme Court's decision focused on secular issues. It determined that the Episcopal Church still controlled the property, as the grant had been made before the Revolution. Although this case pitted a church against a state, no religious values were on the line.

The Court decided a similar case in the same year, again purely focusing on the property ownership issues (*Town of Pawlet v. Clark*). The next case came in 1815 as well, but the Episcopal Church in that case had not fully possessed the property prior to the Revolution. Since the grant had *not* been completed when war broke out, the Court found against the church. The property had belonged to the king, not church land, when the war began, so it reverted to the state.

Freedom of religion, at the federal level, often connected directly to anti-immigration issues and anti–Roman Catholic sentiment that drove public opinion throughout the first half of the century. Alcohol prohibitions were also caught up in these attitudes, but at the state level. Alcohol was considered sinful, and blue laws nationwide, particularly in the Northeast, prohibited its consumption on Sunday. Roman Catholics often opposed these laws, which made for conflict that was, while technically secular in nature, religious at its root. However, the statutes were state, not federal, and their contents and implications varied widely.

In contrast, Protestant versus Roman Catholic disagreements had far more potential to affect freedom of religion. The Whig Party, typically associated with Protestants who had lived in America for their whole—or at least most of their—lives, wanted to restrict the activities of immigrants and Roman Catholics alike. At the federal level, attempts to restrict immigration had no real religious implications. However, the questions raised in the conflicts between the two groups had direct, practical implications for religious freedom.

Where today the courts often rule on whether a behavior is protected by the freedom of religion clause, in the nineteenth century prior to *Reynolds*, the questions were more "religious freedom for whom?" and "to what extent should someone else's religion be allowed to enter the public sphere?" When the federal First Amendment *was* invoked, it typically connected to the government establishment of religion. However, in 1844 a freedom of religion case involving the founding of a charity school in Philadelphia came before the federal Supreme Court.

In the modern era, the debate about religion in public schools centers on whether any religious sentiments can be expressed in such a way as to seem promoted by the school. However, in the nineteenth century, the question wasn't *whether* to have Bible readings in schools. It was *which* Bible to use in the first place. Anti-Catholic sentiment ran high in the country, and the Protestant King James Bible was the preferred text for most city schools. Catholic students, particularly in New York and parts of Philadelphia, argued that this interfered with their right to practice their own religion freely.

Protestants, convinced that Catholics were trying to remove Bibles entirely from public school classrooms (and objecting to the new wave of Catholic immigrants), felt threatened. In fact, these tensions would explode into the 1844 Bible Riots. At the height of the sentiment, not long before rioting erupted, an extremely rich man endowed a school in his will and attempted to limit the religious strife it would encounter. French-born Stephen Girard died in 1831 with an estate in excess of

$7 million. His will stipulated the creation of the school today known as Girard College (which is a K-12 school). He specified that the city of Philadelphia use the school to help impoverished white boys get ahead in life. Because the Bible debate was so heated when he drafted the will, he included a clause prohibiting ministers from teaching at the school. His specific goal was not to repress religion but to shelter the students and teach them morality without the interference of religious fervor.

This provision came under fire, and the case went to the Supreme Court in *Vidal v. Girard's Executors* (1844). Supreme Court justice Joseph Story held an opinion common in the era and still championed by some today. He believed that the United States was a basically Christian nation which allowed the freedom of choice between Christian religions. He felt that governments needed Christian religion to promote morality, and he argued that this was in line with the thinking of the Constitution's framers. He went so far as to compose a disagreement with no one less than Thomas Jefferson, when, in 1824, Jefferson wrote a letter stating he didn't think English Common Law was based in Christianity.[2]

Story's perspectives jibed with the attitudes of many in the era, and the Court might not have permitted the school and its religiously neutral status if Girard's will had not specifically emphasized that he felt no ill toward any religion and did not intend the school as a religious affront. Therefore, in the end, the Court's unanimous decision determined that simply by prohibiting the employment of Christian clergy the school had not prohibited Christian *instruction*. If it had prohibited Christian instruction, then the school would have been viewed quite differently.

This seems a fine line in the twenty-first century, but it was an important qualification in the nineteenth. The school was intended as a charity, and so moral education would have been essential to its function. The degree to which religion and government were intertwined in this era can be seen throughout the language of the decision. Story specifically referred to the United States as a Christian nation, stated that Christianity should not be subject to blasphemy, and called Deism an infidelity.[3] This indicates a tendency, on the part of Story, to believe that religious freedom within the government did not require an absolute wall between church and state.

However, when the question was one of whether a state could enforce essentially prejudicial practices that were unrelated to religion, the Court took a different stance, refusing to apply the federal constitution. Although *Barron v. Baltimore* (1833) had already seemed to state that the U.S. Constitution did not apply against the states, the Supreme Court in 1844 took the explicit step of saying this. In *Permoli v. First Municipality of New*

Orleans, the question was whether funeral regulations which only covered Catholic churches would be allowed. The Court held that if this type of religious freedom was to be protected against state regulation, it would have to be done at the state level, an understanding of the Constitution that continued until 1925.

When the Court heard religious freedom cases relating to conflicts within a church, it also avoided government interference, defaulting to existing religious doctrine when such was available and the views of the church's congregations and religious leaders when no doctrine existed. For example, in the 1820s a religious society agreed to hold all its land in common. Roughly 25 years later, the heirs of one of the original group members wanted the land contributed by their family member back. The heirs claimed the society had acted fraudulently when setting up the communal ownership and sued under contract law. However, in *Goesele v. Bimler* (1852), the Court held that there was no proof of fraud and no right to void. Similarly, in *Baker v. Nachtrieb* (1856), a member left a communitarian society and wanted his share of the property back. Again, the Supreme Court held against the person leaving. In both cases, the Court was obliquely saying that society would not police the relationships between churches and their members.

Church property came up in one other case in the 1850s. In *Smith v. Swormstedt* (1853), the Methodist Church had split in two over slavery. A proviso dating to the 1840s had stipulated that, in the event of a separation, all church holdings would also be divided. However, when the schism actually happened, the division's legality came under scrutiny. The Court upheld the division as legal. Religion did not play a role, as this was considered an issue of contract law.

After the Civil War, one more significant internal church property debate came before the court in the nineteenth century. In *Watson v. Jones* (1872), the question at hand was whether the internal ruling mechanism, in this case of the Presbyterian Church, would be followed or whether the Supreme Court should get involved. Although the issue at stake was actually a matter of contract, later First Amendment cases looked back to *Watson v. Jones*, as the Court's verbiage had clear implications for freedom of religion. The Court ruled in favor of the Church's existing mechanism, in essence determining that, in the matter of a congregation's internal disputes, the state could not contravene doctrinal determinations or otherwise act in a manner that would suggest that the law superseded the Church's established religious practices. The Court ruled by implication in support of the First Amendment, affirming the separation of church and state, but it still used language generally supportive of churches.

The moral issues surrounding slavery divided the nation at every level in the decades leading up to the Civil War. Most abolitionists stood on moral and religious grounds, even as slaveholders defended themselves using the same. The 1857 case of Dred Scott, a slave seeking his freedom under the Constitution, would ultimately have an enormous impact on the First Amendment, though the relationship developed in an oblique way.

Partially, the slavery division was driven by territorial issues. Southern plantation owners believed slavery needed to expand into more and more territory, as slave-grown plantation crops exhausted large tracts of land. These supporters also wanted more senators and representatives from pro-slavery states. However, an increasing body of Northerners also felt slavery's spread would drive up land prices in the West, limiting the amount of land available to new white settlers. As moderate Northerners came to favor—if not slavery's elimination—at least its limitation, Southerners began to worry.

Paternalistic arguments favoring slavery, including those made by widely respected social theorists such as George Fitzhugh, quoted the Bible.[4] And religious defenses of slavery were by no means limited to the public sphere. Congressman J. F. Dowdell tied together the defense of slavery and equality when he wrote, "Let us keep the white race as they are here and now and ever ought to be—free, equal and independent, socially and politically; recognize no subordinates but those whom God has made to be such—the children of Ham."[5] This use of religion to argue against black equality was common in the government, especially as expressed by senators and representatives from slave states.

Religion was also a motivating force for abolitionists, particularly after the Second Great Awakening of the early nineteenth century. They considered emancipation essential to the nation's Godly salvation. Prominent abolitionist William Lloyd Garrison argued that slaves had God-given rights and said denying those jeopardized the salvation of all. Indeed, though such arguments were in the minority, they gained strength and support, to the extent that Lincoln ultimately credited Garrison's impact on the growth of the antislavery movement in the North.

In the mid-1850s, the South and President James Buchanan hoped to use the Supreme Court to settle the slave issue for the last time. The case that resulted was *Dred Scott v. Sanford* (1857). Dred Scott was a slave from Missouri who had gone with his master to Illinois and to the Wisconsin Territory, both jurisdictions that banned slavery. The theory was that if a slave owner voluntarily took his slave for a long time to a state (or a territory) where slavery was banned, the slave became free. However, no federal cases had been put before the Supreme Court when Dred Scott decided to sue for his freedom.

Though it is easy to imagine Supreme Court justices as impartial administrators of the law, whose determinations are wholly unmotivated by human concerns, the fact is that they are human. Throughout its history, the Court has rendered decisions driven by allegiance, rather than impartiality. When the *Dred Scott* case reached the Court, it was made up of five Southerners and seven Democrats. Both sides in the case believed that if the Supreme Court spoke, people would listen. Ultimately, however, the case led to a protracted political battle between abolitionists and slavery advocates for all three branches of the federal government. Moreover, it set the groundwork for part of the Fourteenth Amendment.

Unsurprisingly, the majority opinion favored the slaveholder, but a number of justices wrote dissenting opinions. They primarily argued that in federal territories, the federal government could make laws such as the one freeing Scott and said that state governments could do the same. Essentially, they argued that this was a matter to be determined without the involvement of the federal constitution.

Chief Justice Roger Taney authored the majority opinion, both to render the Court's verdict and to address these dissenters. Taney's ruling first announced that African Americans, even free ones, could not ever be citizens and so therefore could not sue, as only citizens could file federal suits. That would have been enough to end the issue in an immediate sense, but, pursuing the overarching goal of settling the slavery issue, Taney went further. He then considered the issue of whether or not Scott would have been freed by the Constitution if he had been legally able to sue. In what most legal historians argue was a massive overreach of power, the opinion held that since slaves were property under the Fifth Amendment, Congress could not take them away without due process of law (and compensation). By invoking the due process clause, Taney effectively legalized slavery in every state, reversing more than 30 years of legal thinking running all the way back to the Missouri Compromise of 1820. The decision was phrased, in terms of the Constitution's property laws and the Constitution, not in terms of religion; but moral and religious issues lay at the heart of the slavery question. And by applying the Constitution in this way, Taney defined the need for the Fourteenth Amendment following the Civil War.[6]

When the South ultimately seceded, it drafted its own constitution. Although largely modeled on the U.S. Constitution, it differed in some key ways. Beyond the Confederate position on slavery, the South's constitution revealed key religious differences from the document governing the United States. In particular, it included a specific reference to God. At the end of the preamble, the delegates added, "Invoking the favor and guidance of Almighty God."[7] The Confederates placed their belief that God blessed their nation directly into their version of the U.S. Constitution.

While this does not directly impact the religious liberty clause of the U.S. Constitution's First Amendment, it does show a contrasting perspective about the relationship between religion and the state. Confederates felt that religion (and religious liberty) went hand in hand with slavery. The Confederacy existed only for a few months between when its Constitution was ratified and war started, so it is impossible to say exactly how the Confederate States of America would have acted in peacetime. However, its constitutional position regarding the treatment of slavery was clear. Even the United States at this time did not allow African Americans to be citizens due to *Dred Scott*, so it is unsurprising to see them dehumanized and stripped of their individuality, as well, in the South.

After the Civil War, in addition to issues surrounding Reconstruction in the South, the question of loyalty weighed heavily upon people's minds and state governments looked to require former Confederates to prove their dedication to the United States. Loyalty oaths became commonplace, and fines and employment bars ensured compliance. However, some religious officiants argued that the mandates interfered with their ecclesiastical rights and refused to swear oaths.

One priest was arrested and fined for preaching illegally. He refused to pay his fine, and the case went to the Supreme Court in *Cummings v. Missouri* (1866). The Court overturned the fine, holding it and the loyalty oath to be unconstitutional, as such oaths were ex post facto laws that criminalized behavior that had not been illegal when it was done. So, though one of the reasons that many priests and nuns refused to take such oaths boiled down to their free exercise of religion, the Court heard and decided the case based on another constitutional principle.

Immediately preceding the end of the Civil War, the U.S. Congress ratified the Thirteenth Amendment, formally abolishing slavery in the United States. But the law did not answer questions as to the ex-slaves' citizenship, nor did it extend rights to them. The fact that such questions even existed shows the persistent level of institutionalized racism present even in the North. The Civil War might have ended slavery, but African Americans, including those who had been free at the war's outset, were still dehumanized and disenfranchised. As noted in the *Dred Scott* case, the question of citizenship was vital, as only citizens could file suits and seek protections in the federal courts.

To increase the level of complexity, many Southern states still rejected the notion that former slaves had any rights at all, as affirmed by the *Dred Scott* decision. Some used "black codes" in an effort to circumnavigate the federal Thirteenth Amendment and reinstitute slavery in all but name. Though the former slaves were no longer the property of white owners, whose property rights were protected by the U.S. Constitution's due process laws, they were not protected from racism and racist practices. Some black codes were the old slave codes modified, while others were similar laws with the same goal. Vagrancy laws and a variety of other tactics were also used to limit the freedom of blacks.

To combat this, the Congress passed the Civil Rights Act of 1866, which gave rights to ex-slaves and then followed it up with the Fourteenth Amendment. Overall, the Fourteenth Amendment had two clauses with lasting implications for history. First, it conferred birthright citizenship upon all residents, making everyone who was born in the United States automatically a citizen. This reversed *Dred Scott's* proviso that blacks had no access to the Constitution and aimed to force states to treat African Americans fairly.

The second clause identified what rights all citizens were guaranteed. It effectively made permanent the Civil Rights Act of 1866 and then went a step further. It read, "No state shall make or enforce any law which shall abridge the privileges or immunities of citizens of the United States; nor shall any State deprive any person of life, liberty, or property, without due process of law; nor deny to any person within its jurisdiction the equal protection of the laws."[8] Although it would be years before the clause was applied in relationship to the First Amendment, courts would ultimately determine that it meant that the federal First Amendment applied against the states. Because it ultimately impacted the relationship between state laws and the federal First Amendment, it came to change how a state could interact with a group or individual at a legal level.

This was not, however, initially the case. Soon after the adoption of the Fourteenth Amendment, the privileges and immunities clause, modeled after the Fifth Amendment to the Constitution's provision dealing with the federal government, was greatly limited in the *Slaughterhouse* cases of 1873, which dealt with butchers in Louisiana. The city of New Orleans had passed a law allowing only one slaughterhouse for butchers. Independent butchers sued, claiming that their privileges and immunities were violated. Essentially, the Court ruled that the Fourteenth Amendment protected only a few individual rights as privileges and immunities within strict boundaries. This helped the Southern states using the black codes to enforce prejudicial practices. Indeed, these states found numerous ways to avoid Reconstruction's goals, including anti-miscegenation laws that used race as a determining factor for allowing marriages.

Other decisions also limited the reach of the Fourteenth Amendment in the area of civil rights. Congress developed the Civil Rights Act of 1875 in an effort to prevent discrimination in public places. In 1883, however, the Supreme Court overturned the act in a ruling that addressed a series of cases collected under the heading of Civil Rights Cases. Within that ruling, the Court reinforced an earlier ruling, *U.S. v. Cruikshank* (1876), that individuals could sue only the state, not other individuals, for violating their constitutional civil rights and that the federal government could not regulate individuals.

The crowning blow against civil rights came in the 1896 *Plessy v. Ferguson* decision, which held that states could engage in discriminatory practices, as long as they provided "separate but equal" accommodations for the disenfranchised party. Thus, regardless of what the Fourteenth Amendment's writers aimed to do in the area of civil rights, their goals were clearly frustrated by the end of the nineteenth century.

The Fourteenth Amendment's wording makes it clear that it intended to protect both former slaves and other marginalized citizens from government discrimination. But by the end of the nineteenth century, although the amendment had not been legally nullified, whatever personal freedoms that were supposed to be granted had been effectively rendered moot. These efforts to protect citizens from racial bias failed. Later, the Fifteenth Amendment, in an even more explicit attempt to prevent racial discrimination, accidentally undermined itself by limiting protections against voter discrimination to matters of race. By the early twentieth century, most Southern states had developed seemingly nonracial ways to make sure African Americans could not vote, such as literacy tests and poll taxes. Indeed, attempts to enforce the Fifteenth Amendment in the twentieth century (and the twenty-first) have also run into difficulties.

What the Thirteenth, Fourteenth, and Fifteenth Amendments do show is an increased legal respect for the equal treatment of minority groups under the law and a strong backlash that sometimes had religious elements. The efforts to gain equality were either rendered moot or overturned, but this miniscule shift represented a significant change from the Colonial and Revolutionary eras, when most whites either tolerated or accepted slavery without considering the magnitude of suffering it caused. Even the devastating *Plessy v. Ferguson* determination could not escape the word "equal." So, while the Fourteenth Amendment did not directly address religious freedom, its wording would ultimately affect the relationship between the federal First Amendment and state laws. Additionally, the new legal language represented a change in moral perspective that would have later impacts upon attitudes toward freedom of religion in the twentieth and twenty-first centuries.

In an immediate sense, the Fourteenth Amendment was used largely to protect corporations for the first 60 years of its existence, by granting them a form of legal "personhood." If the Southern states were bent on emasculating the racial protections this amendment offered, corporations were equally determined to prevent things like labor laws that would impact their ability to control employees. There is also little evidence that corporations were the main group that those who wrote the Fourteenth Amendment aimed to protect, and as the nineteenth century wore on, businesses subverted several constitutional amendments to serve their own needs. Religious issues were not directly at stake here. However, questions of the relationship between corporations as citizens with constitutional rights to religious liberty would reach the Supreme Court in the twenty-first century.

The practical application of a corporation changed dramatically in the nineteenth century, as more businesses incorporated and grew larger. Because issues in the twenty-first century would include the ability of corporations to wrap themselves in personhood and assert their religious freedom, the historical relationship between the Constitution and businesses is significant.

When the nation was founded, businesses, like governments, tended to be small. Corporations were generally expected to serve the public good in some way, and it was difficult to become incorporated. Many states required the legislature to pass bills before any given corporation could be launched. With the legislature meeting every other year for only a few days, this was obviously a high bar to clear. Bankruptcy law also massively changed in the nineteenth century.[9]

In the early nineteenth century, though, states saw an increased need for businesses and reduced some of the hurdles to incorporation. Corporations also grew much larger and impersonal. No longer were they small businesses handed down inside a family for generations; now they were large factories and mines. Most of these larger businesses started after the Civil War and resisted state and federal attempts at regulations. Indeed, the nature of a corporation changed so dramatically in the late nineteenth century compared to the Revolutionary era as to limit the applicability of any argument that the Founders would or would not have supported the legal treatment of a corporate entity as having personhood.

To gain the most benefit for their own practices, corporations played ends against the middle with state and federal laws. They resisted state regulations by pointing out that only federal regulations applied to interstate commerce. Thus, they successfully argued, as soon as a good left the production facility, that things like railroads could not be regulated, as they were then part of interstate commerce. A series of state railroad rate laws were invalidated on the basis of the federal government having jurisdiction.

On the other hand, the federal government could not regulate child labor laws. Indeed, only state labor laws could be applied to the work inside a factory. For this reason, child labor laws did not become universal until the 1930s. Religion was far more prominent in this era, but corporate efforts to use religion to evade regulations did not generally reach the Supreme Court.

Indeed, though moral and religious questions surrounded the question of child labor, the main child labor case that reached the Supreme Court, *Hammer v. Dagenheart* (1918), cited only secular concerns. There, an attempt in Congress to prohibit child labor was ruled unconstitutional, as the products were never involved in interstate commerce while in production. Morality did have a role in this era. This was more in the Court's holding that Congress could ban immoral products but not products made using an immoral and exploitative process.

Corporations also successfully subverted other laws and regulations in the nineteenth century. They argued that freedom in general should not be limited by government (whether federal or state) and clashed with a number of contract regulations. The most famous freedom of contract case was *Lochner v. New York* (1905), where New York State's maximum work-hour regulation was struck down as violating the freedom of the owner (and, by extension, the employees). The corporation argued that everyone should be free to work for as many hours as they contractually agreed to. The state's stance destroyed that freedom.

Implied here was that these long work hours somehow benefited the employees, who chose to work grueling hours for low wages. The corporations maintained the ironic fabrication of protecting workers' rights in order to maintain exploitative practices. This was most false in the area of mining. Workers, especially mining families, often had to live on company land and in company houses and buy from the company store. Therefore, they were typically so indebted to their employers that they could never quit.

New York did have a religious freedom provision similar to the federal one in nature. New York's religious freedom provision read: "The free exercise and enjoyment of religious profession and worship, with-out discrimination or preference, shall forever be allowed in this State to all mankind; and no person shall be rendered incompetent to be a witness on account of his opinions on matters of religious belief; but the liberty of conscience hereby secured shall not be so construed as to excuse acts of licentiousness, or justify practices inconsistent with the peace or safety of this State."[10]

In spite of the clear moral and ethical considerations, the *Lochner* case remained one of contract law. Partially, that may have been because the situation involved a state regulation and the First Amendment had not yet been used against the states. Although the *Lochner* case was not the only one, it was the most well-known one at the time, and the results in such cases invariably favored companies.

Indeed, when the federal government did manage to pass a law or regulation designed to reign in corporate power, the corporations typically subverted the law and made it work instead in their favor. For instance, the Sherman Anti-Trust Act of 1890 explicitly opposed large corporations (hence the "anti-trust" in the name), and it allowed injunctions to be filed against those who restrained trade. But the injunctions, far from being used against corporations, were typically used against unions.

Among the most famous injunctions subverted by a corporation involved the Pullman Company, which supplied sleeper cars for trains. In 1894, the company cut wages without cutting rents in company towns. When the railroad workers struck against the Pullman Company, the company simply arranged for mail cars to be carried on any train that had a Pullman car, effectively granting the train federal protections. The company then convinced the federal government to appoint a Pullman Company attorney as a special federal attorney.

This allowed the Court to issue an injunction and then use troops to break up the strike. Thirty workers died, the union broke up, and the union head went to jail for six months. Although religious concerns were never articulated in the case, the moral implications of such corruption were clear.

Later, in 1908, the U.S. Supreme Court ruled in favor of an employer who had gotten an injunction against workers, holding them to be an illegal restraint of trade and finding them subject to hundreds of thousands of dollars in damages when wages at the same time were often less than $5 per day. The injunction continued to be used until the 1930s, when the Norris-LaGuardia Anti-Injunction Act finally banned the use of federal injunctions except in limited circumstances. Thus, corporations benefited from federal regulations throughout the nineteenth century by asserting their personhood. They abused both injunctions and the freedom of contract to heavily limit the power of the worker, even though neither was formally defended in religious terms.

While the Fourteenth Amendment gathered dust in the area of freedom of religion, religion was returning to the nation's Supreme Court in the question of polygamy, particularly that of the Church of Latter Day Saints, more commonly known as the Mormon Church. Joseph Smith founded the Church in 1830, and the group's beliefs and practices brought it into conflict with more established religions from its inception. Victims of frequent physical attack, the Mormons found themselves in search of a safer place to live. They relocated to Illinois.

It was there that Joseph Smith initiated one of the Church's most controversial doctrines, when he announced that polygamy was not only permissible but also fully encouraged by God. Though it was generally practiced in private, it, in combination with a variety of other objections, focused public ire on the Mormon Church. Smith was killed by a mob. After this, the Mormon Church splintered, with the majority following Brigham Young out to what became the federal territory of Utah.

Although Utah became a U.S. territory in 1848 after the Mexican-American War, it really was not prime real estate until later. Wagon trains passed through, and eventually the railroad followed, but Mormon authority was largely unchallenged. The vast majority of people in Utah were Mormons, but the federal government still set up rules and regulations.

In 1852, Brigham Young, like Smith before him, announced that the Church would allow polygamy. Plural marriage had been practiced since the days immediately preceding the group's departure from Illinois, and the practice had been steadily, though quietly, growing. Many Mormon leaders had multiple wives, including Brigham Young, who had 55.

Whereas Smith was killed before he could give much public defense of polygamy, Young vehemently defended the practice on religious grounds. A variety of religious arguments were advanced, including one that insisted plural marriage was better for God's kingdom on Earth than monogamy. It helped that those in plural marriages tended to have more children, another important factor in Mormon doctrine.

For that matter, the Church fully regulated plural marriage in Utah, making the practice legal in all but name. Voters in Utah territory were mostly Mormon, so of course the Mormons dominated the territorial legislature and did not object to the practice. And Brigham Young was the territorial governor from 1851 to 1858.

The U.S. government outlawed the practice on moral grounds but found itself unable to enforce the ban. However, this did not mean that it would allow a state with legal polygamy to join the union, even though the territory had more than enough people to petition for statehood.

According to one author, "some 20 to 30 percent of Mormons belonged to a family that practiced the principle"[11] at this time. The practice's controversial nature can be seen in the ways viewpoints and defenses changed over time. Indeed, the number of people involved in plural marriages following Young's proclamation was "more than Mormons acknowledged once polygamy came under fire, but also fewer than their opponents often stated."[12]

Plural marriages were directly connected to the Church's hierarchy. As a man moved up the rungs of leadership, he became increasingly likely to have more wives. Very often, those who took multiple wives had been encouraged to do so by those in positions of highest authority. In addition to defending plural marriage as the best way to maintain religious lives, it was defended as a way to increase order and build stronger families. Mormons tried to contrast the prosperous and good life in Salt Lake City with immoral practices elsewhere in the nation. These arguments, however, really appealed only to existing practitioners of the faith and did not win over many outside of the Mormon Church.

Contemporary historians argued that the high points in civilization did not feature polygamy. Historian Hubert Howe Bancroft wrote, "When Greece and Rome were the foremost nations of the world they did not practice polygamy, nor has the highest civilization ever entertained it."[13] Polygamy, like slavery, was also seen as the enemy of liberty. The South had abandoned liberty, and politicians believed Utah should not be allowed to follow suit. Objections arose even within the Mormon Church. Joseph Smith III, son of the founder, tried to gain control of the Church and went on speaking tours denouncing polygamy.

Opposition to Mormon polygamy had started upon its inception in Illinois and did not relent when the group moved to Utah. Rather, the move placed them outside of the bounds of the federal law, at least from a practical standpoint.

In 1862, Joseph Morrill, an influential senator from Vermont, entered the battle by pushing through the Morrill Anti-Bigamy Act, which outlawed both bigamy and polygamy in the federal territories. Like many politicians, he saw polygamy as an evil parallel to slavery. However, Abraham Lincoln was far more focused on the Civil War. Thus, the first real prosecutions did not occur until later.

When a case did come before the Court, legal enforcement was highly unlikely. Even though Utah was under federal law, juries were comprised of Mormons, and husbands and wives were not required to testify against one another, making conviction nearly impossible. Mormon lawyers maintained that polygamy and bigamy were different practices and should not be lumped together. Whereas bigamy was based on a man lying to his wife about his marital status, polygamy was based in mutual awareness of the plural status. More than that, they argued that polygamy was solely a religious status, not a legal one. The overall battle was between federal interest and both individual and Church beliefs and behaviors. In some ways, it was a battle largely between the government and Mormon Church leaders, as members of the hierarchy were the ones who largely practiced the doctrine and thus defended it.

Then, in the 1870s, Mormons, certain of God's favor, decided to try to get the law on their side, as well. They maneuvered to get a case all the way to the Supreme Court, and George Reynolds, secretary to leader Brigham Young (who would lead until 1877), publicly took a second wife. The Supreme Court ruled on his situation in 1878 in the landmark *Reynolds v. United States* decision. It held that religiously inspired actions could be controlled, the first hint that freedom of religion in the United States had constitutional boundaries. The First Amendment, protecting religious freedom, dealt only with religious beliefs. The Court held that "laws are made for the government of actions, and while they cannot interfere with mere religious belief and opinions, they may with practices."[14] The Court went on to say, in a different quotation perhaps more applicable to present cases: "So here, as a law of the organization of society under the exclusive dominion of the United States, it is provided that plural marriages shall not be allowed. Can a man excuse his practices to the contrary because of his religious belief? To permit this would be to make the professed doctrines of religious belief superior to the law of the land, and, in effect, to permit every citizen to become a law unto himself. Government could exist only in name under such circumstances."[15] The Court spoke forcefully for government power over individual rights, even when the rights of two individuals were not pitted against one another, as would be the case in later high-profile cases.

Mormons in Utah were stunned. It is somewhat unclear why, if not for wholly religious reasons, they expected a victory, as all of the then eight justices of the U.S. Supreme Court ruled against them and national opinion widely rejected them. Regardless, they pledged to continue to follow religion, not the law, and for four years did this, while resisting prosecutions. As noted, prosecutions often failed because both husband and wife refused to testify.

In the 1880s, as the West became a more popular destination for settlers, Congress decided to increase pressure on the Utah territory. Several surrounding territories had become states and so the question became pressing—how and when Utah would be a state and whether it would be the last upper Western state to be admitted. The Mormon Church adhered to its policies, rendering moot the question of any sort of compromise. To make proving the crime easier and wholly eradicate polygamy, the Edmunds Act was passed in 1882. This made it unnecessary for prosecutors to prove a second marriage but instead required them to demonstrate unlawful cohabitation, which meant a man's living with (or supporting) a woman not his wife. "The Edmunds Act further denied polygamists the right to vote, the right to serve on a jury, and the right to hold office."[16] Federal marshals enforced the law and sometimes went along after Church leaders to find them with their second and other wives.

Church fathers used various methods to evade the law, including secret hideouts, but many of them failed. It has been estimated that close to a thousand people were convicted under these acts and others fled to foreign countries. However, the practice itself still did not die out, and so Congress took steps against the Church as a whole. In 1887, Congress passed the Edmunds-Tucker Act, which both made it easier to prosecute polygamists and attacked the Church. It forced the first wife of a polygamist to testify against her husband and also revoked the charter of the Church of Jesus Christ of Latter Day Saints. Once the Church no longer legally existed, the federal government seized the Church's property, other than a few types of things like graveyards and worship buildings. All voters in the Utah territory had to swear that they would uphold the Edmunds-Tucker Act. It was not known how effective this last provision was, but the cumulative effect was significant. At this point, the real battle was between the government and the Mormon Church, or at the very least between the government and those who wanted to do something allowed, but not required, by Mormon doctrine. Idaho, which became a state in 1890, also passed a law removing the vote from anyone who believed in polygamy, and the U.S. Supreme Court upheld these measures.

Ultimately, a solution came in the form of the third president of the Mormon Church, Wilford Woodruff. He had to find a way to rescue the Church, preserve its temples that were under construction, including the main one in Salt Lake City, and restore unity to the faith. He issued a manifesto that urged the Church to obey the law. In later years, he stated that he had experienced a revelation from God that told him to change the Church doctrine but at the time he simply issued the mandate. Some individuals continued to practice plural marriage and continued to have those marriages sealed, but the practice decreased dramatically. In the 1900s, there were hearings, and another proclamation ended the practice after it had dwindled to a slow trickle in the 1890s and the first decade of the twentieth century.

The Mormon Church has tried to step out from under the cloud of inappropriate stereotypes that are still left over from the early days of the Church, many associated with polygamy. Some Mormon fundamentalists broke away from the Church and ran into conflict with federal authorities for engaging in plural marriage. However, most were prosecuted for other practices, like taking underage brides. This issue flared up as recently as the 2010s, in the Western United States with the Fundamentalist Latter Day Saints (FLDS). The FLDS claimed to be an offshoot of the Mormon Church, but the national, more well-known, body disavowed any connections.

As the third quarter of the nineteenth century drew to a close, in 1879, religious liberty seemed, to some, to be decreased by the *Reynolds* decision. At first blush, this seems an unlikely date to connect to future expansions in religious freedom. However, by identifying the boundary between free religious belief and religiously inspired action, the Court created a guidepost for scholars to refer back to. *Reynolds* is typically considered the first landmark freedom of religion case for this reason. It identified the need for balance between religious and personal liberty and the law. Later, equality would also become a factor.

The Fourteenth Amendment set the stage for a number of cases where personal and religious equality would come into conflict. Just as the First Amendment was still coming into its own, *Reynolds* and the Fourteenth Amendment seemed to affect only individual or group relationships with the government, not conflicts between two individuals. Moreover, most of the other issues that would arise in the coming decades and centuries did not yet even exist. Even cases pitting corporations against individuals in religious liberty cases were years in the future.

While equality existed as a legal concept, there was no true definition of what it looked like or whom it might affect. There was no consideration of LGBT rights (or those issues in general), there was very little public discussion of contraception, and women and racial minorities were treated with a high degree of prejudice. Had the legal issues currently facing the United States arisen then, the courts would have decided the cases very differently.

However, the law was still evolving, and to return to those earlier attitudes and behaviors would move society backward. To balance the religious liberties available to minority groups in 1879 against the religious liberties available to them, and to other marginalized groups, today would be anachronistic and problematic.

The early nineteenth century saw the rise of the United States as a nation, but constitutional conflicts were limited, especially in the area of religion. The conflicts that did result were between the state and individuals or the state and the church. They were not between two individuals attempting to exercise constitutional rights in a mutually exclusive matter.

At about the three-quarter mark of the nineteenth century, the Constitution was amended and the first significant religious liberty cases reached the Supreme Court. Both of these developments would continue to shape the history of religious freedom and the law in the rest of the nineteenth and early twentieth centuries.

CHAPTER THREE

Religious Exemptions from the Gilded Age through the 1920s

The relationship between the federal freedom of religion and individual citizens began a slow shift following the 1878 *Reynolds* decision and the Supreme Court's distinction between religious belief and religiously inspired actions. As the nineteenth century became the twentieth, the nation's constitutional concerns shifted. The problems that the Court had addressed in the period before the 1870s, such as, polygamy and anti-immigration sentiments, did not vanish, but they were joined by a series of new issues dealing with anarchists (and opposition to them) combined with fears of sedition and communism. Old solutions lost much of their utility in a changing national climate.

The frontier had largely been conquered by the end of the nineteenth century, when it had previously been a constant social ideal as well as physical presence. Americans turned to managing their nation, and religion, always a part of public life in this era, became intertwined with several popular movements. The legal problems addressed by federal and state courts, along with perception changes following World War I, gave rise to more state and federal power, particularly federal. This growth in turn, oddly enough, helped to create a more robust freedom of religion in the United States.

The rise of the industrial state in the late nineteenth century created huge monopolies and huge problems in American cities. Many cities were dominated by political bosses who had no interest in changing the policies that lined their own pockets. State reform efforts met with mixed success, and companies often relocated when unfavorable legislation was passed and withstood legal scrutiny. For example, many states had regulated child labor by the early twentieth century, but not all. So companies could simply pick up stakes and go somewhere it remained legal. Reformers became convinced that the only way to completely stamp out this practice was through federal legislation.

Monopolies, in particular, could be regulated only at the federal level, due to their inherent role in interstate commerce. Indeed, the federal government was the only entity even remotely powerful enough to take on these enormous companies and trusts with any hope of winning. This is connected to freedom of religion in an indirect but significant way. In time, the reforms caused by these changes led to increased governmental power. This then allowed the Supreme Court to spend more time defending individual liberties than dealing with businesses. Although the cases had not yet become investigations of the relationships between the rights of one individual and another, the changes that began in this era are connected to that ultimate result.

In the late nineteenth and early twentieth centuries, members of the Mormon faith also continued to fight for their own religious rights, forcing the Court to address the boundaries of religious freedom. Both they and a newer religion, the Jehovah's Witnesses, practiced religious proselytization. Prior to 1850, the Mormon Church's activities were mostly confined to Utah. As the century wore on, however, young Mormon men began to travel to fulfill an important part of Church doctrine, spreading the faith. Although some of these missions were international in nature, many took place in the United States. Social and legal opposition quickly developed in response.

The Jehovah's Witnesses experienced similar opprobrium. Charles Taze Russell founded the religion in the 1870s, and for that reason, its adherents were often called the Russellites until the early twentieth century. Russell preached that the world would end in 1914, and, when this proved inaccurate, adjusted the date forward. The group's practices broadened with Russell's death in 1916, and proselytization remained a chief method of spreading the faith. Social opposition arose to the door-to-door canvassing that the faith required, and many were also opposed to the new faith in general. These opinions led to legal opposition, and they wound up involved in more legal cases than the Mormons at the federal level. Though all of the cases specifically examined the rights of individual Witnesses (or, less frequently, Mormons) against the power of the state, municipal, or federal government, the decisions impacted all who engaged in the questioned activity. And none of these cases was designed to weigh the rights of one individual against those of another.

Court cases against these minority groups have been significant to freedom of religion for the entire nation. Even when the laws stricken from the books were generically phrased, it still was typically clear what group was being targeted, and it was almost never the majority religion. Nonetheless, when the Supreme Court strikes down a state or federal law that restricts religious practice, the populace at large gains an increased freedom.

In addition to court cases resulting from legislation targeting minority religions with non-standard practices, political and racial prejudices led to court cases that ultimately supported a broader freedom of religion. One such factor was the rise of antiradical legislation and anti-immigration legislation that led to many battles over personal freedoms by the 1950s. A short look back at anti-immigrant and antiradical sentiments will help establish context.

Racial, political, and religious tension over immigration existed as early as the colonial period. Benjamin Franklin himself inveighed against allowing a large number of immigrants to enter the country. His target was the Germans, who themselves would come to oppose immigration later. Any time a large group was new to the country, it was at risk of a new wave of prejudice. Political parties formed in the 1840s and 1850s to push for immigration restrictions, largely against the Roman Catholics from Ireland, as discussed in Chapter 2.

For the most part, as long as immigration was needed for business, and as long as the immigrants largely came from the northern and western portions of Europe (aside from the Catholic Irish) and held relatively mainstream viewpoints, anti-immigrant activity was limited. However, opposition remained, and radical ideas like anarchism caused widespread concern. National legislation soon followed. Anti-Asian sentiment sparked in the late nineteenth century and extended well beyond the early part of the twentieth century. The first successful and serious push of anti-immigrant legislation resulted in the Chinese Exclusion Act of 1882, which, as the title suggests, targeted only the Chinese.

Other anti-immigrant legislation targeted political and philosophical beliefs and practices. These laws intended to keep certain viewpoints out of the nation, anarchy in particular. Anarchism had heated up as a political doctrine in the latter part of the 1800s, especially in Russia. With the rise of international migration, especially of the poor, the ideal came to America. Though often perceived as violent anti-government agitators, many anarchists were instead interested in workers' rights. They protested poor working conditions and, in an era when the twelve-hour workday and seven-day workweek were not uncommon, long hours. As the need for improvements was great, protests, many organized by anarchists, became more prevalent and more widely tolerated. But in some cases, the backlash against factories, mines, and monopolies went too far. Many workers bought into both the idea that desperate times called for desperate measures and the belief that the owners deserved a taste of their own medicine, which meant that the frequent strikes in this era often came to blows. There was also police repression of these strikes, leading to violence.

One of the earliest anarchist involvements which turned deadly was the Haymarket Square rally in Chicago in 1886. When police moved in to break up a protest supporting an eight-hour workday, someone threw a bomb. One policeman was killed, and the police opened fire. Though accounts differ, it is possible some in the crowd fired back, and the situation devolved quickly from rally to riot. By the end of the crisis, six additional policemen and four civilians had been killed and a seventh officer died later. Estimates of the number of wounded greatly varied. Though the bomb thrower was never identified, and little direct evidence connected anarchists to either the rioting or the police and civilian deaths, eight anarchists were convicted. Four were hanged, another committed suicide, and three more wound up with prison sentences.

In fact, many anarchists were *not* violent, though they could be quite volatile in strikes. Several radical labor unions formed, including, in 1905, the International Workers of the World, also called the Wobblies. It sought (and seeks) to represent workers from all industries. Such unions were considered highly radical, though their methods and ends actually varied greatly, based, in part, on their membership. Though not all of them were affiliated with anarchy, they were often assumed to be, and they were all considered suspect for that reason. Worldwide, anarchist violence was probably worst in Russia, the country that also gave rise to several anarchist philosophers. Ultimately, it was not anarchists but Bolsheviks who assassinated the nation's czar, but the widespread support for anarchy led to generalized suspicions of Russian immigrants.

Immigration reforms in America included an anti-anarchy oath required for admission to the United States. Such changes had no visible effect on the level of support for anarchism, however, and few were turned away for refusing to take the oath. Moreover, there is no evidence of any overseas anarchy supporters shifting philosophies in order to immigrate to the United States. The only real result was that the government later deported some immigrants for engaging in activities supporting anarchism or possessing anarchist materials. (This was particularly true during and right after World War I.) This was one of the first broadly focused (i.e., not aimed at a specific group) immigration controls in America. Such anti-immigrant legislation would, in time, lead to court cases that actually expanded freedom, although the opposite was certainly true at the time. In general, the attempts to tighten restrictions also led to a more powerful federal government, which gave the court more issues to rule on.

Religion certainly factored into anti-immigration sentiment around the country. Anarchist ideals conflicted with America's Protestant main-stream values, so it is easy to see why its supporters were the targets of legal action. However, Protestants were also generally suspicious of those of other religions. Anti-Catholic and anti-Semitic attitudes prevailed and affected immigration concerns. Social class played into the conflict as well, as many immigrants were poor workers, while an increasing num-ber of established citizens lived middle class lives. With the loss of the frontier, the new Protestant middle class had no way to demonstrate its physical superiority and felt emasculated by the laboring class.

Many of today's familiar religious charity organizations were launched in response to these fears. The Salvation Army, now seen more as a thrift store and general charity, started as an organization that aimed to bring salvation to the inner cities, particularly to Catholics. White-collar Chris-tians launched a push to redefine their own religion, with public figures arguing for a robust "Muscular Christianity." This meant that even as the United States modernized, Christianity remained highly visible in daily life at the turn of the century. Among the well-known figures arguing for this new, robust Christianity were Theodore Roosevelt, who himself was a very dynamic figure throughout his life, and G. Stanley Hall, an influen-tial early psychologist.

The goals of Muscular Christianity were at least two. Those in favor, in the words of historian Clifford Putney, "hoped to energize the churches and to counteract the supposedly enervating effects of urban living. To realize their aims, they promulgated competitive sports, physical educa-tion and other staples of modern-day life."[1] Dwight L. Moody was one of the first to combine religion and sports. There was a decided rejection of some aspects of modern life here, and many argued that religion had become effeminate and weak. Muscular Christianity represented the per-fect answer to this, as it included things like the Young Men's Christian Association (YMCA), where the sports of basketball and volleyball were invented.

Society in general was described as being too womanly. Men's lodges sprang up across America with groups like the Odd Fellows joining the older Masons. It was not just the YMCAs and lodges that were involved but also individual white-collar workers, who were involved in a

"Businessmen's Awakening." At a basic level, white-collar Protestant men were also concerned that blue-collar immigrants would be more capable of physical activity, in part because the immigrants were doing physical work. Few of these men actually wanted to work in the dangerous conditions, but they wanted to be manly. Although there is no direct link between court cases and the desire to be active, these are the very attitudes that spurred religion's continued role in life in this era, and Muscular Christianity affected religion's ongoing role in government.

A final religious factor in this time period, and one with more long-term implications, was the development of what came to be called the fundamentalist movement. Fundamentalists argued that there were certain unchanging Biblical fundamentals. Though not all fundamentalists shared the same core beliefs, one of the most common attitudes was that each word of the Bible was literally true. If an idea was not stated in the Bible, then it was not sanctioned by God. While fundamentalism conflicted most in modern society with scientific ideas such as evolution, the divide it created can still be seen in the area of court cases regarding religious exemptions in the twenty-first century. This is because religious fundamentalism typically does not allow for change and re-evaluation. Thus, many modern perspectives, especially those which are all about a re-evaluation of attitudes and rights, may make fundamentalists feel their religious views are under attack.

In the movement's birth in the early twentieth century, fundamentalist doctrines contained the attitudes that would lead to current controversies. For instance, much of the fundamentalist doctrine enshrines male power, which in turn is challenged by the women's movement. Things like birth control, which increases a woman's power over reproductive decisions, are typically unpopular among fundamentalists, even today. Fundamentalism also seeks to preserve a traditional male-female family, and many fundamentalists feel that granting legal equality to the LGBT community threatens that power balance. Many of the efforts aiming to prevent same-sex marriage (and some of the ones aiming to restrict LGBT rights currently) are aligned with the fundamentalist movement.

Finally, fundamentalism, though connected to mainstream Christianity, is not a majority religion. Thus, it is not surprising to find that it has run up against the law at times. However, where other religiously based legal clashes typically see a group fighting for an expanded freedom, those involving fundamentalists often follow a different path. As early as 1925, in the Scopes Monkey Trial, over the teaching of evolution in public schools, fundamentalists have sought legal shelter to continue more conservative practices.

On the whole, fundamentalism maintains some of the same ideas related to Muscular Christianity, where one person's religious beliefs are supposed to influence others. Although this does not amount to the same kind of focus on door-to-door proselytization as in the Mormon and Jehovah's Witness faiths, it does create an environment where members of the faith assert their often anti-modern ideas more than they might otherwise do. While Muscular Christianity has largely faded, the Businessmen's Awakening has gone to sleep, and the YMCAs are now known more for their providing of sporting opportunities, the fundamentalist movement is still very important in the fight for religious freedom in this nation. Much of the opposition to same-sex marriage is rooted in the idea that the definition of marriage should never change and/or is rooted in the Bible, both of which are very much fundamentalist ideas.

While few Supreme Court cases in the period 1880 to 1925 dealt directly with religion, there were some. Although the Constitution did not directly block state infringement upon freedom of religion in this era, religiously based cases still reached the federal level on several occasions. The Court did not use the First Amendment to strike down any federal laws related to religion, but it certainly heard cases with such a focus. Church property, the Sunday-closing laws, and polygamy were the three issues most ruled upon.

Indeed, in Utah in particular, polygamy remained a thorn in the federal government's legal side. As the territory was still under federal law, it was regulated directly by the Constitution, and Congress did make laws directly controlling it. Even after polygamy was legally banned, convictions were still difficult, and the Court had to address a number of connected concerns. In 1881, just three years after the Supreme Court upheld the polygamy ban in *Reynolds*, another polygamy trial reached its docket in *Miles v. The United States*. In that case, the question was whether prospective jurors could be asked about their beliefs on polygamy and whether it was religiously required. There also was the question of spousal privilege. Ultimately, the Court upheld the right to ask prospective jurors their views on polygamy but also determined that the second wife of a polygamist could not be forced to testify against her husband due to spousal privilege. Thus, in an odd twist, even though a second marriage was illegal, it still gave a second wife a layer of legal protection.

The government followed the ban on polygamy with other legal penalties, and those were challenged in court as well. One of the first additional penalties was a ban on voting, both for those convicted of and those accused of bigamy. That law came in front of the U.S. Supreme Court in 1885 in *Murphy v. Ramsey*. The Court, in a 9–0 decision, upheld those penalties, allowing the bans. In the same year, a case, *Clawson v. United States*, came in front of the Supreme Court, where the grand jury had excluded Mormons and indicted a man for polygamy. The Supreme Court upheld that conviction as well. The crusade against polygamy did have some limits, though. In 1887, a case which resulted in multiple convictions for polygamy was limited. In *In Re Snow*, the Supreme Court held that one could be convicted of only one charge of simultaneous polygamy. Thus, if multiple charges covered the same time period, only one count was allowed. Even if a polygamist had multiple wives, it only took one to make him a polygamist, and the others could not be addressed as separate instances, unless he went out and repeated his polygamous marriages after being convicted. These battles mirrored the ones before *Reynolds* in that they examined the relationship between the state and the individual, not one individual and another. The Court in this period was not examining the same types of issues that dominate the current constitutional focus.

The issue of polygamy also came up in other offenses. One man, in ex *Parte Hans Nielsen*, pleaded guilty to unlawful cohabitation and then was arrested for adultery. The legal question was whether the same facts could be used for both offenses (this was again in Utah territory and so therefore under a federal law), and the Supreme Court answered no. However, polygamy remained illegal and other penalties continued to be attached. In 1890, the US Supreme Court, in *Davis v. Beason*, upheld a conviction for perjury when a polygamist had sworn an oath that he was not a polygamist. The oath in question was what is called a test oath, in this case an oath required of prospective voters, who had to swear they were not engaged in polygamy. In this case, the Supreme Court effectively ruled that the oath was legal by upholding the violator's conviction. This meant that the Court believed the Constitution supported the argument that individuals practicing some activities could be banned from exercising their civic duties. In an interesting twist, the majority opinion compared the ban to removing the vote from those who had been convicted of certain offenses. The difference, of course, was that this law did not remove the vote of those convicted but forced people to state that they did not do things they had not yet been accused of, then penalized them for either telling the truth about their activities or lying and saying they did not.

The Mormon Church itself was heavily involved in the battle over polygamy, leading to the laws limiting its involvement, as discussed in Chapter 2. The 1887 Edmunds-Tucker Act outright cancelled the Mormon Church's charter and enacted a number of other reforms aimed at curbing its influence on the issue. It seized Church property to benefit the local public schools, removed the vote from women, prevented children from illegitimate marriages (now including all marriages after the first one for polygamous families) from inheriting, and made sure that all judges were federally appointed. The Church protested, and the case came in front of the U.S. Supreme Court in 1890, in *The Late Corporation of Jesus Christ of Latter Day Saints v. United States.* Much as "late" can describe a deceased individual, it can also be applied to a dissolved business or, as in this case, a religious entity declared illegal. The Supreme Court upheld the law, holding that the treaty adding Utah as a territory to the United States gave the U.S. Congress supreme power over the area and the ability to regulate marriages. Three justices did dissent, suggesting that even though polygamy was illegal, Congress was going too far in seizing church property. It should be noted that most property was not actually seized, as the third leader of the Mormon Church cancelled the Church's support for polygamy shortly after the 1890 ruling.

Polygamy next returned to the Supreme Court the same year, with another case relating to spousal privilege. In 1890, in *Bassett v. United States,* the Court considered whether someone could be convicted based on his wife's testimony. As it had done in 1881, the Court maintained that spouses could not be required to testify against one another, even in illegal marriages, and the conviction was struck down. Though some of these cases named government employees directly, this was only because of their official positions, not because of any of their own privately held views. Thus, these cases placed questions of religious activities against government controls, not one individual's rights against another's. Even this heavy emphasis on polygamy and marriage, which might seem similar to today's focus on marriage, represents a case of individuals (and a Church) versus the state, not one individual versus another.

Polygamy wasn't the only religiously connected issue to reach the Supreme Court in the late nineteenth century. Some of these were really more social in nature than religious, though. These included Sunday-closing laws. Many states had various types of "blue laws," where certain establishments were closed, certain activities were prohibited, and certain products were banned from sale on all or part of Sunday, the established day of rest for most Christians. In three separate instances between 1885 and 1900, the Court evaluated the legality of such regulations.

Some Jewish groups argued that blue laws represented a government promotion of faith that discriminated against them, as their Sabbath was on Saturday. The Supreme Court addressed the issue in in *Soon Hing v. Crowley* (1885), ultimately holding that a mandatory Sunday-closing law was acceptable as a regulation of labor and that it did not promote religion. This could well be an example of legal waffling, as the Court in this period was not generally favorable toward laws regulating labor and working conditions.

Over a decade later, in 1896, a similar case came before the Court, in *Harrington v. Georgia*. Here, trains were shuttered on Sunday, so, in addition to religion, the commerce clause had to be considered. The federal government does not typically regulate local commerce, and its role was typically limited to interstate commerce. The question here did not relate to competition between federal and state or local regulations, though. (In that case, the federal government has usually won in matters of commerce). The Supreme Court ruled in favor of the blue law, arguing that, in the absence of federal legislation on the matter, state regulation was allowed. There was a dissent, but the dissent argued that the federal government's commerce clause power always ruled, and so the issue of religion was not even really considered.

A final Sunday-closing law came in front of the Court in 1900, when, in *Petit v. Minnesota*, a law which closed only certain shops was considered. The law in question prohibited all labor, except that which was needed for the health of the community and "works of charity or necessity" (177 U.S. 164). But barbershops were specifically excluded from the "works of necessity." Thus, barbershops could be banned. The question here was whether the Court would allow the legislature the discretion to exclude barbershops from being considered works of necessity. The Court sided with the existing law, and barbershops remained closed. The issue of religion did not enter into the consideration. Clearly, at least some elements of Sunday-closing laws were widely assumed to be permissible. That was the last Sunday-closing law that came in front of the Court in the 1880-to-1925 period. In all of these Sunday-closing laws, it was clearly an act of the state being opposed by an individual (or an individual acting on behalf of his business) and so it was not a case of an individual versus another individual. This differs from current cases, which look at one individual balanced off against another.

Laws also dealt with the regulation and control of church property and things given to churches, as well as taxation. The first case that came in front of the Supreme Court in this period was *Gibbons v. District of Columbia* (1886), which concerned a federal law in Washington, D.C., that exempted church property from taxation but only if it was in current use. This was upheld in larger part as tax regulations, including exemptions, had been given wide latitude by previous Court decisions. Religion did not seem to be a primary concern. Finally, the Court dealt with a variety of other property concerns, including some that it seemed had no business even coming before the Supreme Court. For example, in one case, *Schwartz v. Duss* (1902), the Court had to consider whether a group could be forced to distribute its property when the group was still meeting and the people suing had never been part of the group. The Court held, not surprisingly, in favor of the group. Here, for the first time, the Court considered cases in which one individual sued another over constitutional rights. Although freedom of religion was not directly addressed, the very fact that the Court heard such cases of one individual versus another opened the gate for later cases in which individuals' religious rights came into conflict.

Most directly related to freedom of religion, the Court also considered what level of control religions could have over their own affairs. This is important because, besides their obvious religious concerns, religious groups also have many worldly concerns, such as paying bills. Quite often, a worldly and religious concern can become intermingled, and these issues have the potential to wind up in court. One such case in the 1880-to-1925 period developed in 1887, with *Speidel v. Henrici*. A gentleman had left a religious community association in the 1830s, but it retained a significant donation he had previously provided it. He came back in the 1880s to sue the group for abuse of power and of the terms of the donation. Although the case included some religious issues, those were never addressed as the Court held that the passage of time without a lawsuit barred recovery. Here again, the Court was effectively addressing a case of an individual versus another individual, and, in this case, religious issues were raised. Though these were not ultimately ruled upon, the fact that the Court heard the case set a precedent for it to hear future such cases.

Another such case was *Church of the Holy Trinity v. United States* (1892), which dealt with whether church hiring could be regulated. In this case, the Supreme Court ruled that Congress, in banning the hiring of foreign nationals, had not intended to include English priests. This eliminated the church's objection to the law and solved the problem without fully resolving whether Congress *could* limit such hiring in the future. This saw a return to the more conventional cases evaluating the relationship between government regulation and church entity. It shows that the Court, in this era, still clearly did not believe the federal First Amendment protected individuals or groups in anything like the modern sense.

However, the legislation from this era with the most long-term effect on freedom of religion actually related to antiradicalism. In addition to fears regarding the spread of anarchy leading up to World War I, the public developed increased desires for federal power. The American public increasingly feared communism as the war came to a close. Russia transformed into the Union of Soviet Socialist Republics, and, as the czars fell to communist rule, the American public became obsessed with the idea that communism would soon endanger the world.

America perceived World War I at the outset in Europe as a nineteenth-century war, nothing more than a struggle between competing European empires. And that was, in many ways, a correct view. However, that attitude posed problems for those who wanted American involvement, as America pictured itself as something different, above such ages-old territorial disputes. President Woodrow Wilson pledged that the United States would remain separate in word and deed, and most people, on the whole, believed that they were doing so. However, the war was not going well for either side, and the United States slowly got more involved. For a variety of reasons, the United States involvement favored Great Britain and France more than Germany (to look solely at the forces involved on the Western Front in France) and by 1917, U.S. involvement seemed imminent. However, President Wilson had run in 1916 on a platform of keeping the United States *out* of war. How could America and Wilson switch gears and stances so quickly from November 1916 (the presidential election) to April 1917, when the United States entered the war?

The answers produced, such as that Germany was now much more of a danger than it had been six months before or that America's honor would not permit itself being offended again, did not satisfy the average citizen, even those citizens who liked the idea of joining the effort and helping Great Britain and France win. Therefore, the American government developed force-based strategies to coerce a supportive attitude. As reason had been inadequate to quell dissent, dissenters were made into lawbreakers. The Selective Service Act of 1917 gave the government the power to raise an army. More than that, the Espionage Act of 1917, on its surface, sought to punish spies. But its vague wording meant that it really could be used to punish anyone who opposed the war. Finally, the Sedition Act of 1918 removed the element of intent-to-cause-harm needed under the Espionage Act, making antiwar speech very dangerous indeed.

The dragnet used by the Espionage and Sedition Acts had far-reaching impacts, with over 2,000 people indicted. And rather than purely targeting antiwar radicals, many of these indictments were used against people who were viewed as socially unacceptable for some reason. Whereas the Second Red Scare in the 1940s and 1950s would focus on leftists, this earlier movement had much broader applications. Anyone who said anything (or was even *thought* to have said anything) against the war could be indicted and convicted. In some cases, people even hired detectives to listen in on private conversations with the express rationale that those who were eventually arrested were a public danger precisely because of their secrecy. Their failure to make public statements was treated as a clear indication of their dangerous nature.

Six cases under the Espionage and Sedition Acts went all of the way to the Supreme Court. Importantly for history, these cases did not all occur in the same Court term (even though all were decided in the same year). In early 1919, the Supreme Court heard the first case under the Espionage Act, *Schenck v. United States*. Charles Schenck was a local leader of the Socialist Party who had printed thousands of pamphlets urging resistance to the draft. In level of danger, this seemed to be a case where the Espionage Act applied. However, Justice Oliver Wendell Holmes was by this time (as the war was already over) having doubts about the overall tenor of the war effort. Holmes thought that the government sometimes overreached and wanted to ban everything that might even possibly have a danger to the war effort. Holmes himself was a believer that the law evolved over time. Nearly 40 years before this, he had written, "The life of the law has not been logic; it has been experience."[2]

Holmes agreed with the case against Schenck and was given the job of constructing the majority opinion. He needed to set up a standard to determine when the government could restrict free speech and settled on allowing such restriction when a definite "clear and present danger" occurred, saying that certain utterances could be banned. He used his famous (and often misquoted) example that "falsely shouting 'fire' in a theater and causing a panic" would not be a protected statement.[3] The rest of the cases in early 1919 were along those lines, as a newspaper writer and Eugene Debs, Socialist leader and often presidential candidate, both had their convictions upheld.

However, Holmes came under criticism from Harvard law professor Zechariah Chafee in the period between the early 1919 Court cases and the later ones, and the nature of the cases changed by the end of 1919. During the next Court term, three more cases came before the Court, and by the end of 1919, Holmes had dissented in two of the decisions. His first dissent came in *Abrams v. United States*, which dealt not with prominent figures but with five Russian Jewish immigrants who were aiming to protest U.S. involvement in Russia. Holmes believed that the U.S. government was overreaching to convict them under the Espionage and Sedition Acts. However, the Court majority felt that the clear and present danger test presented by Holmes in *Schenck* controlled the determination. Holmes, in contrast, felt that these people did not present a danger and so should not have been arrested, let alone convicted. In his dissent, he might also have been trying to answer a previous complaint, that the *Schenck* ruling established only that Schenck was correctly arrested without presenting any guidelines for what kinds of speech *would* fall outside of the government's power. Thus, Holmes's dissent in *Abrams* may have represented an effort to present such guidelines. At the very least, he felt the convictions unwarranted and marked some things outside of government purview, both in general and when the need of the state was not great enough.

Joined by Louis Brandeis, he wrote:

> But, as against dangers peculiar to war, as against others, the principle of the right to free speech is always the same. It is only the present danger of immediate evil or an intent to bring it about that warrants Congress in setting a limit to the expression of opinion where private rights are not concerned. Congress certainly cannot forbid all effort to change the mind of the country. Now nobody can suppose that the surreptitious publishing of a silly leaflet by an unknown man, without more, would present any immediate danger that its opinions would hinder the success of the government arms or have any appreciable tendency to do so.[4]

Holmes went beyond that, though, to say that in general more speech was the answer, not less:

> Persecution for the expression of opinions seems to me perfectly logical. If you have no doubt of your premises or your power, and want a certain result with all your heart, you naturally express your wishes in law, and sweep away all opposition. To allow opposition by speech seems to indicate that you think the speech impotent, as when a man says that he has squared the circle, or that you do not care wholeheartedly for the result, or that you doubt either your power or your premises. But when men have realized that time has upset many fighting faiths, they may come to believe even more than they believe the very foundations of their own conduct that the ultimate good desired is better reached by free trade in ideas—that the best test of truth is the power of the thought to get itself accepted in the competition of the market, and that truth is the only ground upon which their wishes safely can be carried out. That, at any rate, is the theory of our Constitution. It is an experiment, as all life is an experiment.[5]

Essentially, this dissent argued for a free trade in ideas and an open area for people to freely discuss things. This concept was not clearly iterated in the Constitution, but as Holmes believed more in experience than permanent rules as a basis for the law, this should not surprise anyone. Of course, Holmes did not believe in a total freedom, just more freedom than the majority was willing to give to Abrams (and that the majority had been willing to give to Schenck in the original formulation). However, this did create some area of relatively unregulated space from the federal government, and this was seen as part of Americans' fundamental liberty.

This, however, was still a battle between the federal government and an individual. It also did not reach the states. Holmes's test here would also suggest that experience and rationality should be the underlying basis used, and one would wonder if Holmes would allow one individual to use his religion (which cannot be rationally proven) to clearly and illogically restrict the equality of another. This, also, was still a battle between the state and a person, rather than between two individuals, as is the case in most legal battles today that come under scrutiny of the First Amendment's freedom of religion, particularly in the most hotly contested areas.

If this was an area free from federal regulation, and if Americans were supposed to have some of the same liberties (in terms of freedom of restraint) from the state government as the federal government (through the Fourteenth Amendment), it would seem that a similar area should exist in terms of state regulations. The case cementing such a thought process, though, did not come to fruition until the 1920s, relating to a case that began in the 1910s.

In 1919, Benjamin Gitlow was the managing editor of *The Revolutionary Age*, a communist publication. He was arrested and charged with publishing an article called the "Left Wing Manifesto." While the level of interest curtailing radicals had increased after World War I, the state law he was charged under was passed in 1902. He was accused of aiming to overthrow the government of the state of New York in a violent manner. After his 1920 conviction, he was sentenced to a 5- to 10-year jail term. He served two years of it before being released on bond pending his appeal, and his case reached the U.S. Supreme Court in 1925. Although the Court upheld his conviction under a "bad tendency" test, where anything that might have a tendency to cause bad things to happen would be banned, its decision held enormous importance for the relationship between the federal First Amendment and the states. It ruled, "For present purposes we may and do assume that the rights of freedom of speech and freedom of the press were among the fundamental personal rights and 'liberties' protected by the due process clause of the Fourteenth Amendment from impairment by the states."[6]

Holmes and Brandeis dissented, holding that Gitlow did not present a "clear and present danger," which they held to be the correct test, not the bad tendency test. However, their dissent agreed that the First Amendment, as applied through the Fourteenth Amendment, *did* prevent the states from infringing on the freedom of speech, the freedom of the press, and other basic rights and liberties. Suddenly, the freedom of and from religion existed at a national level. States could no longer infringe on this basic right without violating the federal Constitution. In reality, this relationship would have to be tested, though, to be upheld by the Court.

Those arguing today for a so-called Religious Freedom Restoration Act want to restore, or at least reset, religious freedom to what it was at one time. One might want to return to 1925 as a baseline for religious freedom and restore the religious freedom to that level, with the states not allowed to restrict whatever religious freedom existed in 1925. Religious doctrines have greatly changed since then, but that level of religious freedom might be restored. That level would be low, though, as it did not include any protection of religion against state infringement, as the Fourteenth Amendment had not yet been applied against the states in the area of religion. Thus, this would probably not be the year, but if it was, and if any balancing needed to occur, we would need to balance that religious liberty off against what the people of the time thought about other rights. In terms of equality, the other side of the balance, that level was low too. The prevalence of the Ku Klux Klan in the 1920s should indicate that this was not a heyday of rights for African Americans and women. LGBT rights were not even considered and reproductive rights were at a low point. Thus, neither side in the debate would likely want to use the 1920s as the baseline. The rights of some groups would be difficult to balance as the ideas supporting their equality were not even fully considered yet.

This also points out that the current debate over religious exemptions is somewhat shifting the overall discussion, or attempting to. Politically powerful groups and corporations have generally not used the law and the First Amendment to accomplish their goals. It usually is the "little guy" or the minority religion, like the Jehovah's Witnesses or, in most instances, the Mormons. This is not to suggest that the Mormons have been the subject of more court cases but just that the Mormons are the majority in some places. Thus, the current use by corporations of the First Amendment to accomplish their goals (or the goals of their owners) is unique in American history in the area of religion.

Now, it should be stated that corporations did use the law to accomplish their goals, but that was more in the late nineteenth century when other parts of the Constitution were mostly used. The law in general has also changed to more protection of the individual since then. With this attempted shift back to defend some corporations and the religious goals of its Founders, America should ask itself multiple questions. First, does America want the rest of the law to shift back as well? Second, will this change on one part of the law force a change in other areas as well? Third, what is the point of the Constitution? Is it to protect the powerful or the relatively powerless? Fourth, how parallel are past battles, as most of those were a church against the government or an individual against the government, not an individual verses another individual? While some might argue that today's cases deal with corporations often, the way that corporations are winning is that corporations are being given rights because of their being treated as individuals.

CHAPTER FOUR

Sherbert and *Yoder*

While the 1925 *Gitlow v. People of New York* decision initiated the process that would end with the full application of the First Amendment, including the freedom of religion clause, against the states, change came slowly. After all, in an immediate sense, Benjamin Gitlow lost his case. The Court ruled on several cases related to the First Amendment in the next several years. But it had to test its own ability to enforce the Fourteenth Amendment against the states before it could delve more deeply into *how* the relationship worked. Then its focus shifted to address corporate concerns once more before finally being brought to bear on the First Amendment's relationship to state laws in the area of religion, in *Cantwell v. Connecticut* (1940).

Several cases which related to the First Amendment in areas other than religion but brought no immediate change to the status quo involved fears of communism. In 1927, the Supreme Court heard *Whitney v. California*, which tried someone for organizing a branch of the Communist Party and asked whether someone's free speech rights were affected by a general ban on the Communist Party. The Supreme Court held that they were not, although Justice Louis Brandeis wrote an eloquent concurrence arguing for free speech. It was nearly a dissent, but the doctrine allowing free speech had not fully evolved yet. The next major First Amendment case involving the states did not come until 1931, when the constitutionality of California's Red Flag laws was tested, as that state had banned the display of red flags, which it considered a sign of anarchism. The Supreme Court struck down the law in *Stromberg v. California*, because it was considered too vague. The opinion held that the law could criminalize legitimate activities. This was a significant case as it was the first time that the

Supreme Court had struck down a state law as a violation of the Fourteenth Amendment's liberty provisions. Both of these cases dealt with free speech, not freedom of religion, but the Supreme Court in *Gitlow*, as noted, had lumped all of the parts of the First Amendment together. Both of these cases, as well, were those of the individual versus the state, as the whole question of individual rights was being considered (although religion did not directly play a role).

The Supreme Court in the 1930s did not consider as many First Amendment cases as in more recent decades, because much of its attention was on economic issues. This shifted late in the 1930s for a couple of reasons. The first was, oddly enough, not directly related to freedoms at all but to government regulation. In the 1930s, government regulation on economic activity increased as an attempt to deal with the Great Depression. Until 1937, there was continued Supreme Court resistance to such regulation being constitutional. In that year, in *West Coast Hotel v. Parrish*, the Supreme Court upheld a minimum wage regulation, and that was the start of the end for Supreme Court opposition to general governmental regulation of the economy. This meant that relatively fewer such cases would be heard by the Supreme Court, opening up the docket for more cases on civil liberties. The standards were also switched. Before the 1930s, regulations of civil liberties were generally upheld and seldom made it to the Supreme Court and, conversely, economic regulations often made it to the Court and were struck down. After the 1930s, the reverse was true: civil liberties regulations were more often struck down while economic regulations were upheld.

This was codified in the 1938 *Carolene Products* decision. (It is technically *United States v. Carolene Products* but is better known as *Carolene Products*.) In perhaps the most famous footnote in Supreme Court history, Justice Stone wrote, contrasting specific areas of the Constitution to the general restraint that the Court was going to give, that "there may be narrower scope for operation of the presumption of constitutionality when legislation appears on its face to be within a specific prohibition of the Constitution, such as those of the first ten amendments, which are deemed equally specific when held to be embraced within the Fourteenth."[1]

The *Carolene Products* decision also raised the scrutiny level for laws which applied to specific parts of the first ten amendments. Among those types of legislation which were noted as perhaps needing extra scrutiny were those "directed at particular religious . . . minorities" and legislation showing "prejudice against discrete and insular minorities."[2] The footnote was more about suggesting areas of future inquiry and protection than noting areas which were being protected in the case at hand or at the present time. This somewhat opened up a whole new area of protected liberties, or more accurately, signaled to lawyers an area that the courts would be more interested in examining. This helped to lead to civil liberties cases in the late 1930s and the 1940s. This also is of current interest as the Supreme Court was protecting minorities. Most of those groups using the Religious Freedom Restoration Act are not usually thought of as minorities, in religious terms or otherwise.

While the *Gitlow* decision and the cases that it spawned worked their way through the courts, there were also a series of decisions being reviewed by the U.S. Supreme Court under the federal constitution. One of the more interesting areas in the 1925-to-1938 era was dealing with private schools. Part of contractual rights and charters in the late nineteenth and early twentieth centuries was the right to not be overly regulated by government. A charter, once granted, was supposed to be unalterable, but it could be changed in the public interest. The question, of course, was when such a change was allowed. In 1925, the Supreme Court decided *Pierce v. Society of Sisters*, which dealt with an Oregon law that required students to attend public school. The law was mostly aimed at getting rid of Catholic schools. This was struck down as a violation of the rights of private schools and was also seen as violating parents' right to raise their children how they pleased. Children's rights were not considered here, nor were religious issues, and thus it was only the issue of the state versus the parents in the area of charters. Two years later, in 1927, the Supreme Court ruled in *Farrington v. Tokushige*, which held that a law passed in a federal territory (in this case Hawaii) could not prohibit the teaching of a foreign language as it violated due process. Part of due process was that things which are not dangerous should not be universally banned. Both the owners of the schools and the parents were being seen as having been denied their due process rights. Obviously, both of these decisions touch on religion, in their impact, had the laws been allowed to stand, and in their purpose, although the Hawaii law was both a cultural and a religious statement. *Farrington*, like *Pierce*, did not consider the rights of the children and was also only the state versus the parents, not individuals versus individuals.

Religion also was a motivation for actions undertaken that resulted in lawsuits. For example, in *United States v. Schwimmer* (1929), the Supreme Court upheld the U.S. requirement that a person swear an oath to be willing to defend the country. The person in question was a pacifist and wanted to become a U.S. citizen. Oddly enough, as a woman, she could not be drafted but still was required to be willing to take up arms to defend the country. This was a 6–3 decision with Justices Oliver Wendell Holmes and Brandeis among the dissenters and noting that pacifist sects such as the Quakers had long existed in America. Oddly enough, unlike some other naturalization and immigration requirements, becoming a pacifist after becoming a citizen would have been allowed, whereas what Schwimmer did, in the other order, was not. Two 1931 decisions upheld this idea. Another decision in the same time period that dealt with conscientious objection was *Hamilton v. Regents of the University of California,* which dealt with the requirement that all males at a state university had to take training with the ROTC (Reserve Officer Training Corps), which trained men to be officers. It was held that this requirement did not violate one's right to due process. This case was decided more as an establishment clause case (did forcing one to take ROTC create a religion?) rather than as a free exercise case, which would seem to be more on point. These decisions all continued the trend of the decisions being about people trying to protect their own individual rights versus the state.

One trend that continued from the pre-1925 period and has continued up until the present is the desire of the Supreme Court to remain neutral in internal church disputes. In *Gonzalez v. Roman Catholic Archbishop* (1929), the Supreme Court ruled unanimously that it would not interfere in a church dispute over who should have been appointed to a church office.

Other civil liberties issues that have continued to the present day also arose in this period but were disposed of on different grounds than they would be later. A continuing issue is how much the state may help private schools (which are very often religious). In 1930, a case, *Cochran v. Louisiana State Board of Education,* came to the Supreme Court challenging the subsidization of private school textbooks but not on First Amendment grounds. It was challenged as a taking of private property, which should have been, in the eyes of the plaintiff, illegal under the Fourteenth Amendment (this was a state law). The program was upheld, though. Very few lawsuits on this basis have ever been upheld, as legal programs are generally allowed to be funded. The question in any case, courts hold, is whether the program is legal, not whether the tax to pay for it is illegal. Taxes, in turn, have to be challenged as illegal taxes, not as legal taxes for programs that people hold to be illegal. There is also obviously the question of whether the person can challenge the law, what is called *standing.* Those not directly affected by the law are not allowed to challenge it, particularly not when advocating against a tax to pay for a program (as was the case here). The legislature is given a wide berth to provide for programs that are otherwise constitutional.

Another cause of increased litigation was the rise of the Jehovah's Witnesses. The ideas of the Witnesses had been around since 1870 but moved into the courts only after the World War I period. World War I era draft cases for the Witnesses had not ended positively, but then again few groups had won in the courts and those that had received a favorable hearing from government tended to be long-established groups like the Quakers. Their increased prominence led to many different cases, and they serve as an example of a second point worth making.

Many groups (in fact most) that came in front of the court in the area of freedom of religion (and most in the area of freedom from religion) throughout history have been "disfavored groups," including groups like the Witnesses. They have not been groups that would win elections and gain power in the traditional way, and thus they have not been likely to be protected by the political process. That was part of Stone's point in *Carolene Products*, that "discrete and insular minorities," to use his phrase, needed more protection by the law as they were unlikely to find it any other way. However, recently, as will be seen later, those groups that are winning elections at the state and local levels have been using the courts as well.

In the late 1930s and early 1940s, the Jehovah's Witnesses frequently went to court. This was for a variety of reasons, including that they were some of the first who went door to door distributing religious literature. They also were a newer sect and so were not even as accepted as the Mormons. One of the early cases was *Cantwell v. Connecticut*, in 1940. This was the first time that the U.S. Supreme Court used the First Amendment to strike down a state statute dealing with religion as violating the freedom of religion clause. In that case, a city, New Haven, Connecticut, passed a licensing law which required people to get a license but then allowed city administrators to deny a license if the "cause did not seem to be in good faith," to quote one summary of the case.[3] The Court in *Cantwell* did not wholly deny the right of the state to regulate religion, but the state could not discriminate between religions or viewpoints. The state could regulate only time and place issues and could not ban a religion through those regulations. This is clearly again a case of an individual challenging a law of the state. (Cities are grouped with states legally and so are covered by the Fourteenth Amendment.) This is obviously different from modern cases dealing with one individual's rights in conflict with another's.

Tied in with the belief that religion should be treated in a nondiscriminatory fashion was the intersection between speech and religion. After all, a religious speech is both speech and religion. How do the two areas intersect? Distribution of religious literature is both freedom of the press and freedom of religion. Two of the first cases after 1925, which affected religious freedoms, and where the side favoring religious freedom had won, had that intersection. (As noted before, the Court dealt with several cases that looked at freedom of the press alone, but as this is a book on religion, they will not be considered here.) In *Lovell v. City of Griffin* (1938) and *Schneider v. State of New Jersey* (1939), the distribution of religious literature, in both cases by Jehovah's Witnesses, was at question. However, the Court disposed of both on freedom of the press grounds, holding that it was unconstitutional to require written permission. In this case, it did not matter whether the material was sold or given away—licensing was required for both instances. This licensing came from the state and city, as shown in the title of the cases.

Freedom of religion also came up in a variety of other cases. In the case of *Chaplinsky v. New Hampshire* (1942), a Jehovah's Witness was distributing literature and talking and a crowd gathered. The police did not protect Chaplinsky, but after a mob formed, the police arrested him. Upon his arrest, Chaplinsky insulted a policeman and he was arrested for using "offensive" words. Chaplinsky, rather than dealing with the religious elements, argued that the charge was vague. The Supreme Court, though, held that "fighting words" were outside of the protection of the First Amendment, similar to how libel and slander is. The definition of those terms would continue to be fought over, which proves that just because the Supreme Court holds something to be inside (or outside) of the First Amendment's protection does not end the issue. This also was a case between the city and the individual as it was a city official that arrested Chaplinsky.

One area dealt with in the earliest cases was the flag salute. With the prospect of World War II looming, many communities created flag salutes to foster national unity. These communities assumed that all patriotic Americans would be willing to honor the flag in this way. The Witnesses, however, believed that the flag was a graven image and that worshipping graven images was banned by their religion. (Christianity generally banned the worshipping of graven images, but different branches considered different things to be graven images.) An early case in that area was *Gobitis v. Minersville School District*, from 1940. While the case was important for the public due to the fact that World War II had started and the United States seemed poised to enter it, it had actually started long before. In 1935, forced flag salutes had been going on in Germany under the Nazis; the leader of the Jehovah's Witnesses, Joseph Rutherford, denounced the practice, and, in turn, a young man in Massachusetts named Carleton Nicholls refused to salute the flag. While some might think that a forced flag salute in the United States was different from that in Nazi Germany due to the different manner of saluting, it was not until the 1940s that the U.S. flag salute was done with the hand over the heart (except for the military), as it is today. In the 1930s, one saluted the flag with one's hand out, similar to the Nazis.[4] In Pennsylvania, just north of Pittsburg, in Minersville, Lillian and William Gobitis, one in fifth grade and one in seventh, decided to follow Carleton. The state had passed a flag salute statute but had not made the practice mandatory. The principal viewed their defiance as a threat to discipline and so pushed the school board to ban the practice. The school board attorney concluded that they could do this and so did it. The children were then expelled. They started attending a school solely for Jehovah's Witnesses children, and their parents got ready to appeal their sentence. The suit challenging the expulsion did not start until 1937.

In the federal district court, which did not decide the case until 1938, the Gobitis family won, but the school board appealed. At the circuit court level, the Gobitis family won again. In a twist of fate, this case almost did not go to the Supreme Court as the school system was thinking of dropping the case. However, patriotic groups wanted an appeal, believing that allowing students to not salute the flag would be a threat to law and order. This case was thus somewhat of a parallel to current cases with one group versus another (if you consider the Gobitis children a group), but freedom of religion was used to protect a set of rights rather than restrict another group's rights (unless you consider promoting law and order in a vague way a right). However, it was not a full parallel as it was a group versus a family, not an individual versus another individual. At the Supreme Court level, the school board (and the patriotic groups) won, and Justice Felix Frankfurter wrote an opinion arguing that the flag salute was more about patriotism than religion. While Frankfurter felt that religion had protection, religious beliefs do "not relieve the citizen from the discharge of political responsibilities."[5] The fact that these were children who did not yet have political responsibilities did not seem to enter much into the opinion. This was written, at least in part, with an eye toward what many expected would be America going to war in Europe or the Pacific and the belief that the nation needed to unite. Interestingly enough, Frankfurter quoted Justice Holmes as saying "We live by symbols" and ignored the fact that worshipping graven images as symbols was the exact thing that the Gobitis family was objecting to. There was one dissent—that of Justice Harlan Stone, who believed that religion should triumph—and it was an 8–1 decision.

The nation usually does not pay that much attention to most Supreme Court decisions but seemed to do so for this one. Perhaps it was also that the nation, like the Court, was paying attention to the storm clouds of war approaching and did not want any dissent. But the timing also indicates that there were some who saw the Court giving the public permission to attack the Witnesses and one report at the time noted that there were "hundreds" of attacks. This reaction caught some of the Court off guard, and the justices started to rethink their action. In a concurrence on the *Jones* decision (discussed later), three justices indicated a desire to reverse the *Gobitis* decision and that *Gobitis* had been wrong (even though all three had agreed with that decision at the time). Two new justices also joined the Court, and there were enough votes to hear a challenge to the law.

In the next flag case, *West Virginia State Board of Education v. Barnette* (1943), three Jehovah's Witnesses students from near Charleston refused to salute. Walter Barnette was the lead named plaintiff. This was a 6–3 decision for the students, which was quite a shift from the 8–1 decision the other way just three years prior. This issue had both freedom of speech and freedom of religion at play. The freedom of speech issue was whether anyone could be forced into a public physical display or whether speech included physical actions—if it did, then the freedom of speech should prevent the forced flag salute, as obviously freedom of speech also included the general right to remain silent and not have speech forced. The Court here focused on the freedom of speech issue, but its language also applied to religion. However, this case was clearly between a state entity (the board of education) and a set of individuals. Thus, it was not really in parallel to modern cases in that those are usually (especially when they are controversial) between one individual and another, with religion being used to justify one individual's treatment of another.

Frankfurter had argued for allowing patriotism to be forced in 1940. But three years later, the war tide was turning in favor of the Allies and people were also beginning to wonder how much freedom should be restricted in order to win freedom abroad, at least in some areas of life. Justice Robert Jackson wrote the main opinion and, in response to Frankfurter and others' arguments that this was needed, looked back to the Civil War and noted that "it may be doubted whether Mr. Lincoln would have thought that the strength of government to maintain itself would be impressively vindicated by our confirming power of the State to expel a handful of children from school."[6] Jackson also answered the argument that the Supreme Court should not run every school and that the local boards would prevent abuses by noting that "there are village tyrants, as well as village Hampdens [referring to John Hampden, a hero in the English Civil War], but none who acts under color of law is beyond reach of the Constitution."[7] Finally, Jackson turned to the whole issue of what should protect American liberties. Should it be the Supreme Court, as Jackson was arguing, or should it be the legislatures, which the Court (under Frankfurter) had held only three years earlier in *Gobitis?* Jackson answered his own question by holding that the answer had been given at the start of the Constitution and that the only way the Bill of Rights would stand was to have the courts involved. "The very purpose of a Bill of Rights was to withdraw certain subjects from the vicissitudes of political controversy, to place them beyond the reach of majorities and officials, and to establish them as legal principles to be applied by the courts. One's right to life, liberty, and property, to free speech, a free press, freedom of worship and assembly, and other fundamental rights may not be submitted to vote; they depend on the outcome of no elections."[8] This might seem to be a ringing defense of individual liberty, and it was, but only against the power of the state.

This forcibly removed from political consideration the liberties of the country and pointed out that one should not have to worry about who controlled the legislature in order to enjoy one's liberties. After noting this, Jackson turned to some regimes in history which had tried to create national unity through compulsion and failed. He wrote:

> Probably no deeper division of our people could proceed from any provocation than from finding it necessary to choose what doctrine and whose program public educational officials shall compel youth to unite in embracing. Ultimate futility of such attempts to compel coherence is the lesson of every such effort from the Roman drive to stamp out Christianity as a disturber of its pagan unity, the Inquisition, as a means to religious and dynastic unity, the Siberian exiles as a means to Russian unity, down to the fast failing efforts of our present totalitarian enemies. Those who begin coercive elimination of dissent soon find themselves exterminating dissenters.[9]

Jackson was saying here that the very goal of unity would be corrupted and that instead of unity all you would achieve was tyranny.

Jackson closed with one of the most stirring defenses of individual liberty the Court has ever issued. He wrote, "If there is any fixed star in our constitutional constellation, it is that no official, high or petty, can prescribe what shall be orthodox in politics, nationalism, religion, or other matters of opinion, or force citizens to confess by word or act their faith therein."[10]

Frankfurter, in response to Jackson, retreated back to his original defense of the power of the state to promote unity and general judicial deference. In his dissent he noted his own sympathy, that "one who belongs to the most vilified and persecuted minority in history [i.e., Jews] is not likely to be insensible to the freedoms guaranteed by our Constitution. Were my purely personal attitude relevant, I should wholeheartedly associate myself with the general libertarian views in the Court's opinion, representing, as they do, the thought and action of a lifetime. But, as judges, we are neither Jew nor Gentile, neither Catholic nor agnostic."[11] As far as religious freedom, though, he held it to be limited, noting, "The constitutional protection of religious freedom terminated disabilities, it did not create new privileges. It gave religious equality, not civil immunity. Its essence is freedom from conformity to religious dogma, not freedom from conformity to law because of religious dogma."[12] This debate in many ways is still going on today—when does religious freedom end and when can one be forced to conform to law in spite of religious ideas. These cases, like most others in the early years of the application of the First Amendment to the states, were between individuals and the government, not two sets of individuals. These cases also, as the Court noted in *Barnette*, did not interfere with anyone else's rights (besides those forced to salute the flag)—it was merely whether or not the government could force one to salute the flag. The pledge in question did not contain the words "under God," which many might expect religious dissenters to object to—that was not added until the 1950s as part of a larger anticommunist crusade.

Jackson, with his opinion in the *Barnette* case, started the discussion that continues to this day in terms of what the nation should do when an individual's rights collide with other interests. While in *Barnette* it was a stated national interest, it today is the interests of those who want their marriages and personal relations treated the same as another's. In *Barnette*, Jackson stated that the state cannot compel belief, but today the nation faces another question. It is at what point, or whether, the state can compel equal treatment when that treatment conflicts with an individual's beliefs?

Refusal to salute the flag also came in front of the Supreme Court via a conviction for advocating refusal to salute the flag, in *Taylor v. Mississippi* (1943). Mississippi had passed a law making it illegal to advocate not saluting the flag, and the Supreme Court struck down this law. The Court held that while doing something with an evil purpose might be banned, merely communicating ideas and beliefs could not be held to be illegal.

Jehovah's Witnesses also came in front of the Court because of their treatment by local authorities. Many places did not want Witnesses to go door to door in their community and so passed a wide variety of local ordinances. Some were blatantly discriminatory and aimed against the Witnesses while others were more neutral in their application, and still others simply banned all people going door to door. One case in the early 1940s was *Jones v. City of Opelika* [Alabama]. Here, a black man was arrested under a city ordinance that prohibited the selling of books without a license, and these licenses could be revoked at any time. The license was required whether the books were commercial or religious. The requirement was probably what allowed the license to be upheld as the Court ruled that religious activity, when it was commercial, could still be regulated as commercial activity. This decision, in 1942, stood only for a year, as in 1943 another case was heard. That case, *Murdock v. Pennsylvania*, held that Jehovah's Witnesses did not have to apply for a license. It did not overrule licenses in general but just held that the First Amendment's nature of the activity (selling religious material door to door) was more important than the selling part and that the Jehovah's Witnesses' First Amendment rights were overly restricted by the regulation. Both of these cases were a municipality versus an individual.

Another Jehovah's Witnesses case also came from Alabama, in *Marsh v. Alabama* (1945). There, a white woman had been arrested in a company-owned town, which added a complicating factor, as the company had posted a notice prohibiting solicitation. The Witnesses suggested that the notice had been posted solely against them. The Supreme Court held for Marsh, noting that just because this was a company town did not mean that the town could trample upon people's constitutional rights. Even in company towns, "the channels of communication (should) remain free," wrote the Court.[13]

World War II and the subsequent Cold War also greatly affected religion and governmental treatment of it. Many who were conscientious objectors were widely dismissed as un-American. The issue of whether conscientious objectors should be penalized was in question in *In Re Summers*, a case from Illinois (1945). Illinois required all members of the bar to be willing to serve in the state militia, something Clyde Summers was not able to do as he was a conscientious objector. The federal government had granted Summers conscientious objector status, but the state was not willing to accommodate. In a close vote, 5–4, the Supreme Court upheld Illinois's holding. Pacifists of established religions had long had accommodations given by the draft, but one question here was whether or not they were required in general and another was whether state privileges, like the right to practice law, were guaranteed. The dissent pointed out that Illinois had not drafted people into a state militia since 1864 and that whole religions, like the Quakers, would be removed from the state bar if this were upheld (and widely applied). Summers later moved to New York State, was admitted to the bar, and became a leading expert in the area of labor law. This case, like all the ones before, pitted an individual against the state.

The Cold War and World War II also played a larger role in the issue of equality and religion. First, the Cold War, particularly in the area of race, convinced the U.S. government that it needed to publicly commit itself to the cause of equality. In order to convince the newly emerging nations around the world that America believed in racial equality, the U.S. government needed to identify itself prominently with the idea of human rights. Second, World War II caused many to think about who deserved equality and the bulwarks of society that were used in the past to prevent equality of all. The court system came into play defending the equality of all with the case of *Brown v. Board of Education* (1954), which declared racial segregation of public schools unconstitutional. The Supreme Court, J. R. Pole writes, "endowed on American society an obligation to put to an end the manifold practices which had made separation an institutionalized ingredient of American life."[14] Of course, what creates separation and when that creates inequality continues to be debated.

This issue repeatedly came in front of the courts. Some rose out of World War II, which had more support than previous wars from the populace, but the support was not universal. With more than 10 million people serving (and many more classified by the draft system), even a tenth of a percent who challenged their classifications would constitute 10,000 cases in the system. Ministerial exemptions were established but were administered by civilian boards in order to make sure that only legitimate claims were upheld. As in later wars, one way that some non-ministers avoided the draft was to enroll in seminaries and other ministerial training schools. (The majority of those in such schools in all wars have been legitimate students, particularly so in World War II.) As with the overall support for the war, the number of fraudulent students was also lower in World War II for a variety of reasons. In *Eagles v. Samuels*, a student had enrolled in 1941 in a ministerial training school and then apparently not attended again until his exemption was revoked. He challenged the revocation on a number of grounds, but freedom of religion was not one of them. It was suggested in the opinion that both his actions and the overall school might have been a scam to get out of the military. The student lost his case. Even though the area was different than previous cases, the same types of parties were involved—the state (in this case the federal government and the selective service system) and an individual.

At times the conscientious objection issue mixed religion and other constitutionally protected issues. For instance, a case in 1950, *Gara v. United States*, mixed free speech with the freedom of religion issue. While the Supreme Court, as it was equally divided, was only upholding a lower court ruling, the lower court held that while a person might believe that it was his duty to resist the draft, he could not counsel others to do the same. This is one of the few areas where someone can do a legal act but not counsel another to do the same. Part of this might be due to the fact that a conscientious objection to war is supposed to be something that someone comes to over time and is a belief that remains over time, though not something quickly arrived at.

Conscientious objectors returned to the courts in the 1950s in several cases. Two in 1953 and 1955 focused on tangential issues. In one, the main issue was what amount of material is the U.S. government required to produce at hearings on conscientious objectors. The court held that the U.S. government is not required to produce everything, and the issue of freedom of religion did not appear to come up. The other concerned the level of pacifism required for a conscientious objector application. A Jehovah's Witness said that he was willing to fight, and so the system denied him a deferral, but the system ignored the fact that he was willing to fight only with spiritual weapons and only in a spiritual war. However, in 1955, two convictions were reversed because the government failed to provide defendants sufficient evidence from the FBI case files for national security reasons. In all of these, other than the Jehovah's Witness case, the religion issue was not directly reached. The year 1955 was the last time a conscientious objector case reached the Supreme Court until 1965, in the *Seeger* case.

The Cold War did play a role in another case, though, with the Supreme Court considering a test oath in the early 1950s. In California, Los Angeles required an oath of loyalty to the government in order for a church to receive a tax exemption. As some churches are pacifist and some oppose oaths in general, this would seem to be discrimination, as certain churches would receive tax exemptions and others would not. The Supreme Court agreed and struck down the requirement.

Polygamy also returned to the courts in a variety of ways in the late 1940s. These were not direct challenges to whether or not polygamy was illegal but more discussions of when polygamy led to violations of other laws. In 1946, the Supreme Court had to consider whether having someone in a polygamous marriage, even if presented as a "celestial marriage" (i.e., one that is religious without state recognition), allowed for a kidnapping charge, and the Court held that there was no evidence that the wife was being held against her consent and so it was not a kidnapping. However, the next year, in *Cleveland v. United States* (1946), convictions under the Mann Act, which held it illegal to entice a woman to go across state lines for immoral purposes, were upheld in cases where women moved in order to have polygamous marriages. Thus, this was not kidnapping, but one could be convicted under the Mann Act. Even in the cases of the Mann Act, the only parties considered were the state and the people involved, as the woman involved did not have her rights considered.

Sunday-closing laws came in front of the Supreme Court in 1961 with several cases and then dropped off the Supreme Court's radar, it seems, after that. In 1961, the main case was *McGowan v. Maryland*, which looked at a law banning certain kinds of business on Sundays. The Court differentiated between the law's origins, which were to promote church attendance on Sunday, and the law's current purpose, which was, in the eyes of the Court, to promote a uniform day of rest. Several companion cases were heard at the same time, including *Braunfeld v. Brown*, which argued that the law's effect discriminated against Jews, as Jews who were practicing took Saturday (sundown Friday to sundown Saturday, technically) as a day of religious rest and the laws thus forced observant Jews to close their businesses for two days as opposed to one for Christians (observing or not). The Supreme Court in *Braunfeld* held that the purpose was now secular, as it forced people to take one day off, and so any burden that resulted was acceptable. In dissent, Justice Harlan argued that the law interfered with a free exercise of religion and so should be struck down. His, however, was the only vote. Three other dissenting votes argued that the overall burden should be balanced off against the state's gain and stated goal, which foreshadows future balancing tests. Thus, only four justices voted to uphold it as a whole, but it was allowed as those in dissent could not agree on what parts of the law violated the Constitution. Once again, though, this balancing was between the state's interest and the individual's, not an individual's versus another individual's.

Licensing of religious tracts and religious proselytization continued to be a big issue before the Supreme Court. Licensing laws generally did not fare well before all courts in this era. In 1951, two licensing laws were struck down. The first fell because the Supreme Court held that it did not have clear criteria about when a speech would be allowed and when it would not and so was arbitrary. The second allowed local officials discretion over the permits and so was struck down. Licensing returned to the Supreme Court in 1953 in two cases. In one, a regulation allowed for a religious service but prohibited any religious speeches. This thus forced regulators to decide what was a religious speech and what was religious services and was struck down as being discriminatory. In another case, *Poulous v. New Hampshire*, a regulation was allowed that required payment of a sliding fee for a permit as it was not discriminatory and did not allow local officials any room for discrimination. Again, this was a case of the state versus the individual.

Religious property appeared before the Court along with the question of who would control internal church affairs. This tied in with the Cold War. As New York State wanted to remove foreign Soviet influence, it passed a law recognizing the local church structure in the United States, rather than the Russian Orthodox Church, headquartered in the Soviet Union (while the Soviet Union banned religion, the Russian Orthodox Church still managed to have its headquarters located there), as the controlling agent. As the international body had not renounced that control, this was not allowed by the U.S. Supreme Court in *Kedroff v. Saint Nicholas Cathedral* (1952). Eight years later, the issue returned to the Supreme Court as the State Court of Appeals had allowed what was originally forbidden by the Supreme Court. Regardless of who ordered it, the U.S. Supreme Court was not going to allow the state to interfere with the internal affairs of the church.

Potential religious fraud was considered as part of the freedom of religion issue. In *United States v. Ballard* (1944), the question was whether or not a jury could consider either the truth of a religious belief or the sincerity of the religious belief. Both are obviously problematic. This case arose from the I AM movement, which believed in reincarnation and the wife and son of the founder were indicted for asking for donations. They were convicted and appealed, and their convictions were overturned as the truth of a religious belief was held to be in the religious realm by the Supreme Court. The question of how sincere a religious belief is, the Supreme Court suggested, should be allowed to go to the jury. As the convictions were on the basis of the truth of a religious belief (and the sincerity), the case was sent back down to the Circuit Court of Appeals, and the conviction was upheld. After that, the conviction was challenged again on nonreligious grounds and it was overturned. Here, the case might seem parallel to the present with one individual's belief against another, but it was a federal trial on fraud charges, rather than someone trying to sue based on fraud.

In the early 1950s, a new chief justice was appointed to the Supreme Court, and he would come to greatly reshape both civil liberties and how the U.S. justice system treated them. Earl Warren would seem to be an odd candidate to promote human rights based on his political background, but he did just that. Warren had been involved early on in antiradical efforts after he joined the prosecutor's office, and he backed the effort in World War II to imprison Japanese Americans. This detention and subsequent internment came while he was attorney general of California. Once Warren became chief justice in 1954, his attention was on other matters, but he did turn to defend civil liberties. His first case concerning civil liberties was *Yates v. United States*, in 1957, which dealt with what level of freedom should be given to those in the Communist Party. Previously, anyone who had been in the Communist Party was subject to possible arrest, but the *Yates* decision allowed advocacy of illegal ideas, as long as that advocacy was theoretical. Thus, people could join the Communist Party (or other disfavored groups) as long as they did not advocate for any illegal acts to be performed. Much of the Court's cases in the latter part of the 1950s did not touch on individual freedoms. The 1960s, though, saw a different story.

Both individual freedoms and those touching on the freedom of religion (and the freedom from religion) were handled in the 1960s. Unlike today, the most controversial cases concerned the establishment of religion issue. Bible reading in school had long been contentious and had been adopted in the 1840s and 1850s in part to make sure that any Catholic in the schools would be exposed to a Protestant Bible. Catholics for their part frequently established their own schools, thus somewhat defeating the original goal. Some battles turned so intense that all mandatory Bible reading was cancelled in public schools. A second wave of Bible-reading promotion was started in some places in the 1950s. Once again, the concern was not morality, but politics, as the goal was to prove to Americans that no one supported communism. The idea was that the best proof that one was not a communist was that one was a Christian, or at least religion. All communists were supposed to be atheists under this theory, and the only answer to atheism, the idea further held, was religion. Some protested the idea in the 1960s, but few had in the 1950s, as no one wanted to be associated in any way with anything that smelled of communism. In addition to Bible reading, some states, including New York, added school prayer, and the New York State Board of Regents came up with a suggested prayer. This led to *Engle v. Vitale*, in 1962, which struck down the school prayer. President Kennedy urged the nation to support the Court's ruling. Kennedy had remarked that, in the words of one biographer of Warren, "Americans should go to church and pray there and at home, not in school."[15] This was important as the Supreme Court had been embattled in the 1950s ever since it had issued the *Brown v. Board* decision, and the arch-conservative John Birch Society regularly erected billboards urging people to "Impeach Earl Warren." While national criticism was somewhat muted, and there were no serious attempts to impeach Warren, many in the nation still criticized (and criticize) the Supreme Court for "taking God out of the public schools"; even though religion was not the real reason behind putting prayer and Bible readings into many of the public school systems, anticommunism was.

In 1963, the Supreme Court followed this up by striking down a law requiring the start of the school day with a reading of Bible verses, in *Abington Township v. Schempp.* In both cases, the state was not supposed to take a stand on religion. By the 1960s, the idea of a "wall of separation" between church and state was growing clear. The strengthening of this wall led to increased personal freedom of religious choice for many, as the state avoided taking a direct stand on which religion was best. That idea of a wall of separation came from Jefferson's letter to the Danbury Baptists. While this caused a lot of opposition, the nineteenth century (as noted in Chapter 2) shows the wisdom of this approach of creating the wall of separation. A lack of separation resulted in the Bible Riots of the 1840s and a great deal of religious tension.

Another case in the 1960s that dealt with state-established religion was *Epperson v. Arkansas,* from 1968. This case dealt with an anti-evolution law that Arkansas had put into effect in the 1920s. The law had been rarely enforced but was tested by Susan Epperson, a teacher of biology at Little Rock High School. Instead of trying to remove the law, the state defended it, and the case ended up in the U.S. Supreme Court. There, the justices struck down the law, holding that the state cannot pick which religion to favor, which it was clearly doing through the law. None of these dealt with freedom of religion, but the cases do show that religion was frequently in front of the Supreme Court.

These cases in the 1950s and 1960s dealt with the freedom-from-a-religious-establishment part of the First Amendment. This was also the more controversial part of the 1960s, as many religious conservatives charged the Warren Court with removing God from America. However, there were also cases in the 1950s and 1960s that dealt with the freedom-of-religion part of the First Amendment, which is the focus of this book.

With the Vietnam War, the issue of the draft became critical in the 1960s again. Many religions express opposition to war, and so many religious people feel that they should not be forced to serve in the military. However, the 1960s saw the question of whether this view should be moved beyond traditional religion, or perhaps beyond religion at all, and whether the First Amendment allows this distinction. The *Seeger* decision also notes how one must be careful not to assign too much significance to the timing of a case, particularly in terms of why it was brought. The *United States v. Seeger* case was decided in 1965, just as the Vietnam War was heating up. One might assume that this request for an exemption was somewhat related to the Vietnam War as the United States was nearly two years into heavy involvement. Daniel Seeger, however, had started his process in 1957, in the middle of the Eisenhower Administration and while the United States was relatively uninvolved, especially in terms of the traditional military, overseas. Seeger basically informed his draft board that he refused to sign up for the draft as he had "concluded that war, from the practical standpoint, is futile and self-defeating, and that from the more important moral standpoint, it is unethical."[16] That request, though, mentioned nothing about religion, and in response to a separate question, Seeger defended "his 'religious faith in a purely ethical creed.'"[17] This was not a spur of the moment or a whim, as best can be told. Seeger attached a seven-page justification for his views and cited a wide variety of thinkers in his answers.

Seeger lost his case at the bottom two adjudication levels of the draft system, won at the hearing board, lost in U.S. District Court, and then won at the Appeals Court level in the Second Circuit Court of Appeals. One difference between the U.S. District Court and the 2nd Circuit was how each court read the previous *Torcaso v. Watkins* case of 1961.

Torcaso dealt with a Maryland law that required the swearing of belief in a Supreme Being in order to hold governmental office. A notary sued to get a commission and the Supreme Court in *Torcaso* held that the law placed the government on the side of one type of believers, those who believed in a Supreme Being, and against all others, and thus struck it down as a violation of the establishment clause.

There was a question on the draft form that asked if the applicant believed in a Supreme Being, and Seeger's lawyer tried to argue that that question was illegitimate based on *Torcaso*. The District Court read *Torcaso* narrowly and held that as draft exemptions were not required, the U.S. government could give them to whoever it wanted to (and thus withhold it from whoever wanted). The Appeals Court, however, held that religious sincerity, not a specific belief, was the key and that there was no doubt that Seeger was religiously sincere. The Appeals Court struck down the Supreme Being test.

The case then went to the Supreme Court, which took a very narrow view but still upheld Seeger's exemption from the draft. The Supreme Court thus ruled the same way as the Appeals Court but for quite a different reason. The higher court decided to keep the Supreme Being test but to read Seeger's application fairly broadly. The decision, written by Justice

Tom Clark, held that Seeger's ideas "occupy the same place in his life as the belief in a traditional deity holds in the lives of his friends, the Quakers."[18] The logic was that since the belief occupied the same place as a belief in a Supreme Being, it was parallel enough for the test to be upheld and for Seeger to meet it. Outside influences may have played a role here, as antiwar opposition was heating up and the Court did not want to create a completely new way for people to oppose the draft or try to avoid it. They might have been seen as doing this by ruling in Seeger's favor, but the justices seemed to be trying to satisfy both sides by helping Seeger while still ruling that one had to be religious in order to get a draft exemption. Thus, even though Seeger was not motivated by Vietnam, the decision in his case may have been shaped by it. However, this case clearly was one of the government versus the individual.

One reason why there is not that much attention paid currently to the military and religion is that there is no draft and no prospect to reinstate one. While there is a Selective Service System and men turning 18 years of age must register, there is little if any support to revive the draft. Calls for this move during the Iraq and Afghan wars in the 2000s and 2010s met with resounding silence.

Many other cases about religious freedom came up in the 1960s, and they had a significant impact on future debates. Among them was *Sherbert v. Verner* (1963). This case dealt with unemployment compensation. Adeil Sherbert was a Seventh Day Adventist who worked Monday through Friday for a corporation. She worked successfully, but the corporation moved from a five-day workweek to a six-day week (including Saturdays). Adeil refused to work on Saturdays due to her religion. She was fired and, once fired, she was denied unemployment compensation as that compensation was only for people who were willing to work. The requirement of work allowed exemptions for anyone who had "good cause" to not work. In the mind of the state, her reason did not amount to good cause. (The state did limit the good cause exemption to religion, but Sherbert's reasoning was not compelling to the state.) The Supreme Court held that this denial of unemployment compensation was a substantial burden on her religion and that there was no compelling state interest that required the rule. The only governmental interest here was preventing abuse of the unemployment system, as claims for exemptions that were without merit would cost the system extra monies. This case created what came to be known as the *Sherbert* test, requiring a compelling state interest where a law substantially burdened a religion.

This test stayed largely in place for laws infringing on the freedom of religion for the next 27 years, from 1963 to 1990, when *Employment*

Division v. Smith (also sometimes called *Oregon v. Smith*) was decided. In many ways, the test created in *Sherbert* is still the core of the debate, as it has become enshrined in the Religious Freedom Restoration Act, and many people seem to think of it as the correct test today. (More discussion of the act and the test will come in a later chapter, but it bears mentioning here.) However, this case clearly was one of one individual versus a government rule. Most cases today, which some people argue should apply the Sherbert test, are those of one person's rights versus another's. *Sherbert*, though, is not parallel to the cases dealt with today. There is no indication that Adeil Sherbert was trying to shape the behavior of another person or to justify her treatment of another person because of her religion. Even if the *Sherbert* test is the right one for determining when an individual's religion can be burdened in pursuit of a general governmental objective, it does not mean that it is the right one for determining when one person's freedom of religion outweighs another person's right to equality (or any other individual right).

Another case dealing with regulations of religiously motivated behavior was *Wisconsin v. Yoder* (1972), a case dealing with Amish school children in Wisconsin. Local school officials in Wisconsin wanted them in school, in large part because the amount of funding a district received, as in other states, was dependent on the number of pupils attending. There was also a mandatory attendance law, but it is suggested that this was of less concern for those at the local level. The issue also came to a head in the 1960s, with new Amish families moving into the area. There had been mandatory attendance laws before, but high school was relatively new for all. Without high school being mandatory, Amish parents who wanted their children to stop attending after the eighth grade had no problem pulling their children as that was when school ended anyway.

It was more than a few families' decision to pull their children out of school which prompted this issue. On the one side, local school districts wanted the children in school to receive funding, and they also wanted to enforce uniform rules. It was feared that if an exception was made in this one case, there would be a flood of requests. On the other side, groups opposing state education supported the Amish. The leader, for instance, of the coalition that funded the case was a Lutheran minister. Caught in the middle were the Amish, who were bombarded by both those who wanted mandatory school attendance and those who wanted to weaken state education. The Amish also as a group opposed using the law to solve differences. Even in the most scholarly accounts of the trial, the Amish voice is mostly silent, such as in Shawn Francis Peters's *The Yoder Case: Religious Freedom, Education and Parental Rights*.[19] The children at question never had their views directly asked at all. The state was not requiring the students to attend the state school but just to attend some school, and other Amish children were attending a school set up by the Amish on a farm. This became a case only because Yoder's children (and a few others) refused to attend the Amish school and because the state wanted all the Amish children (including those who attended the Amish school) back in the state school. Two lower courts upheld the verdict, and then it headed to the Wisconsin and U.S. Supreme Courts. The state court ruled that the parents' religious freedom was being infringed and so held for them. That court was guilty of a bit of hyperbole, holding that "the impact (of forcing schooling) may result in the extermination of their religious community."[20] However, the court ignored that alternative schooling was already available for the students and even being used by some. The one dissent noted this and commented that the majority "completely ignores the personal liberties of the Amish children to avail themselves of educational opportunities beyond eighth grade."[21] Four justices (of the six in the majority) did join a concurrence, which basically limited the ruling solely to the Amish.

Wisconsin appealed and the U.S. Supreme Court held that the state had not demonstrated enough of a compelling interest to restrict the Amish's religious freedom by requiring the extra two years (after eighth grade) of schooling. Justice William Douglas partially dissented in noting that the children had not been considered, but Chief Justice Warren Burger's majority opinion noted that the children were not the ones arrested. While that is true, it did not follow that their interests were not relevant.

One author summarized Yoder thus: "Their [the Amish's] victory was important because it acknowledged a communal exemption. The Amish as a longstanding and serious religious community were granted a constitutional exemption. In other words, the courts acknowledged a religious group's communal character and on behalf of the state found a constitutional claim of free exercise against Wisconsin's compulsory school attendance laws."[22] *Yoder* is thus one community (the Amish) against the larger society. That is wholly different from today's battles, which are one individual (or one corporation as the extension of that individual) versus another individual in a question of which person's individual rights will be allowed to triumph.

As some commentators have noted, the respectable nature of the Amish, their quiet ways, and their simple request to educate their children the way they want to helped to gain public sympathy for their cause (even though such factors are not supposed to be part of constitutional analysis). In an interesting twist, Yoder himself left Wisconsin and headed to Missouri, due in large part to the notoriety that came from the decision—notoriety that most Amish would not have wanted as the Amish shun attention as prideful.

By the end of the 1960s, and by the time of *Yoder*, understanding of human rights had increased. Civil rights, legally, had largely reached their current legal level, and public support had increased for those rights as well. Women's rights had been increased with the Civil Rights Act of 1964 but had not reached their current level. Reproductive rights would soon be increased, with the *Roe v. Wade* decision of 1973 (and in some ways were then above the level that they are at in the present). However, contraceptive technology was different in 1970 compared to in 2016. In the area of the rights of the disabled and those who need accommodation, many different rights have been added since 1970, including the Americans with Disability Act of 1990. The largest change, however, came in the area of LGBT rights, as the late 1960s and early 1970s saw the start of the civil rights progress for that group. Thus, if society is going to return to 1970 as the baseline for religious freedom, LGBT groups would greatly lose rights, and those rights are ones favored by most people. Such a loss would be devastating to that community.

During the 1960s, many civil rights acts were passed and at least one came to have a direct impact on religion. This was the 1964 Civil Rights Act, which forbade discrimination on the basis of religion but allowed some exceptions. One was for a religious corporation. Bette Evans writes, "Congress recognized the special needs of religious institutions to take religion into account in making employment decisions. Hence, Section 720 of the Civil Rights Act provides that these prohibitions shall not apply 'to a religious corporation, association or society with respect to the employment of individuals of a particular religion to perform work connected with the carrying on of such corporation, association or society of its activities.'"[23] However, courts have generally given more leeway to these organizations when religious functions of the corporation are involved. However, the corporation needed to be religious. A regular corporation, however held, was outside of that section.

As the 1980s began, the issue of religious exemptions that got its start with *Sherbert* and *Yoder* moved to take center stage. It gained prominence first though by their being denied, rather than their continued use.

CHAPTER FIVE

Smith, RFRA, and Its Limitations (1980–1995)

An overview of religious freedom from 1980 to 1995 starts with President Ronald Reagan, as he reinjected religion into politics, and his appointees were important in shaping many of the religion cases to follow, both those of the free exercise variety (considered in this book) and those of the establishment variety (generally not considered here). This was a fairly busy decade and a half for the Supreme Court, although free exercise clauses were not the top religious issues to get billing. Among the individual religious freedom issues considered were unemployment compensation, literature distribution, conscientious objections, taxes (in several different forms), and religious practices. The topic winds up with the ban on peyote in Native American faith practices that resulted in the *Smith* case and then finally with the federal Religious Freedom Restoration Act (RFRA) of 1993. The RFRA enacted the standard associated with *Yoder* and *Sherbert,* both of which held that religious freedom could be restricted only when there was a compelling governmental objective and the means used was the least restrictive. However, this balancing was in terms of a compelling government objective.

The distribution of literature might have been thought to have been settled in previous cases, including *Marsh v. Alabama* (1946) and *Jamison v. Texas* (1943), but it still came in front of the Supreme Court. In 1981, the Supreme Court considered the case of *Heffron v. International Society for Krishna Consciousness,* whose adherents are also sometimes known as the Hari Krishnas. The Minnesota State Fair wanted to limit the society to its booth and not allow them to freely roam distributing literature. The limits were on sales or distribution of literature, as well as requirements that fairgoers first show interest before the society spoke to them. The majority, in a narrow decision, upheld the regulations. A dissent argued that the regulations on sales were reasonable as an antifraud measure but that distribution should be allowed as with other groups, including political candidates, who were allowed to roam and speak. One dissent, authored by Justice Brennan, thought that the regulations were not "narrowly tailored" enough to accomplish the government's stated objective. It should also be noted that the society was willing to wear name tags and to only approach those who showed interest, and thus the debate was over what type of regulations, not whether or not to regulate.

The Hari Krishnas returned to the Supreme Court some 11 years later (1992) in two cases, both dealing with the same set of ordinances. In this case, the question was what restrictions an airport terminal could place on the distribution of literature and on solicitation of funds. The court below had split in who won and so the cases were *Lee v. International Society for Krishna Consciousness* and *International Society for Krishna Consciousness v. Lee*. This was also a narrow decision and the society won again (in one case) while losing in the other. The Supreme Court ruled 6–3 in *Lee v. International Society for Krishna Consciousness* to uphold a ban on solicitation in the terminal but struck down the ban on leafleting, as it was not reasonable because it was overbroad. The key difference is that the solicitation included the issues of sales and fraud while the pamphleting was merely a dissemination of ideas. Only Justices Sandra Day O'Connor and Anthony Kennedy were in the majority both times, as Justices Antonin Scalia, Clarence Thomas, Byron White, and Chief Justice William Rehnquist voted to uphold the entire set of regulations. All three of these cases were clearly between the state, as it was the one regulating the fair and the airport, and a religion, the Hari Krishnas. In the 1970s and 1980s, many regulations targeted the Hari Krishnas, as they were the current focus of laws aimed to restrict what some saw as an illegitimate religion. In some ways, the victories by the Jehovah's Witnesses and the Mormons (in areas outside polygamy), together with the rise of newer religions, increased opposition to the Hari Krishnas in the 1970s because of their nontraditional nature. In this way, the treatment of the Hari Krishnas mirrored that of previous minority groups, and this was in part due to the fact that the Hari Krishna's activities, circulating and requesting donations, were somewhat similar to the methods of the Jehovah's Witnesses and the Mormons. There were also some factors which caused the authorities to pay increased attention to the Hari Krishnas, including their doctrine, which was far removed from Christianity, and their Asian origin, both of which clashed with some people's attitudes about which religions should be tolerated in America.

Besides attempts at regulating newer religious practices, there were also other issues that continued from the past, including the issue of conscientious objectors. In 1985, the Supreme Court considered the Selective Service System, or draft system. One registrant had not enrolled and did not enroll again after the system asked him to. After this, he was prosecuted and he claimed selective prosecution. The majority held that he had not proven this selective prosecution and so upheld it. The dissent noted on procedural grounds, that the government refused to allow discovery and held that the case should be sent back to allow that discovery. Once again, this was clearly between a governmental entity (in this case the federal government) and a person's religious interest, not between two individuals.

Taxes also came up in a variety of forms dealing with religion and the free exercise clause (and religion in general). In one case, the federal government had chosen to treat churches differently from other organizations under the federal unemployment tax. The question for the Court was whether employees of a school which did not exist independently of the church were allowed to be treated in the same way, and the answer the Court delivered was yes.

Taxes generally applied came up in *United States v. Lee* (1982), which dealt with Social Security taxes for an Amish employer. This case also has parallels in current debates over government regulation of religious practices and ideas. Edwin Lee objected to paying those taxes as he thought that Social Security (and his support of it) violated his religion. However, the Supreme Court held that when an employer ventures into the world of commerce, he is subject to uniform laws and Social Security taxes. The court held, "Not all burdens on religion are unconstitutional. . . . The state may justify a limitation on religious liberty by showing that it is essential to accomplish an overriding governmental interest."[1] This seemed to agree with the *Sherbert* test (and *Yoder*), but it should be noted that it is still the governmental interest versus the religious person. (It should also be noted that here, unlike with *Sherbert* and *Yoder*, the state won.) Those in favor of RFRA often forget that the state does win sometimes even under RFRA-type tests. This has parallels in both the *Hobby Lobby* case (to be discussed in Chapter 6) and in the area of same-sex marriage (to be discussed in Chapter 7) as the Affordable Care Act is legal (as of the time of this writing) and equality is mandated under many state statutes for same-sex couples. Both of those areas will be discussed more later.

Sometimes, religious communities came in front of the Supreme Court the same way any other community would and their religious nature was largely secondary. For instance, in *California v. Grace Brethren Church* (1982), the issue was one of jurisdiction and whether the federal courts could hear a challenge to a state tax. The tax here was on unemployment, but the relief was denied as Congress had before prohibited federal district courts from entering injunctions in this area.

While not dealing with an individual, tax regulations took center stage in 1983, when Bob Jones University discriminated on the basis of race and claimed religious justification. This university was a very prominent fundamentalist Christian school, and it held that the Bible prohibited interracial relationships. The university also acted to ban interracial marriage and dating as well as those who supported such ideas. It admitted African Americans who would follow the ban. The IRS denied Bob Jones's tax-exempt status, which meant that anyone who donated to them would not be able to take a tax deduction. The Supreme Court upheld the IRS, ruling that the state had a compelling interest in eliminating racial discrimination and generally left it at that, holding that this interest outweighed whatever burden was placed on the school. The Court did note, though, that the university was a school and not a church and so should be treated differently. The school, nearly 20 years later, did reverse its policy. This is important, as it goes along with the idea that if the government has a compelling interest it can act to eliminate discrimination.

This differs somewhat from some of the current cases, where specific individuals are claiming a right to be free from governmental control, but is similar to others, like *Hobby Lobby v. Burwell* (2014), in that corporations are claiming freedom from government. (The law treats corporations like individuals, but one needs to differentiate between the claim of an individual and the claim of an entity; however, the courts chose or choose to read the "personhood" of a corporation.) The *Bob Jones* case though begs the question in either instance of whether those who would favor a vibrant RFRA would want the *Bob Jones* case reversed as the university claimed a religious reason to discriminate. This case also demonstrates that even under a compelling government interest test, once again the state might win, as it did in *Bob Jones*.

Taxes again, this time in the form of state taxes, were at the forefront, as the question was whether a state could allow a tax deduction for a private school and the Court held that it could. Deductions were also at issue in 1989, when members of the Church of Scientology attempted to write off monies given to the church. The Court considered these payments for religious services rather than donations. Donations are supposed to be given freely, not in return for services or anything else, and as the payments to the Church of Scientology resulted in services being rendered the Court held that they were not deductible. The Church charged its members for certain things and this arrangement was not held to be a religious donation, making it nondeductible.

Taxes sometimes combined with other issues, even inside religion. Those included taxes, or the lack thereof, on religious publications. The Court struck down a scheme to exempt only religious publications from sales taxes and then held, a few years later, that sales tax and use tax on religious items were not a prior restraint on religion. In this case, the ministry in question, Jimmy Swaggart Ministries, was a large televangelist one, so there was a large amount of material (and tax) in question and the publications were being sold widely.

The final tax and religion issue of this period dealt with funds given to missionaries. In this case, the parents of Mormon missionaries gave them funds and the amount was suggested by the Mormon Church. The parents claimed a tax deduction as they viewed the mission as charity, but the Supreme Court disagreed. Perhaps the most surprising thing about this case was that the District Court and Court of Appeals had both denied the deduction, and the Supreme Court agreed to hear the case. The Supreme Court decision was unanimous, which begs the question of why the case was deemed important enough to be heard. None of these issues seems exactly comparable to cases heard under the RFRA (and the government has generally been given a wider degree of latitude with taxes) but, even if they were, these cases prove that the government has generally won cases concerning taxes, and that would suggest that RFRA-type laws would not lead to the side claiming religious liberty to always win.

Some areas that might not be thought of as related to religion also came in front of the Court. One of those was in the area of a driver's license photo. A woman in Nebraska refused to have a photograph on her driver's license, and this refusal came from her belief that photographs were graven images. She extended this to having no photographs of herself. While this was not a belief of any church she was associated with, it was a sincere belief as she had no pictures inside her house of anything she considered a creation of God, including animals. The Supreme Court allowed her, by affirming a Circuit Court of Appeals decision, to get a driver's license in spite of Nebraska's general requirement that photographs be taken. The Supreme Court was evenly divided, so it did not issue a ruling, but the lower Court of Appeals did not rule that it was a compelling state interest to force the issue and held that so few people will seek such an exemption that it will not be an issue. Thus, the state did not always win when a compelling government interest test was used, but clearly here again it was the state versus an individual.

In *Bowen v. Roy* of 1986, the Supreme Court considered the case of a Native American who refused to supply his child's Social Security number in return for state aid. The Court held that the state could use the Social Security number and then remanded the case to a lower court. The agencies had been willing to fill in the number for the parents, but the parents opposed this as they thought that any use would rob the child's spirit. After remand, the federal government agreed both to not use a Social Security number and to remove the one that they had already assigned.

In a religion case which was more about free exercise than establishment, the question came up about what level of protections would federal law give a Jewish congregation. The synagogue, the Shaare Tefila synagogue in Silver Spring, Maryland, sued those who had desecrated it under federal law prohibiting racial discrimination and allowing lawsuits. The lower courts had dismissed the claim as Jews are no longer seen as a distinct race. The Court allowed the claims, though, both because Jews were seen as a distinct race at the time that the statutes were passed and because those who harmed the synagogue viewed the Jews as a different race. In this case, bias was in the eyes of those who were biased, not those who were receiving the bias. This is not really parallel to the current cases, as the federal government was protecting a religion rather than regulating it. Also, this is not parallel as there is no right to desecrate a place of worship, and so there is no balancing here, unlike in current cases, like *Hobby Lobby*, where a corporation, acting as a person, wants to use religious ideas to restrict contraceptives, or the same-sex marriages cases, where one person's religious rights are balanced off against another person's equality.

The Court also concerned itself with when a religious group could be restricted from using an area and how the question of equal access would be handled. This impinged on the area of religious freedom: if a public school (and many of these questions were in the areas of public schools) opened the area to some groups, did it need to open it to all, including all religious groups? In *Widmar v. Vincent* (1981), a school opened up a forum for all student groups, and the question was whether or not a religious group could be excluded. In a 7–1 vote, the Supreme Court held that the group could not be excluded. It should be noted that the decision was largely reached on free speech grounds, not a freedom of religion ground, as the Court held that all regulations of speech have to be content neutral and the regulation here clearly was not. In 1990, the Supreme Court upheld in *Board of Education v. Mergens* the Equal Access Act, which applied this rule to all schools, holding that the rule did not violate the establishment clause. In this case, a student group was suggested for a high school, and the group had religious content. The school board denied the group access. The Court held that this denial was unconstitutional as the forum had to be administered in a content-neutral way. These equal access cases were viewed as more speech than religion related, and so are not parallel to most current cases.

Religious practices were also the subject of controversy in the Supreme Court. In Florida, one city tried to ban the practice of one church which practiced ritual animal sacrifice, in the case of *Church of Lukumi Babalu Aye v. Hialeah* (1993). As it was clearly illegal to ban a single religion, the city tried to mask the act as aiming to control the killing of animals. The act prohibited all sacrifices for rituals and so focused on the general practice, not the particular religion. The Supreme Court did not buy the distinction and offered a rare unanimous decision. The act regulated only the one church and so was discriminatory against that religion and hence religious freedom generally. The act had also not shown a compelling government interest that would have justified this burden on religion.

Government regulation of religion also arose in *Goldman v. Weinberger* (1986). That case dealt with a psychiatrist in the U.S. military who was also a rabbi and an orthodox Jew who had worn a yarmulke inside against military regulations in order to observe his Jewish faith's requirement to keep his head covered. (He also wore one outside, but as it was under his uniform cap, it was not an issue.) It should be noted here that the employee had been in the military for a significant amount of time before the military banned his yarmulke. This goes both to refute that the ban was needed for military efficiency and to suggest that Goldman might have been targeted for something he did, not for wearing his yarmulke. This case, oddly enough, was not decided under a compelling government interest test as deference was (as has often been the case) given to the military. The military only had to show that there was a rational basis, and the military here argued that the wearing of the same cap by all sponsored unity.

While not a Supreme Court case, one issue of religious freedom dealt with how much of a duty could be imposed on a religious counselor. The case was decided in California, and it was *Nally v. Grace Community Church of the Valley* (1988). The case arose from a suicide, but the question was whether there was a duty to send the person to a professional psychiatrist, and when the person was not sent, was the church responsible for his death. The California Supreme Court ultimately ruled that the church did not have a duty, in large part because the California legislature did not impose such a duty. The Supreme Court, in part because the state had not acted, largely stayed out of the dispute. Had the legislature acted, the U.S. Supreme Court might have gotten involved. A larger consideration of this case is needed than most, as it is one of the few that deal with practices that resulted in someone dying.

In this case, a troubled young man joined a community church and came to the church asking for help with a variety of psychological issues. The church (Grace Community Church of the Valley) had come to have a very literal interpretation of the Bible and hold that God was the only one who can solve mental health issues. Ken Nally joined the Grace Community Church of the Valley and asked for help from its counseling program. The program held that the cause of all problems was sin and if sin could be removed, the problems would leave as well. It should be noted that even though some of Grace's counselors were ministers, none had any formal training in counseling.

Nally had become involved with Grace in the early 1970s, when he was having difficulty with school. He had sought counseling at Grace, and one element of contention for him was that his family was not interested in joining that church. His family was Catholic, and he tried to recruit his mother to join, but she refused. He had convinced his mother to attend counseling for some problems that his mother and father were having but his mother, Maria, was not interested in the church's solution of throwing his father out until he found a job.

Ken, though, continued his relationship with the church and sought counseling on several occasions. In late 1978, one counselor broke off his relationship with Ken but did not refer him to any other professional. Right before this occurred, Ken had mentioned having suicidal thoughts. Also, in counseling sessions with his girlfriend, Ken had asked if people who commit suicide find their way into heaven. The church, to Ken, appeared to say yes they still could, even though the church later defended their position as an opposition to suicide mixed with one not losing admission to heaven by committing suicide. The church was saying that they were opposed to the act, but did not think God condemned the person who did the act.

In early 1979, Ken attempted suicide and while in the hospital after a pill overdose, he confided in his minister and another person that he would try again. Once discharged, Ken then moved out of his parents' home and committed suicide. Ken's family found out about the previous suicidal thoughts only after his death and came to blame Grace and then ultimately to sue the church the next year.

Grace Community Church was part of the larger fundamentalist Christian movement, which holds that there are certain fundamental principles of the Bible that all true religion was based on. Among those principles was the fundamental inerrancy of the Bible and a 6,000-year-old earth. The battle between Grace Community Church and those outside was portrayed to the members of Grace as a battle between those who were saved and those who were not. Grace portrayed itself not just as the best way to be saved but as the only way. Fundamentalism also moved into politics, by presenting itself as the best way to avoid communism and thus the best way to be American. In the 1970s, fundamentalism was also behind the rise of Jerry Falwell and his politically active Christian evangelist Moral Majority. Thus, while this case looked like it was just between Walter Nally (Ken's father) and Grace Community Church, it was seen by many as being between the forces of fundamentalism and those of modernity.

Fundamentalism is often thought of as being mostly rural, but it long had had a strong foothold in Los Angeles, and other early fundamentalists, including Aimee Semple McPherson (broadcasting from Los Angeles from 1923 to 1944), had been active there. The initial case did not directly attack religion but argued that the behavior of the lead pastor and his counselors was outrageous, to use the legal term, as they should have known that the young man was suicidal, and yet they refused to act. Among the difficulties the plaintiffs, Ken's parents, had was finding an expert witness to testify, as this was one of the first cases where a church was sued. However, expert witnesses were found and the case proceeded. Even though the church claimed religious sanction, it relied on its insurance company for counsel in the case.

Part of the problem in this case was that none of Grace's counselors was formally trained as a psychologist or psychiatrist, and so this got into the question of what level of training mental health professionals should have. These people had some level of training but were not formally trained at the doctoral level or, often, even certified.

At the trial court level, the judge found that there was no possibility of liability as there was no accepted level of care. For there to be liability, one must know, or should have known, that he (or she) was doing wrong. Without that standard of care, that knowledge would be impossible.

However, the appeals court held that Nally did have a chance, or at least enough of a chance, to avoid what is known as a summary judgment. That ruling is used (and was used in this case) to dismiss a case as unwinnable. The appeals held that there was a chance for Nally to win by proving there had been a standard of care and so the trial court had been wrong to rule for the church based on a summary judgment. The appeals court held that a tape made by one of the church counselors which had directly stated that suicide was a way for God to call a believer home, along with the church's knowledge of that tape (and Ken's history of suicide attempts), suggested that they should have done something different or that their failure to do something different was reckless. This was based on California law, not federal law, and under California law, even though there was no duty to prevent suicide, one could still be held civilly liable if one failed to prevent suicide in a reckless manner. The case was decided on a 2–1 basis, with the dissent holding both that the case of action that the majority upheld was not recognizable under California law and that the Nallys in the lower court had not presented this course of action. Part of the difference between the two sides came in how strictly the law was being interpreted and the willingness of the court to allow clergy to be sued. The majority read the law broadly and were not opposed to allowing clergy to be sued in some circumstances, while the dissent read the law narrowly and feared that suing clergy would open a "Pandora's box" of lawsuits.[2]

The case went to trial in 1985 and, surprisingly enough, it only took one day to seat a jury. The Nallys' attorney had the difficulty of proving that there was a standard of care to be observed and that the defendants had not met that standard. The church, on the other hand, aimed to make another defense, in addition to disproving the two claims that the plaintiffs advanced. They aimed to prove that the limited secular professional help that Ken had got had not committed him to an institution, and so they were liable if anyone was, which in turn removed the liability of Grace Church.

The case also differed depending on whose side you were on. Walter Nally saw this as solely about one minister's failure. As one writer said, "for Walter Nally this was about one clergyman in particular."[3] For the church, it was seen as part of God's plan and as God being on trial. The lead minister, John McArthur, commented, "There's a certain amount of identification with Christ when we suffer reproach in his name. He too was falsely accused. If we have to go through this, if this is what the Lord has chosen for us, I guess he has a purpose in it. I just believe my life is in the Lord's hands—I serve him."[4] This misses, of course, the Nallys' whole argument, as there is no way to impose any standard of care on McArthur's conduct if what he says is true, without testing religion as well, as any standard imposed would test the deity of the person's religion. One of the defendants testifying said that he knew that Ken had expressed a desire to kill himself again once he left the hospital, but didn't feel like he needed to tell (or so he claimed) the hospital staff because he figured that they knew already. Of course, this same defendant also stated that only Biblical counseling was necessary, which would make a rational person wonder if he had any real desire for the secular hospital staff to know, as that would increase the chance that Ken would, voluntarily or involuntarily, have to engage with non-Biblical counseling. Rea, the main counselor who met with Ken, also admitted having no formal training. The defense's answer to this was to cast doubt on the family and try to prove that whatever problems Ken was having, they came from his family, including his family's lack of interest in becoming members of Grace Church and lack of interest in following the counseling suggestions.

After calling the counselor, the plaintiffs turned to an expert to try to create a standard of care that the church and its counselors should have followed. The defense objected, stating that this was allowing one's beliefs to be tested. Freedom of thought, in religion, and statements about it have long been allowed, but freedom of action is not. That was the dichotomy that was first announced in *Reynolds v. United States* in 1879. The judge generally agreed but did allow testimony as to the general standard of care imposed upon ministers and others, which allowed the plaintiffs to make their point that they wanted to make in general. Testimony was also allowed on the general duty to refer, meaning testimony as to when a person is supposed to send someone to more qualified professional help, and testimony was allowed on the whole idea of outrageous (to use the legal standard again) conduct, the idea that some things are so outrageous that they should be penalized even if not otherwise banned. After calling some other witnesses, the plaintiffs called Ken's mother to testify about her interactions with Ken and that she had been reluctant to hospitalize Ken.

The plaintiffs then called a second person from Grace who had counseled Ken, Richard Thompson. It was he who had made the tape that stated that suicide was acceptable, and counsel for the two sides tangled over what would be allowed. They first fought over whether or not the tape would be allowed, and it was denied as it had been made after Ken's death and so there was no chance that he had heard it. They then clashed over whether Thompson could be questioned about one of his books. The defense said no and that all that was relevant was what Thompson had told Ken, and the plaintiffs held that the book was relevant as it showed their attitude toward suicide. At the heart of the issue was whether the book showed belief, which could not be questioned, or action, which could be. In terms of psychology, here was the issue. "To teach psychiatry is bad is belief, to actively discourage psychiatry crossed the line into action."[5] Thompson adamantly argued that he had no standard of care that was due and his only responsibility was to God. The case closed with a few more witnesses.

At the end of the plaintiff's case, the judge granted a motion to dismiss, as the defense filed a large brief arguing that without a "compelling state interest," the religion of the defendants could not be regulated. The plaintiffs in turn argued that this was about the conduct required of anyone religious or not, when they undertake to counsel someone. The judge ruled for the defense, holding that while a standard might be required, it was not the job of a court to establish such a standard. The case was then appealed again to the state Court of Appeals. That court held that the case should be reinstated, as there was a duty to be imposed, but it was not a duty on religious counselors. It was a duty that was imposed upon all non-therapist counselors. The court held that when one agreed to enter a relationship as a non-therapist, one took on the duty to refer. As far as religion was concerned, the court fell back on the difference between belief and action, set forth both in *United States v. Reynolds* in 1879 and *Cantwell v. Connecticut* in 1942. (Both of those were decided by the U.S. Supreme Court, as noted earlier.)

The case was then referred to the state Supreme Court, which had turned more conservative (the California state Supreme Court was a popularly elected body), as had much of California in the 1980s. The court agreed to hear the case, and both sides reprised previous arguments, although the defense relied more on arguments that this lawsuit was trying to create a new tort. (A tort is where someone injures you and you sue, and there had been great debates over torts in the 1980s.) The defense argued that this was not a new tort but instead a new defense to the traditional tort of negligence. Not surprisingly, both sides presented positions on the tort issue that would allow them to win overall.

The plaintiffs argued that the defendants had held themselves out as able to treat mental illness. This was important because if a counselor does not hold himself out as competent in treating an area of mental problems and a person goes to see that counselor knowing that, then there is no liability as there was no representation that one was competent. This is particularly true for unlicensed professionals, as was the case of the defendants here. The plaintiffs also said that the religion issue was not the key but the standard should be the same for all unlicensed counselors who hold themselves out as able to treat mental illness. There was a substantial amount of discussion of when this duty started and whether or not facilities that offered crisis hotlines would also have a duty to refer from those lines. The plaintiffs suggested that they did not, as there was not the same sort of relationship. The defendants held, on the other hand, that there had been no relationship established and that there was therefore no duty to refer. The defendants also tried to use the religion issue to skirt liability. The underlying debate, as noted, was whether or not this action would allow a new tort to be created.

In 1988, over nine years after the suicide and eight years since the litigation began, the California Supreme Court ruled in favor of the defendants. They held that the Church had set itself out only as a spiritual counselor, not as a professional counselor (and definitely not as a licensed counselor). As there was no relationship, the court then looked at general liability and held that there was no requirement to act and so therefore no lawsuit. It should be noted that religion did not play a large role directly in the decision, and therefore there were no grounds to appeal to the U.S. Supreme Court. The U.S. Supreme Court could have been appealed to only if there had been a question under the First Amendment of the Constitution in the Court's holdings. A concurrence by two justices held that there was a duty and that the duty was allowable under the First Amendment as there was a compelling state interest but that the defendants had met their duty because at least some of the defendants had suggested that Ken seek professional help.

Thus, the Church won and was allowed to be immune from lawsuits. The case connects to current debates in terms of how much leeway spiritual counselors (and churches in general) should be allowed to have. The current standard federally (and in many states) is that of the RFRA or a similar state statute. By allowing restriction of religious freedom only when there is a compelling governmental objective, RFRA and its companion state statutes would seem to agree with Nally.

Nally is the last case that was decided by a state supreme court that dealt with professional counseling. Quite a few other cases followed, but all of those dealt with sexual misconduct on the part of the clergyman. While the standard is supposed to be the same for conduct throughout generally, it should be admitted that courts often, even if not admitting it, are less likely to defend people who committed a crime versus those who just committed some level of possible misconduct. This is particularly true in the area of sexual misconduct of the kind that often was at the heart of clergy abuse cases. Of course, also, any sexual abuse is wrong, while pastoral counseling, even that which doesn't work, or is flawed, at least starts out with good intentions. Pastoral counseling also generally starts with at least some level of consent on the part of the person being counseled. Some of those cases did result in holdings that abuses occurred, but the conduct in these cases was much more egregious than that in Nally's case.

The most important case, in terms of how it shaped the current debate over religious exemptions from laws, came up over the matter of Native American peyote use. Peyote first surfaced as a drug on the public radar in the 1970s. This matters as some Native American religions had (and have), as part of their spiritual ceremonies, the ritual taking of peyote. Without the use, the ceremony was not complete. The decade here does matter. While peyote had been used before that, it took the American Indian Movement in the 1960s and 1970s to force reconsideration of Native American rights (among other issues). Peyote had been widely criminalized and Native American religions in general were denigrated. The latter is important because either peyote had to be rehabilitated from its status as a drug or the overall religion had to be honored. To draw a comparison to another religion that had some parallels, no one in the 1970s would begrudge the Catholic religion's use of alcohol in the communion service, even though alcohol was (and still is) considered a drug. Even during Prohibition in the 1920s, use of wine in religious ceremonies was not banned.

By the early 1980s, some states had relaxed their rules on the use of peyote, but the federal government still considered it an illicit drug in general. The case arose out of Oregon and an antidrug program. That state, it should be noted, outlawed the drug's possession but did allow people to make the argument that they could possess it for religious purposes. Alfred Smith, who worked as a drug counselor, was a Klamath Indian and participated in a ceremony of the Native American church, a recognized religious body. It should also be noted that peyote had been used for centuries by Native Americans and had been used in the religious organization that Smith frequented for nearly a century. This is significant because it demonstrates that Smith was not using religion to avoid drug charges. This was just as established as many other churches, a factor that plays into consideration in most people's opinions about the case. It should also be noted that peyote was, at the time, heavily regulated and generally illegal.

Smith then was confronted by his employer after a coworker had been fired for use of peyote and admitted his own use (thus this all started over his telling the truth). He was fired and then applied for unemployment compensation. This was denied as he had been fired for misconduct. It should be noted that Smith had been sober for 26 years at the point he was fired and had been involved with the church for 5 years.

The lower Oregon state court overturned the denial as a violation of Smith's (and his coworker's) freedom of religion. They then wanted the unemployment commission to reconsider. This might have ended the issue, but the state attorney general, Dave Frohnmayer, saw this case simply as a drug case, and he also was interested in running for governor and saw taking an antidrug position as being popular with voters. To allow drug use and then allow unemployment compensation did not sit well with Frohnmayer. He then asked the state Supreme Court to review the case.

The state Supreme Court also overturned the denial, but instead of looking at it purely as a freedom of religion argument, it looked at it as a place where the state interest (avoiding fraud in unemployment compensation benefits) was not outweighed by the interest of the person in freedom of religion. This put it squarely in the area of the *Sherbert* and *Yoder* cases, where the state interest had been balanced off against the individual's. The state Supreme Court also chose to not investigate if the use of peyote had been illegal because illegal acts were not relevant according to the state's own unemployment guidelines—they only looked if the act had been committed in connection with employment. After reconsideration was denied by the Oregon Supreme Court, the attorney general asked the U.S. Supreme Court to consider the ruling.

In 1988, the Court spoke, returning it to the state so that they could decide whether the use of peyote in ceremonies was illegal.[6] The Oregon state Supreme Court took up this issue the same year, mostly ignoring this question. It did hold that the use of peyote was legal under the First Amendment but also noted that a criminal case was not being considered here. The state Supreme Court also seemed to not answer the question posed by the U.S. Supreme Court. Doug Frohnmayer won a third term as attorney general easily but wanted to continue the battle, viewing this solely as a drug issue. It should be noted that three years earlier, in 1985, the state had agreed to grant Smith and his coworker unemployment benefits, which meant that the practical issue had already been settled. The state had also agreed to allow any future applicant for unemployment benefits to use religion as a defense if a similar case arose.

Frohnmayer appealed the case to the U.S. Supreme Court again, fearing his ability to prosecute drug use in other areas and regretting, at least publicly, the need to limit Native American use of peyote. He believed that he had to uphold the law on peyote or else give up the ability to prosecute other drug cases. Some accounts have suggested that Frohnmayer might have been able to find a way out if he had been willing to, though. The state, based on what the U.S. Supreme Court had said the first time around, presented the case as an issue of criminal law now, not unemployment insurance, even though no crime had been alleged. While one might blame Frohnmayer for focusing on the illegal drug use, he was taking his cues only from the U.S. Supreme Court. Frohnmayer argued that reducing drug use was a compelling interest. Those supporting Smith argued that the case should be one of unemployment compensation and not one of drug use and that there was not a strong enough compelling interest in unemployment compensation. (This was supported by several unemployment compensation cases heard by the U.S. Supreme Court all the way back to *Sherbert*.) There was tension on both sides, as the Native American church feared losing in the U.S. Supreme Court, and Frohnmayer, who now was running for governor, was getting bad press. However, a settlement could not be negotiated that would satisfy Smith, Frohnmayer, and the Native American church. Thus, the case proceeded to the U.S. Supreme Court.

Oral arguments produced few surprises, but Frohnmayer did differentiate between wine in a communion and peyote, suggesting that peyote was more dangerous. When Craig Dorsay, the attorney for Smith, presented, he was questioned about the difference between use of marijuana and peyote and did not produce as strong an answer as he might have hoped. The real surprise came in the decision, which was a 6–3 vote in favor of Oregon.

It actually might be better stated that the real surprise (and the outrage) came from the holding. Antonin Scalia, rather than holding that the state had met its burden of proving that the law and holdings were justified, decided to rewrite the First Amendment, in the eyes of many. In the first part of his opinion, "he rationalized that according to his interpretation of the Court's free exercise jurisprudence, neutral, generally applicable laws had never been limited by the free exercise part of the Constitution."[7] Scalia went on later to explain why the *Sherbert* ruling (and the line of cases resulting from it) did not hold here. He also suggested that the *Sherbert* ruling should not hold as much in general.

Scalia first held that the freedom of religion only came into play in terms of actions, not beliefs, when the laws were not generally applicable. He made much of the fact that this was a criminal law here that made peyote use illegal for everyone. Scalia had little to say about the fact that the law being challenged had not been the peyote law until the U.S. Supreme Court forced the parties to pay attention to it upon their return to the court. One might note that the unemployment compensation law was also generally applicable, but Scalia apparently chose to focus his defense on the drug law, not the more relevant unemployment compensation system. This takes away the comparison to *Sherbert*.

After noting that generally applicable laws were never allowed to be violated under the guise of a free exercise of religion, Scalia returned to several cases that had allowed such violations and distinguished them. In Scalia's mind, such cases involved religion and another constitutional liberty. In this case, two were better than one. For instance, the *Yoder* case involved both the freedom of religion and the right to educate.

He finally turned to the *Sherbert* case, which had started the whole line of cases. *Sherbert*, he held, was not applicable as it was only an unemployment compensation case. In *Sherbert* and several other unemployment cases, no law had been violated. (It was just the question of proper granting of unemployment compensation.) Adeil Sherbert, for instance, merely wanted to not work on Saturday as it was her holy day. The conduct in Smith's case was criminal and this made all of the difference for Scalia. Of course, no one was charged with violating the law in Smith's case, but this made no difference to Scalia.

One author summarized Scalia's overall point about the heightened scrutiny this way: "Scalia essentially argued that the higher level of scrutiny used in the unemployment context was the exception rather than the rule."[8] Scalia did make two other points, though, one to argue that allowing these exceptions would create anarchy (although one would think that preventing anarchy would be a compelling government interest and thus allowed) and that any religion which felt abused could use the democratic process, which ignores the whole point of the Bill of Rights protecting minorities. Scalia's ruling, unlike those in later sessions of the Court, did note some areas where allowing religious exemptions might prove dangerous: "list[ing] a number of laws that might be challenged should the courts continue to make exceptions to generally neutral laws: payment of taxes, health and safety regulations, drug laws, social welfare legislation, child labor, environmental protection, and laws providing for the equality of the races."[9] This list should be of interest to those favoring an RFRA-type law as those supporting a law would need to suggest which of these laws that Scalia lists should be allowed to be challenged (and why those not allowed would be excluded). Scalia did not, though, list any rights that might be challenged by allowing the First Amendment's freedom of religion provision to trump them, but that might be largely due to his narrow reading of human rights (and wide reading of government power) in general. Thus, Scalia's opinion is of little use when comparing it to later decisions like *Hobby Lobby* and the cases surrounding LGBT controversies.

Scalia in many ways was more a nineteenth-century conservative than a twenty-first century one, holding that only those rights recognized by the Founders were legitimate. Thus, peyote use could be banned (and would generally not be favored as it was not at the time of the founding).

He in general read the constitution very narrowly and that was the case again here.

Carolyn Long's book *Religious Freedom and Indian Rights: The Case of Oregon v. Smith* suggests that Scalia's main mistake was in reshaping this case from an unemployment compensation case to one dealing with the drug laws. The case could have been narrowly dealt with under the unemployment compensation system, either upholding the allowance of the benefits (which the Oregon Supreme Court had done) or denying them, holding that the benefit to the system of not allowing drug users to get benefits for being fired for that drug use outweighed whatever burden was put upon religion. Scalia's First Amendment analysis was where Sandra Day O'Connor moved away from him in her concurrence.

There were five votes to go with Scalia, and O'Connor concurred in the holding, but sharply criticized what Scalia had given as the reasoning. Her opinion was actually much longer than his. O'Connor first pointed out the obvious, that a generally applicable law does restrict religious conduct. She wrote, "It is difficult to deny that a law that prohibits religiously motivated conduct, even if the law is generally applicable, does not at least implicate First Amendment concerns."[10] She also pointed out that most legislators would paint a law as generally applicable even if it was aimed at only one religion.

O'Connor went on to deny that there was any legitimate point to describing cases as hybrid cases and held that the Court had always used the compelling government interest test or at least had examined it. Just because the Court had found that some areas were beyond the test, such as the military, did not deny its validity. O'Connor closed with a restatement of the point made earlier, that the purpose of the Bill of Rights is to guarantee freedoms without having to rely on the democratic process. However, O'Connor still joined the majority as she felt that the government had a right to prohibit dangerous drugs. Of course, it helped her case that the government had placed this substance in the same drug class as cocaine and heroin, drugs dangerous to health and with a high chance of abuse. O'Connor also ignored the fact that this had been an unemployment compensation case until the Supreme Court forced the changed focus. O'Connor's concurrence thus would have allowed the test suggested by RFRA but still allowed the state to win.

Harry Blackmun wrote a dissent, which was joined by Thurgood Marshall and William Brennan. The dissent went somewhat along the same lines as O'Connor's opinion in that it criticized Scalia for departing from the established norm. It added that it was incorrect for the Court to have considered the state ban on peyote as the state had not considered it and that Scalia and others prided themselves on judicial restraint, or not deciding things until they had to. He also agreed with O'Connor that the U.S. Supreme Court should defend minority religious interests rather than leaving it to the legislative process. Blackmun differed from O'Connor in that he felt that the state had not proved that peyote caused any harm and that the state had not demonstrated that it usually enforced the peyote laws, particularly against those in religious ceremonies. If the state did not enforce the laws, the state (and the U.S. Supreme Court) could not hide behind a need to universally enforce the law, or the claim of harm, as it was obviously not happening without the enforcement. In one final twist, Justice Kennedy had been apparently considering a concurrence (or joining O'Connor's), which would have produced only four votes for Scalia, meaning that his opinion would not have been as significant. However, Kennedy did not issue that concurrence. Kennedy, it should be noted, was relatively new to the Court, only joining in 1989. (The case was decided in 1990.)

Scalia's opinion produced outrage. Both sides were surprised at the breadth of the ruling. Scalia was also widely criticized, both for lowering the amount of protection given to the freedom of religion and for engaging in "judicial activism," a term which means, at the very least, going out of one's way to strike down a state decision (or federal or state law). Conservatives liked to paint only liberals as doing this.

A coalition quickly formed to try to get a law passed effectively overturning *Smith*. While Congress cannot directly overrule the Supreme Court, it can pass legislation that creates remedies and sometimes the Supreme Court allows these. The effort resisted on Section V of the Fourteenth Amendment, which gave Congress power to enforce the Amendment—the question was whether it could both increase rights and fix problems or just fix problems. The coalition decided both and tried to draft a bill restoring rights to where they had been pre-*Smith*. The bill was introduced in 1991 but did not pass. The bill was reintroduced the next year with a companion bill aimed at protecting Native American religious freedoms even more, because, as many people noted, even with the compelling interest analysis Smith would have lost, as O'Connor concluded. Oregon did pass a bill allowing people to use religion as an affirmative defense answering a drug charge.

It took until 1993 for the RFRA to pass. Part of this was due to concerns over abortion, as many pro-life people feared that RFRA would allow more access to abortion, as some pro-life people feared that those who were pro-choice would argue that their pro-choice religion includes a belief in the right to an abortion. There was also concern over whether or not prisoners could use the legislation to sue. However, the Supreme Court in 1992 reaffirmed the language of Smith in the *Church of the Lukumi Bablu Aye v. City of Hialeh* ruling, and this spurred those in the coalition who were left to keep fighting.

RFRA was summarized by one book, Barry W. Lynn's *The Right To Religious Liberty*, as "require[ing] that any law substantially burdening religious exercise be (1) in furtherance of a compelling governmental interest and (2) the least restrictive means of furthering that compelling governmental interest."[11] This aimed to restore the language from before the Smith case, but it was unclear what specific language (*Sherbert*, *Yoder*, some other case, or some combination) should be used, and no particular case was used as the model by the law. It was just clear in rejecting *Smith*. RFRA was applied to the states through Section V of the Fourteenth Amendment, which gave Congress the power to enforce the Fourteenth Amendment. It should be noted that it was 1994, before peyote use in religious ceremonies was protected at the federal level.

In 1997, the U.S. Supreme Court, in *City of Boerne v. Flores*, struck down RFRA because it limited the states by preventing them from passing laws unless those laws were justified by a compelling interest. The decision allowed RFRA to still restrict the federal government. The Supreme Court held that the use of Section V had overstepped Congress's bounds because interpreting the Constitution was supposed to be something left to the Supreme Court. It should be noted that most of the Supreme Court accepted this limited view as even those who dissented wanted a revision of *Smith*, which the majority had used to write *Boerne*. However, even though RFRA only limited the federal government, many states copied the language of RFRA into their state statutes. Thus, while RFRA did not control the states directly, its language was still the model.

The federal RFRA (and the state versions), even after *Boerne*, did not provide clarity, however. Two authors, Christopher L. Eisgruber and Lawrence G. Sager, wrote, "Not surprisingly, RFRA precipitated more confusion in the courts. As we have seen, it restored a test that talked tough but packed no punch in practice. Congress said nothing to clarify the meaning of this schizophrenic standard. Instead, it bluntly asserted that the test had proven 'workable' in the past. Saying this did not make it so, of course."[12] Thus, there continues to be the question of whether the test is workable or not.

Even if one accepts the balancing test of RFRA, there are still issues to be decided. Restoration of religious freedom sounds great, but what level of religious freedom is to be restored? The *Sherbert* level? The *Yoder* level? The level that existed exactly before the *Smith* decision? Within each of those, there is also a society baseline that is being applied, even if that is not stated. After all, for the state to balance the state or federal interest versus the religious individual, it must have some fixed level of religious freedom, which is a level at a certain point in history. In turn, the rights of others, when in conflict with religious liberty, would also be set at that year. Does society return to the 1960s, which was implied in *Sherbert*? There are gender considerations in *Sherbert* that would not be considered the same way 30 years later (at the time of *Smith*) or more than 50 years later (the present). Finally, even if a level is agreed upon (let's say for the sake of argument the pre-*Smith* level), what type of balancing do the courts do? After all, RFRA does not say, restore religious freedom and let it reign. It says restore religious freedom and have it balanced off against the interests of the state. Do we view state interests (and concerns and other peoples' interests) as the state interests and concerns of the 1990s or those of today?

Smith also begs the introduction of another point. The *Smith* case is not parallel to most of the current cases. Whether examined as an unemployment compensation case or examined as a drug case (this book argues it is the former), it is an individual against the state—a classic religious freedom and First Amendment case. Most current RFRA cases are one individual versus another, with the state being somewhat in between, if the state is directly involved at all. That is quite different, just how different will be seen as the discussion here moves into the first decade of the twenty-first century.

Finally, there is a significant irony here. RFRA was created to protect an individual's religious interest against the state. One man, Alfred Smith, stood against the might of the state. One man's religious interests stood against an unconnected (in many people's minds) drug control aim of the government. However, by 2016, powerful corporations were using that same law to restrict individuals' contraceptive freedom and equality, thus in many ways turning RFRA's one against the mighty mantra on its head.

CHAPTER SIX

From RFRA to *Hobby Lobby*

The Religious Freedom Restoration Act (RFRA) of 1993 was passed in order to counter the *Oregon v. Smith* decision, and it requires governmental laws which substantially burden religion to be justified by a compelling government interest. Even then, the least restrictive means must be used by the government. However, this act only balances off the interest of the individual whose religious freedom is allegedly limited versus that of society. It seems to ignore any other interested parties, such as if there are other people affected, including those who are on the other side of the scales of justice. For instance, if a person claims to be allowed to discriminate against participants in a same-sex marriage because his religion requires it, RFRA only looks at the interest of the state and the interest of the person claiming a right to discriminate—it ignores those wanting to participate in the same-sex marriage ceremony. Such a lack of consideration is nothing new, as previous cases have also ignored important third parties. In the area of the establishment (not free exercise), the prayer in the public school cases (such as *Engle v. Vitale*) ignored everyone besides the children being told to pray. Historian J. R. Pole writes, "Oddly enough, although these opinions dealt with the susceptibilities of children, they failed to notice the difficulty for the nonconformist or irreligious teacher who might be assigned the duty of leading the class in prayer."[1] Thus, many decisions in the past really dealt with different issues than the ones considered today. This should not surprise us as the Supreme Court generally tries to limit its holdings to the area of law forced by the case at hand (and to the type of parties covered by the case at hand). However, not even all the parties covered by the case are represented.

As America as a country claims to be equal for all members of society, discrimination allowed by law destroys that equality. Pole describes John Rawls, a twentieth-century American philosopher, in this way: he "described self-respect as 'perhaps the most important primary good.' He [Rawls] defined self-respect as an ability, within one's powers to fulfill one's intentions."[2] Not being able to marry equally would seem to be the antithesis of that self-respect and so also the antithesis of the "most important primary good."[3] Rawls (and Pole) thus emphasize two central questions that RFRA asks: what interests should be balanced and what should be the overall goal?

After the *City of Boerne v. Flores* (1997) case, where the federal RFRA was upheld but only to apply to the federal government, several states, feeling their own constitutions inadequate, passed their own versions, mostly seeking to protect religious minorities who felt that previous laws discriminated against them. These laws were passed in part because they sought to do what the federal RFRA had tried to do, but had been prevented from, by *Boerne*.

However, the RFRA acts in the early wave were relatively uncontroversial, especially when compared to the second set. The other difference between the first and second set of RFRA acts on the state level was that the first set of acts were aimed at (and used against) state interference with religious freedom in the pursuit of general state interests. They were thus similar to the national RFRA, which had been sparked by *Oregon v. Smith*. There, a Native American's right to use, in a religious ceremony, a substance banned by federal law had been at issue. This prompted the act's weighing of the individual right versus a general governmental objective. Unlike later RFRAs on the state level, it was not one individual's right versus another's.

It should be noted that there were religious protections of an individual's freedom of religion in many state constitutions as of 1995 and some of these did go beyond those of the federal Constitution. This was allowable under federal law as long as the protection did not lead to the establishment of religion. The focus here, then, is on the impact of the federal RFRA and its state counterparts.

The federal RFRA was trumpeted (and has been trumpeted) by its supporters as a solution to the issue of religious freedom, but its passage in 1993 did not end the debate over religious freedom. RFRA also was not the only question to be considered by the Supreme Court. Equal access questions, among others, also occurred in the Supreme Court, and the focus of the Court somewhat shifted to the state level after RFRA was held to apply only to the federal government.

Equal access continued to be a point of contention in the courts. *Mergens* (1990) and *Widmar* (1981) did not end the issue. The Supreme Court in 2001, in the case of *Good News Club v. Milford Central School*, considered whether a school could prohibit a resident from using school district resources after hours based on the subject of its activities. The district banned religious services and claimed that it did this in order to avoid establishment clause violations. The Court held for the club, holding that this was viewpoint discrimination, which is not allowed. This case was the club versus the school, or the religious group versus the state, and so is not directly parallel to what is being discussed under some of the legal battles currently going on.

The issue of licensing and control of speech also returned to the Supreme Court. Thus, many of the issues in front of the Court were not new ones. The issue in licensing dealt with door-to-door canvassing by the Jehovah's Witnesses (a group, as we have seen, that had been to the Supreme Court on more than one occasion before). The case was *Watchtower Bible and Tract Society v. Village of Stratton* (2002), which dealt with a village in Ohio that required all canvassers to personally register and be willing to display a permit. The Jehovah's Witnesses said that this violated their freedoms of religion and speech as well as the freedom of the press. Villagers could avoid solicitation by posting a "no soliciting" sign or by filing a form with village officials. The form would allow or ban solicitation by the group and the one church listed was the Jehovah's Witnesses. The Supreme Court held for the Witnesses as it is not acceptable to force people to register before they engage in First Amendment activities. The right of individuals to post no solicitation signs was upheld, though. The Jehovah's Witnesses had been less often at the Supreme Court in the 1980s and 1990s than before, perhaps in part as municipalities adjusted to the idea that they had to accommodate (or at least work with) the Witnesses, a significant shift from previous attitudes.

This ordinance was interpreted somewhat in the vein of RFRA, even though it was a state ordinance. The Court held that the statute's stated interest of fraud, crime, and privacy did not justify the law. The decision also held that the statute was overbroad and so was not narrowly tailored. On both of the prongs of RFRA (although it was not directly used as it had been struck down against the states in *City of Boerne*), the statute was ruled unconstitutional. However, this was again the case of a group against the state (in this case a city, which is interpreted legally to be part of the state), not the case of one group (or one individual) versus another.

This decision in the area of free exercise continued the pattern of the last 60-plus years, when those who were winning decisions before the Supreme

Court were generally religious minorities. (Religious minorities had been the main group to use the free exercise clause before that, but as the focus here is Supreme Court decisions, the analysis here only goes back to when the free exercise clause was used to strike down a state statute.) Thus, as recently as 15 years ago, the free exercise clause was mostly seen as a way for those without significant political power to have their rights recognized. That debate and issue has now shifted and those with significant political power are using the same clause. While those in favor of religious exemptions might ask what is wrong with that, the issue here is not what is wrong or right with that but just to note that there has been that shift. We are not dealing with 200-plus years of history (since the passage of the Bill of Rights) or roughly 150 years of history (since passage of the Fourteenth Amendment) or even 90-plus years of history (since the First Amendment was first applied against the states). We are dealing here with the recent past. Those who would suggest that history is mostly on their side in the area of religious exemptions need to realize that the First Amendment has mostly been used to protect minority interests, and that is in agreement with the overall history of the Bill of Rights, as it was put in to protect groups and individuals against an overly strong federal government. That history of protecting minorities is much longer than the history of RFRA. It was then extended to protect individuals against the states. It was not put into place for those who win elections to find another way to accomplish their goals.

The goal of RFRA was to protect minorities in another way—it was to protect minorities from the power of the state. Its goal was not to protect minorities (or anyone) in their goals to accomplish things that would be illegal for anyone to accomplish for a nonreligious reason. Neither was its goal to allow anyone to use their religious liberty to restrict another person's otherwise protected constitutional liberties.

The Supreme Court considered one case dealing with financial assistance and the issue of religion in this period, that is, since passage of the RFRA, which was *Locke v. Davey*, decided in 2004. In this case, a student in Washington State went to college on a scholarship which prohibited study in ministry. This was held to be allowable, as Chief Justice Rehnquist believed that the scholarship lay in an interstice of the First Amendment—neither affected by the free exercise clause nor prohibited by the establishment clause. In a rare split, Justices Clarence Thomas and Antonin Scalia disagreed with him, holding that the program violated the free exercise clause and so should not have been allowed (in most cases on religion, Rehnquist, Scalia, and Thomas all agreed).

The issue of controlled substances was also considered by the Court. In *Gonzales v. O Centro Espirita Beneficente Uniao do Vegetal* (2006), the

Court considered the use of hosaca tea in a religious ceremony, which contained a banned substance. The Supreme Court held that the federal government had not shown a compelling governmental interest in banning the tea and so failed to meet its burden. The Court here used RFRA. As this was a federal law, RFRA was still used, as it still limited the federal government even though it did not limit the states. It should be noted that the government here lost in a relatively spectacular fashion, losing on a preliminary injunction, which held that there was no way that the government could win its claim, even if the evidence was considered in the best light for them. Both *Gonzales* and *Locke* were cases again that dealt with the state versus the religious freedom of the individual.

The religious climate of the early 2000s played a role in two other issues that came to dominate the period, universal health insurance and marriage equality. The overall milieu will first be examined here and then the two issues at hand. With the rise of the war on terror, and other factors, religious conservatives and fundamentalists reasserted themselves somewhat. They pushed for (but failed to achieve) a federal constitutional amendment banning same-sex marriage, and their influence was seen in George W. Bush's abstinence-only sex education policy, for instance.

Universal health insurance, which is what sparked the case of *Burwell v. Hobby Lobby* (2014) in many ways, is in many ways much older than the Affordable Care Act (ACA). The reason this history is important is that much of the visible public opposition to national health insurance is now couched in religious terms. While there may be religious objections, one must wonder if all the support for those objections is solely based in religious freedom concerns or if there is somewhat of a continuation of the debate over national health insurance here as well. The overall debate over health care, it should be noted, was not generally couched in religious terms.

There also are differences between medical insurance and other insurance that should be noted. All other forms of insurance (other than life insurance) do not cover risks that occur on a daily basis. Auto insurance truly is needed only when one uses an automobile. Now one generally does not want to wait and buy insurance the day of renting a car, but one could do that every time one rented a car (and never owned an automobile) and be legally responsible and fully covered. Ditto with homeowners or renter's insurance, if one from time to time had nothing he or she wanted to insure. One never has a day when health insurance is prevented from possibly coming into play.

The mandate under the ACA required buying health insurance. There was a political debate over it, as some people resisted federal interference and others just wanted to save (and for the healthy not buying insurance was cheaper than buying). However, without a mandate, only the unhealthy would buy insurance, which in turn would not create enough funding for the plan. A final note to consider is that without a mandate, many people would wait to buy health insurance. This will drive up costs and in turn encourage waiting even longer before buying insurance. Young and healthy people would not buy it and the older and more sick people could not afford insurance without some sharing of the risk. The only way to share costs equally is to have a governmental mandate. Also, of course, preventive care saves money, but the only way that many people will use preventive care is that if it is covered by their insurances. These are all practical considerations though, not legal ones and not First Amendment concerns. A bit of history, though, is needed for the overall debate.

Insurance was called for on a national scale in some European countries in the nineteenth century and was carried out, at least in terms of life insurance, in some lodges and organizations in the United States as early as the nineteenth century. Health insurance was added to the benefits given by some states in Europe as early as 1883 (Germany had up to 13 weeks of sick leave as of that date), but the United States did not have calls for it on a national scale until Franklin Roosevelt in 1935, as part of the Social Security Act. The United States had more employer-offered plans, along with plans done through fraternal organizations, with the employer plans growing especially quickly after World War II. The American Medical Association (AMA) opposed national health insurance, feeling that it would cut into their fees, and so it was removed from Social Security. Harry Truman returned to the issue in his Fair Deal, which he called for after winning the 1948 election. Some reforms were passed from time to time, but the farthest reaching was the one that declared benefits to be generally untaxed, leading to many insurers offering benefits, particularly during World War II. The federal government was generally left to deal with issues that fell through the cracks, like early efforts to somewhat deal with mental health.

In the 1950s, medical care came up again, but the AMA had successfully linked governmental-provided medical care with "socialism," and the 1950s were the height of the Red Scare. Anything linked with communism in any way was not going to be adopted. The AMA, say its critics, was more interested in preserving bottom lines, as doctors and hospitals feared governmental medical care would cut profits. Also, Dwight Eisenhower, president during most of the 1950s, aimed to look inactive and to avoid rocking the boat in any serious way. Both of these factors prevented serious medical reform. However, evidence was growing in the 1950s and early 1960s that serious medical reform was needed. Michael Harrington's *The Other America* (1962) examined poverty in America. One of the primary areas of need, he said, was in medical care, both for the poor and for the elderly.[4] There was a growing segment of the elderly, as people started to live longer, and the elderly were becoming more politically active. The elderly also started to do better financially, which made them more of a politically important voting bloc. The election of John F. Kennedy in 1960 brought a consideration of new ideas and Kennedy called for medical reform, similar to the call earlier made by Harry Truman. However, medical care for both the elderly and poor seemed to be issues going nowhere until Kennedy's assassination in 1963. Very little of the formal opposition, it should be noted, was based in religion, either in the 1950s or in the 1960s. As a matter of fact, many hospitals were church based (at least nominally).

Reform became possible after Kennedy's assassination and Lyndon Johnson's ascension into the White House. Johnson wanted government to be more involved in providing a social safety net and had the political skills to make that happen. This led to his calling for both Medicare and Medicaid. Medicaid helped the poor, being run by the states and funded by the federal government, mostly, while Medicare helped the elderly of all classes. With these two programs, the poor would be covered by Medicaid and the old by Medicare and everyone else by their employers. However, many jobs lacked insurance, even in the 1960s. The assumption was that anyone who would work in those jobs would be either a spouse or a minor dependent (and so covered under someone else's plan) or poor (and so covered under Medicaid) or old (and so covered under Medicare). No thought was made for anyone else, such as the self-employed, part-time workers, or those working for firms that did not provide health insurance, or at the very least, it was held to be politically unfeasible. The assumption also was that employers would continue to offer health insurance and that most employees would work full time. Unions were also assumed to be strong enough to force companies to grant health insurance. All that changed in the 1970s and 1980s, along with the escalating cost of health care.

Health care's costs increased faster than inflation for most of the 1960s, 1970s, and 1980s. This problem was increased by large numbers of uninsured, who were forced to use emergency room facilities for primary care, and the costs of that care were much higher than it would have been had that care been delivered by a doctor. This health care price inflation was increased in the early 1980s as social services in general were cut. New medical technology also sent prices skyrocketing. All of this forced the for-profit hospitals to start to look for profits elsewhere, raising prices on other things and in turn forcing an increase in insurance costs for both employers and employees. Non-profit hospitals just passed along the costs where possible or relied on the government to cover the uninsured. Employers in turn tried to cut costs by limiting access to insurance, which in turn drove up the percentage of those who were uninsured. While the 1980s did not see a great concern with social issues, it did see a focus on practical economics return, particularly in the late 1980s.

Bill Clinton's presidential campaign in 1992 focused on the economy, and one issue he promised to tackle was the rising number of uninsured and the cost of health care. Domestically, this seemed to be a good time to tackle such a project, as the Cold War had ended and some people were calling for a "peace dividend" to be spent on the American people. Also, a variety of different groups had studied the issue and had put forth plans. Most groups called for an individual mandate combined with an employer mandate in some cases. (Both of these would prove to be controversial later under the ACA of 2010.) For instance, the conservative Heritage Foundation continued to call for an individual mandate, and the Health Saving Account that is currently in place in some workplaces was based on a conservative idea. Whether or not to have governmentally mandated health insurance is painted today as a Democratic-Republican divide but very often was not in the early 1990s. There were (and are) at least five forces in play (in no particular order): the individual insurance companies, those who favor allowing the marketplace to control everything, those who favor a national health system (a universal system or a kind of "Medicare-for-all"), those who favor doing nothing, and those who want something in the middle. Doing nothing was the default for the 1980s, and the situation of rising health care costs and rising numbers of uninsured was getting worse.

After winning the election, Bill Clinton turned to his wife, Hillary Clinton, and asked her to lead a task force to produce a health care bill. The final result was a mammoth proposal that very few people understood. The proposal was opposed for multiple reasons, above and beyond the fact that it mandated health insurance. The proposal was in the center of the insurance spectrum, requiring enrollment, requiring employer coverage, and setting standards for what insurance had to cover. Some opposed it not on the merits but because it was proposed by the mere wife of a president. There also were political reasons for opposing the bill. Some assumed the bill's success and then argued that the bill would allow the Democrats to claim the allegiance of the middle class. It should be noted that if people assumed the insurance reform would fail once adopted, that politically (but not nationally) those opposed to the Democrats would want the bill to pass. Political opposition rallied, national TV ads were run against the plan, and the bill failed.

After that failure, the issue passed off the national radar but did not improve. Millions were moved off of their employer-subsidized insurance plans and onto government plans, as they were poor, or onto plans they bought themselves, or just did not have insurance. Some individual issues were dealt with, as prescription drug coverage was added to Medicare (Medicare part D, it is now known as). However, no national solution was found. In 2009, President Barack Obama made health care reform one of his priorities. He heavily highlighted it in his campaign and after being elected, he put it second on his priority list (after fixing the economy).

In 2009, in the first Obama presidency, Democrats, who controlled both houses of Congress, introduced a health care plan. Unlike the 1990s, when the White House directed the effort, Barack Obama allowed Congress to take the initiative. Obama figured at least that the Democrats in Congress would be less likely to oppose his efforts if they had a hand in crafting the proposal. It worked at least for passage and the ACA was signed into law in 2010. This did not, however, lessen the identification of Barack Obama with the act and it is often referred to as Obamacare. The Supreme Court in 2012 affirmed the constitutionality of most of the act (backing the mandate but throwing out the federal government's ability to penalize states for not expanding Medicaid to less impoverished persons and families), as did Barack Obama's reelection in 2012. All of this background shows that the opposition and debate was done in policy terms, not religious terms.

Opposition to the ACA mentioned many different things, but religious freedom was not usually one of them. People opposed the act as it was argued that it would force them into governmental exchanges, opposed the mandate to buy insurance, and opposed various provisions.

Provisions of the act were challenged, as noted, in 2012, but the main claims then were the individual mandate and a provision forcing states to increase the number of people covered by Medicaid, the medical plan that covers the poor. It should be noted that there was not a direct government mandate to buy health insurance. The only way any government mandate can be accomplished is to make it illegal to not do so. That was not what the ACA did. It instead gave people a choice—buy insurance or pay a tax penalty. This tax penalty was challenged as an illegal mandate, but the Court choose to view it more as a tax and the taxing power has always been interpreted widely by the courts, giving latitude generally to the federal government, particularly since the 1930s. The Medicaid expansion, on the other hand, was struck down as it was viewed as illegally coercing the states.

Between the June 2012 ruling and the presidential election in November, the mandate and insurance exchanges of the ACA came into effect. This did not stop efforts to repeal the act as a whole, as the House of Representatives (under Republican control after the 2010 midterm elections) scheduled and had multiple votes to repeal it, some of which ended in vetoes by the president and some others of which died in the Senate.

Some other issues also need to be discussed here, as they have an impact on opposition to Obamacare and the battle over religious exemptions to Obamacare (and more widely religious exemptions in general). They also impact how we view these battles. At least part of the opposition to Obama and his programs is based on race. This was seen in the wide scale discussion of his birth in Hawaii. Many people, in what came to be called the "birther movement," believed that he had been born in Kenya and so was not a "natural-born" citizen and so could not be president. As his mother had been a citizen, the courts were unclear if this would have been the case, but it was irrelevant as all credible evidence pointed to his having been born in Hawaii. This level of interest suggests that part of the issue may have been racial as there was no similar interest in other candidates who had been born outside of the United States. It is possible that this dislike of Obama on racial grounds carried over to his programs in general and to Obamacare, which is probably his most visible program. How, though, would this play into the religious exemptions to Obamacare debate? While those who are the plaintiffs in front of the Supreme Court may be wholly interested in the religious aspects, it takes a lot of money and time to bring a case to the Supreme Court and very often groups band together to do this. This is seen in many different issues. Now, does this disqualify the objections? Perhaps so, and perhaps not, but it definitely does color our understanding of the issues if the disagreement has all of these factors in it.

Finally, there are the overall political issues. As noted before, part of the opposition to Bill Clinton's health care reform proposal in 1993 was based in the belief that a successful reform would create a permanent political advantage for Democrats. In a similar vein, it is not impossible that part of the opposition to Obamacare is political and part of the support for religious exemptions is as well. Once again, if true, it does not discredit the overall objections but just shapes our understanding of the debate.

The background to the *Hobby Lobby* case also bears scrutiny, as it entered the debate in 2012. The *Hobby Lobby* case doesn't cover all clauses of the ACA but just some specific contraceptives and contraceptive methods that were required to be covered by insurance plans under the ACA. The reason for the objection was because among the contraceptives were those that prevented an already fertilized egg from implanting in a uterus and the company believed that life began when an egg was fertilized, these contraceptives were a form of abortion to some ardent anti-abortion advocates. It should also be noted that this applied only to what the Court called closely held corporations. Closely held corporations, defined as corporations with most of the stock held by fewer than five people, were treated as an individual and a person by the courts. If corporations are people, they then can be protected against governmental legislation in some cases under the Fourteenth Amendment, just like people. But exactly how common a closely held corporation is differs among experts, with some suggesting that most corporations are closely held and that more than half of the people in the United States work for closely held corporations. These corporations are ones where only a few people own more than 50 percent of the stock. Oddly enough, personal service corporations cannot be closely held corporations. Whether personal service corporations could also fight successfully for this exemption has yet to be seen. In a final irony, the corporation provided two of the contraceptives until 2012 when the ACA was upheld in the courts. It was only after the ACA was upheld and a religious liberty advocacy group approached Hobby Lobby that Hobby Lobby actually looked more carefully at its own health care plan.[5]

The case was heard by the U.S. Supreme Court in 2014, in *Hobby Lobby v. Burwell*. Sylvia Burwell was the secretary of Health and Human Services under President Obama at the time. As that division of the government oversaw the ACA, she was the one sued. Hobby Lobby was a corporation lead by David Green, a Pentecostal Christian, who opposed part of the contraceptive mandate because it, in his opinion, required providing contraceptives that acted as abortion agents, including what is often known as the "morning after pill" or "plan B," which prevents fertilization of eggs. Whether or not this is the equivalent of abortion is debated but was believed to be the case by Green.

In a 5–4 decision, the corporation was not forced to provide coverage as the Supreme Court held that there was a less restrictive alternative that could be used to provide the same coverage. This alternative was, in the opinion of the Court, that the corporation could inform the insurer that it objected and the insurer would in turn pay for it or that the government itself could pay for it. A similar work-around was already in place for religious organizations that objected to covering contraceptives, and this is what the Court based its opinion somewhat on. However, some of the religious organizations had not accepted this work-around, as the organizations still saw this as supporting or allowing abortion and so the model used had not been as successful as the Court thought it would be. The Court applied some of RFRA and held that the issue of whether or not a compelling government interest was introduced did not have to be reached, as the issue of whether or not this was the least restrictive means could easily be reached. On that question, the Court held that this was not the least restrictive means. RFRA, and some of the Court cases before RFRA, such as *Sherbert v. Verner* (1963), of course, holds that when there is a substantial burden on religious freedom the least restrictive means must be used and there needs to be a compelling governmental interest; the courts have held that either prong can be decisive.

The Court also held that some of RFRA needed to be considered and that RFRA did treat nonprofit corporations as persons and so should hold for profit-making corporations in the same way. The decision held that the corporation was a person and thus those who held most of the stock could impose their views, similar to how it would have been if a person had acted directly. The Court did consider how broadly this rule should be applied, and four justices in the majority argued that RFRA was the only standard and that other things such as bans on employment discrimination due to race are not allowed as these are laws with narrow proscriptions. Tax laws were also required to be followed. Thus, in an interesting twist, the federal government could tax and provide health insurance for all but could not force an employer to provide health insurance. One justice, Anthony Kennedy, argued that this case applied only to the specific set of facts here and the narrowly tailored and existing remedy of the opt-out. As the procedure was already being used for non-profits, it could also be used easily for certain types of for-profit corporations. As RFRA applied, the whole free exercise of religion, oddly enough, did not need to be reached. RFRA is read here as not defining the free exercise of religion but limiting the federal government more than the free exercise clause would.

The dissenters, not surprisingly, disagreed and looked at a wide variety of different issues. There were actually two different dissents. The first, by Justice Ruth Bader Ginsburg, argued strongly against the majority. It first argued that the previous courts had been right in holding that for-profit corporations did not qualify for protection under RFRA. It also argued that corporations should not be held to be persons under the law for religious freedom as religion is something that a person does, not something that a corporation does. The main dissent also pointed out that the Court was not fixing a problem but creating another one. By allowing this one exception, it encouraged some corporations to challenge others. This was, in turn, inviting huge amounts of litigation. This part of the dissent seems to have been proven true, as efforts to enact the very work-around got enmeshed in the issue of what constitutes a burden on religious freedom. Corporations have argued that even informing an insurer that they are not going to cover contraceptives constituted a burden on their religious freedom. Ginsburg also noted that burdens should not be imposed on third parties in pursuit of one's own religious interests, and she stated that this was what was occurring here.

There was also another dissent, by Justices Elana Kagan and Stephen Breyer, who argued that the claim against the contraceptive mandate falls on its own merits. Kagan and Breyer held that, as Ginsburg did, the contraceptive mandate is justified as a necessity and so therefore allowable under RFRA.

One interesting note here is that *Hobby Lobby* in some ways effectively reverses a long-held doctrine. Before, shareholders had been separated from corporations in a number of important ways. One was that shareholders could not be held liable for the mistakes of the corporation. If there was a corporate shield between the corporation and the shareholders in that way, it would also stand to reason that there would be a corporate shield in the other way, shielding the corporation from the values of the owners. However, this case seemed to hold the opposite. One must assume, though, that if Hobby Lobby lost a criminal case and the corporation's officials were sentenced to jail, the main stockholders would not want to join them there. Some even noted that the Court might choose to extend that criminal liability, even though in the past it had chosen not to, due to the separation between corporation and owners.

One might think that this solved the issue, but then a religious college, a kind of corporation, refused to file the form claiming that filing the form was still helping its employees gain contraceptive coverage that it objected to. Thus, any aid, in any way, would violate this belief system, or would seem to. That case was reached in the 2016 case of *Zubik v. Burwell*, where six religious colleges and other non-church religious institutions objected to the notification provisions and wanted to be treated like churches, which had been exempted. The Supreme Court in the summer of 2016 held that the insurance companies could generally offer the coverage without any interaction with the challengers and so the case needed to be reconsidered on that basis; therefore, there were more arguments at a lower court ordered.

The success of *Hobby Lobby* on the federal level with RFRA and how much attention it received both impacted other areas and leads to the question of how limited the case really is. While there were only four contraceptives at issue, is the case limited to only certain contraceptives? The Supreme Court was somewhat silent on this, other than Kennedy's concurrence noting that this ruling is limited to the four contraceptives being challenged here. Could all contraceptives be challenged as, after all, some major religions, such as Catholicism, want no artificial contraceptives to be used? Could other things be challenged, like a 40-hour workweek or bans on child labor, if this seemed to violate a corporation's rights? What about gender roles? Other than taxes and laws banning racial prejudice, the Supreme Court was very short in its ruling about what was prohibited (in terms of what items were not considered here), deciding to leave it up to RFRA and future cases. That is problematic in that many noted that RFRA was not passed to deal with corporate rights but to deal with individuals whose religious practices were impacted by state and federal law, which many hold to be a quite different thing. The Court did comment that the laws prohibiting racial discrimination would still be upheld, but there are a lot of other laws that were not discussed by the majority. As this comment was not needed to rule, one must wonder whether the language would be controlling for future decisions.

These rules are also supposed to be limited to closely held corporations, but this language is in itself an expansion from previous doctrine. This in turn means that it could be expanded. Also, of course, if corporations gained power from being closely held, in that they did not have to provide health care coverage or follow other laws, one would expect corporations to do exactly that. The abuse by corporations in the late nineteenth century noted in an earlier chapter indicates that some corporations will restructure themselves to lessen costs (and/or to accomplish other goals).

There also needs to be a comparison to the original goals of *Smith* (and RFRA), which were to protect an individual against the powerful federal government. Part of the point of the Bill of Rights was to protect individuals who could not win their rights in other ways, as through the political process. Protecting large corporations seems a quite different matter. Also, of course, the rights of those who wanted the coverage are not being considered. In the *Smith* case, there were only the two parties involved— the government and Smith. Here, there are at least three—Hobby Lobby/ David Green, the federal government, and the employees.

One should also note that this decision does not solve the issue either—it just moves the issue from being one of whether or not parts of the ACA is acceptable to one of what RFRA holds. Now, the question becomes, What does RFRA allow and ban and who does RFRA control on a corporate level? After all, if the rule that non-profits were covered allows closely held corporations to be covered as well, then why not all corporations?

RFRA at the federal level was not aimed at radically transforming federal law but merely aimed at putting the law back to where it was before the *Smith* case. Religious exemptions advanced by organizations are relatively rare. Martin Lederman noted, "Historically, claims for exemption from commercial regulations were idiosyncratic, brought intermittently by plaintiffs who rarely engendered sustained assistance or political support. By contrast, dozens of plaintiffs, including major corporations, reputable and well-established educational institutions (including the University of Notre Dame and Catholic University), and even some Roman Catholic archdioceses, have raised RFRA claims in the contraception cases."[6]

Previous cases which allowed religious exemptions need to be read with a keen eye. This is not because they were wrongly decided but because they are not wholly parallel with what is being considered today in a number of different ways. The goal of the early cases such as *Yoder* and *Sherbert* was also to prevent the state from infringing on one individual's religious beliefs and (sometimes) actions, whereas here in *Hobby Lobby* it is often protecting a group's actions and in the modern times it is groups against individuals or corporations versus individuals, not individuals against a governmental law or action. While legal doctrines are meant to be relatively permanent, they are generally applied mostly in parallel cases.

The Supreme Court did deny some requests for exemptions. *Sherbert* and *Yoder* are often discussed by those who want to argue for religious exemptions to be generally applicable laws, but a more parallel case to the ones heard today might be *United States v. Lee* (1982), which dealt with an Amish employer who felt it a violation of his religion for his employees (all of whom were Amish) to take Social Security benefits (which in turn meant that he should not have to pay into the fund). The Court did not consider whether legislation might create a less restrictive means but just whether the tax was justified. Law professor Martin Lederman notes, "The Court has never granted an exemption on the grounds that theoretical supplemental legislation might ameliorate the harm to state interests."[7] Thus, the exemptions sought by those opposed to the ACA did not exist before the *Smith* case, making it impossible for them to have been *restored* by the RFRA. The *Lee* case was in the early 1980s and thus was in the middle of the period that many cite as the era that RFRA (and state level

RFRAs) needs to return the law to. *Lee*, however, is not fully parallel as the interests of the federal government here (in being able to fund Social Security and work efficiently) and the interests of Lee are being balanced. In most cases today, one individual's interests are balanced off against another's. This book hopes that most would give more weight to a person's individual interests than the state's interests, and so those favoring religious freedom should be less likely to win than under the *Lee* case (where those interests lost anyway).

One might think that granting some of these exemptions would "settle the waters" and make America a more peaceful place. However, others are not so sure. Law professors Douglas NeJaime and Reva B. Siegel write, "Some, tacitly acknowledging the democratic contests in which complicity claims are entangled, urge religious accommodation in the hopes of peaceful settlement. Yet the complicity-based conscience claims asserted in these contexts are often not simple claims to withdraw. As we show, complicity claims can provide an avenue to extend, rather than settle, conflict about social norms in democratic contest."[8]

This would also be a diversion from history. NeJaime and Siegel continue: "In adjudicated religious liberties law, when accommodation has threatened to impose significant burdens on other citizens, courts have repeatedly rejected the exemption claims. The underlying intuition seems to be that one citizen should not be singled out to bear significant costs of another person's religious exercise."[9] *Hobby Lobby* is one of the first cases to hold that one citizen should be burdened with another's religion, at least in modern history.

In 2014, after Hobby Lobby's success in the *Hobby Lobby v. Burwell* case, a second generation of state RFRA acts, worded similarly but with different agendas, were passed or considered. These acts aimed to use religious freedom to accomplish political goals, particularly in the area of opposition to marriage equality. Some interest existed in using the *Hobby Lobby* decision to fight contraceptives, but that was generally on the federal level under RFRA (and so did not need new laws). The focus of the efforts was in the area of opposition to marriage equality, and that is the focus of the next chapter.

CHAPTER SEVEN

Marriage Equality and Beyond

The *Hobby Lobby* case and the debate over whether or not the Religious Free-dom Restoration Act (RFRA) required the government to allow exemp-tions to generally applicable laws (covered in Chapter 6) was one of the larger issues in religious freedom in the early twenty-first century. The other big issue in terms of religious liberty (at least that is how it is cur-rently phrased) that exploded in interest in this time period, 1995 to the present, is marriage equality. The issue has been around in America for the better part of 50 years, even though it really seems to have dominated the news only for the past few years. In the 1970s, the first attempt was made at a same-sex marriage in Minnesota, which the Minnesota Supreme Court denied as a right. The U.S. Supreme Court, in turn, decided that there was no a federal question and so decided not to hear the case. (This chapter is not intended to be a full review of LGBT rights or of marriage equality in general but just an overview.) The issue lay dormant until the early 1990s, but other developments occurring at the time were important. The LGBT movement began to coalesce and became more visible in this time, partly in response to the AIDS crisis. Advocacy groups and legal help organizations, including Lambda Legal, PFLAG (originally Parents and Friends of Lesbians and Gays, and now just PFLAG), and GLAD (GLBTQ Legal Advocates and Defenders), also formed. The national attention on the issue also freed many to be openly identified as LGBT, which was vital for public perception about the issue. Many in the 1970s and before assumed (wrongly) that no one they knew was LGBT, and the public self-identification of many as LGBT in the 1980s and 1990s and beyond changed that.

The issue of marriage equality returned to the national consciousness in 1993. Marriage, it should also be noted, is a fundamental right. Law professor Kenji Yoshino notes, "The US Constitution contains no reference to the 'right to marry.' Yet even the staunchest textualists in our judiciary agree it is a fundamental right, meaning the government cannot restrict it without a compelling interest."[1] (The first legal precedent came out of Minnesota, where the plaintiffs, wanting to marry, lost, and that was back in the 1970s, after which it vanished from the national radar.) The Hawaii Supreme Court held in 1993 that the state constitution required allowing gays and lesbians to marry. For a time, this seemed like it would open up the question nationally as states generally recognized marriages performed in other states. However, Hawaii voters in 1998 reversed that decision by a constitutional amendment, before the case finally reached its ultimate conclusion in the state Supreme Court. (The original decision had been made in the middle of the judicial process.)

The nation took notice, though, and Congress pushed through the so-called Defense of Marriage Act (better known as DOMA) (1996), which contained two important provisions. The first defined marriage federally as between one man and one woman. The second allowed states to not recognize marriages in other states, which reversed a full century of states agreeing to do that. The latter was more important for same-sex couples, as being married in one state brought little comfort if that marriage was not recognized in one's home state. After all, the whole idea of having one's marriage recognized in one's home state was what brought about the *Loving v. Virginia* case in 1967, which declared state bans on interracial marriages unconstitutional.

While DOMA might have seemed to settle the issue, it only really returned it to the state level, and states had to decide what to do with the issue, and as each state has a different political climate; each state acted differently. Some states legalized marriage equality eventually, either through the legislature (rarely) or through the courts, while others enacted either civil unions or domestic partnerships, and others acted to ban gay and lesbian marriages. These bans took place through amendments to the constitution of the state, through ballot initiatives, or through new laws. The civil unions and domestic partnerships gave various benefits of marriage without using that term. (And, as other states did not have the same status, these other states were not required to even consider recognizing them.) Vermont was the first to grant a civil union with the same benefits as marriage, in 1999. In the early 2000s, it seemed like those defending marriage equality were constantly on their heels, losing most state votes and being trampled in national debates. In the 2004 presidential election, one of the main charges leveled by President George W. Bush against his opponent, John Kerry, was that Kerry supported marriage equality nationwide. Kerry had not, for the record, made this a part of his campaign. Bush also pushed for a federal amendment banning recognition of same-sex marriages in other states (which would have turned the federal law of DOMA, which could be struck down by the courts, into a part of constitutional law, which cannot be struck down by the courts). In a split decision of sorts, Kerry was defeated, but Bush did not get his constitutional amendment, as it failed to get the two-thirds vote needed in Congress, even though it did get a majority.

At around the same time, in 2003, Massachusetts became the first state to allow same-sex marriage as the state Supreme Court held that the Massachusetts constitution required marriage equality. (The legislature could have rewritten the law but did not, which meant that the courts effectively ordered marriage to be equalized for same-sex couples.) In 2004, same-sex marriages started in Massachusetts. Massachusetts then forced states to decide (and the federal government to decide) when a state had to recognize another state's decision to legalize same-sex marriage. This also encouraged the forces favoring marriage equality to continue the fight. After all, it took 12 years to get the first full victory, and this one victory encouraged them to continue.

Massachusetts was one of the few states to move in this direction, though, as the 19 states which considered constitutional bans or statewide bans without changes to the constitution in 2004 or 2006 all passed those bans. California was the largest one, and in 2008 it added a ban on same-sex marriages. State laws could be overturned by state courts generally if they conflicted with the state constitution but state constitutional amendments could not, and as the federal government had left the issue generally to the states, state constitutional amendments, along with DOMA, seemed to end the issue.

Opinion on the national level started to shift, though, as shown by two political developments. In 2004, George W. Bush attacked John Kerry successfully on the issue of marriage equality in his reelection campaign and brought a constitutional amendment to ban the practice to a vote in the U.S. Senate. Bush's reelection showed how the nation stood, in part, at that time. By 2008, this started to change. Thus, the period 2004 to 2008 was the high-water mark for opponents of marriage equality, even though it did not seem so at the time.

There were some partial victories, though, with some states adding civil unions for same-sex couples, along with the lone example of Massachusetts allowing marriage, and these encouraged same-sex marriage activists to continue to fight. Civil unions, defined generally as a legal union with most or all of the same rights as marriage but with a different name, did not satisfy those who wanted full equality. This partial victory encouraged people to keep fighting. The reason that same-sex-marriage advocates felt that civil unions were not enough was that if a marriage and a civil union were equal, only one term, "marriage" (and only one classification), would be needed. It also caused many people to think about it, which did push some to shift their opinion. Many gays and lesbians also started to reveal their sexuality to their colleagues, which further encouraged thinking, a process referred to as "coming out." Many people who opposed marriage equality but who had long-term friends whom they suddenly found out were gay had to reconsider their position. This caused many to evolve. In 2008, in Connecticut and then, in 2009, in Iowa, the courts recognized same-sex marriages in their own states (and by implication those performed in Massachusetts).

Vermont granted marriage equality in 2009, and Vermont was a first (remember they were first in 1999 as well, to try civil unions), achieving marriage equality through the legislature. Every state before that had been ordered to do so by the judges. This meant that a majority of the representatives in a state wanted marriage equality rather than judges finding that marriage equality was deserved. Iowa was also important, because Iowa was seen as part of the "heartland of America," where "average" people lived.

After 2009, in some ways the focus almost split. In many different states, litigation ensued to check whether ballot initiatives and laws were constitutionally sound. In other states (and in some states both occurred), efforts were made to legalize marriage equality. In still others, further efforts were undertaken by those opposed to further codify their opposition. Some states where a majority was opposed to marriage equality even debated ending all marriages altogether in order to avoid recognizing same-sex ones.

One of the more important states, both politically and in terms of size, was California, and it had passed Proposition 8 in 2008, which stated that marriage was between a man and a woman and amended California's constitution. This proposition was soon challenged in federal court after it was passed and a full trial ensued, with expert witnesses being heard on both sides. Those against Proposition 8 won both at the trial court stage and at the Ninth Circuit Court of Appeals. The arguments against Proposition 8 were that it discriminated and that the legislation did not pass muster because all legislation must have some rational basis rather than being grounded solely in hatred. Whether subjected to merely needing a rational basis or subjected to heightened scrutiny as it discriminated against a protected group, the proposition failed at the trial court level as it infringed on the U.S. Constitution, and even state ballot measures are not allowed to do that.

The U.S. Supreme Court declined to decide the question over Proposition 8, holding that those defending the measure did not have standing, as the state refused to defend it, and a private group was defending it. Generally, only people directly involved in the matter (or suffering a loss in terms of a lawsuit) can directly defend a matter. The state of California decided to not defend the ballot measure, leaving its defense up to a group of organizations opposing marriage equality. Those against Proposition 8 won at the state Supreme Court. The U.S. Supreme Court then held that those groups supporting Proposition 8 did not have legal standing to support the measure, meaning that they could not defend the measure. With no one to defend it, this meant that the measure was defeated due to the state Supreme Court decision, and same-sex marriage was restored in California. (It had existed for a time between the legislature's enactment of same-sex marriage and the proposition). These developments all occurred in 2013.

At the same time the U.S. Supreme Court heard the Proposition 8 question, it also ruled on the DOMA, which had been passed in 1996. The act both refused federal recognition of same-sex marriage and allowed states to deny recognition of same-sex marriages performed elsewhere. In *Windsor v. United States* (2013), the Supreme Court dealt with whether a person married in a same-sex marriage would be treated differently for estate tax purposes than a person in an opposite-sex marriage. DOMA required this (and allowed states to not recognize a marriage performed in another state), but the Supreme Court struck it down entirely as a violation of federalism, as the federal government was intervening into an area usually left for the states (marriage). The overall issue was, for the moment, left to the states. Justice Anthony Kennedy's opinion did heavily hint, though, that he, if forced to choose solely on constitutional equality grounds, would side with those favoring same-sex marriage.

After the 2013 *Windsor* decision, the same-sex marriage issue really started to heat up both on the state and the federal levels. Many courts had relied on DOMA to settle the issue in their own state, because if the state in question did not have same-sex marriage and it was not required to respect marriages in this area performed in other states, then that seemed to answer the question. However, with DOMA out of the way, courts had to fully consider the issue. Many county clerks in areas that favored marriage equality, even if the state as a whole did not, started to issue licenses. These actions were done for personal reasons, as some favored allowing same-sex couples to marry and some probably acted for political reasons as well. This forced states to have to try to decide what level of autonomy to give county clerks and for states (and judges) to avoid hiding behind DOMA.

The year 2013 also saw several polls with over 50 percent of people favoring same-sex marriage for the first time. Thus, in five years, between 2008 and 2013, the nation had gone from having only one state with marriage equality (Massachusetts) to more than half of its people polled favoring it. However, 2013 still saw less than 15 states, as of the middle of the year, with marriage equality. As we are dealing with constitutional rights here, one might wonder what the popular opinion toward such items had to do with their constitutionality. Formally, it had little to do with constitutionality and informally quite a bit. To paraphrase the famous fictional commentator Mr. Dooley, the Supreme Court does read the election returns (and the political polls). Rising national support allowed the Supreme Court as well to shift over time.

The year 2014 opened with many keeping an eye on the Supreme Court, wondering if that would be the year that the full question of marriage equality would come before it. However, 2014 was a year of incrementalism rather than a year of sudden major change. By the middle of 2014, every state with a same-sex marriage ban was experiencing litigation over it. The political climate was also changing. Not only was support for same-sex marriage growing but also there was an increasing number of politicians who were willing to support it, or at least not oppose it. For instance, in the summer of 2014, when Pennsylvania's same-sex marriage ban was struck down by the courts, Tom Corbett, the Republican governor, decided to not seek a reinstatement.

As far as same-sex-marriage litigation is concerned, the summer of 2014 might very well be called the summer of the appellate court. The Fourth, Seventh, and Tenth Circuit Courts of Appeal, covering 11 states, all ruled against bans on same-sex marriage. Those rulings did not immediately go into effect because those states that had been directly affected appealed their cases to the Supreme Court. It was October before the Supreme Court ruled on those appeals, deciding not to hear them. That meant that those 11 states now had same-sex marriages, raising the number, by that point, to 30. November saw the Sixth Circuit Court uphold a ban on same-sex marriage, meaning that the Supreme Court would have to weigh in sooner or later. It was April 2015 before those cases were heard by the U.S. Supreme Court, and, in June 2015, the Supreme Court ruled in *Obergefell v. Hodges* that people across America have the right to marry, regardless of whether they want a same-sex or opposite-sex marriage. The ruling was 5–4.

Those opposed to same-sex marriage then moved to invoke the RFRA on the state level where those acts existed and to pass them where they did not. The federal government was not directly affected, as it did little to affect same-sex marriages (there are very few federal marriages, for instance, as those would be only in federal territories), and federal officials had to follow *Obergefell*. One concluding note would be that 2016 saw little change, as Justice Antonin Scalia died in February and without a replacement (eight justices meant possible ties), the Supreme Court was reluctant to issue broad rulings and so passed the few times when issues related to sexual discrimination (and most other big issues) came in front of it.

Nationwide marriage allowance, and even acceptance, in the courtroom did not equal acceptance in all areas. In some states, those opposed to same-sex marriage simply stopped issuing marriage licenses. In Alabama, judges were allowed to *not* perform ceremonies or issue marriage licenses (this was a holdover from the previous century in a vestige of segregation, as this discretion allowed judges to discriminate legally) and the judges often carried out this allowance. As a way to get around equal protection claims, judges stopped issuing the licenses to all couples, not just same-sex ones. It should be noted that in Alabama the chief judge of the Supreme Court, Roy Moore, at first declared the Supreme Court's decision in *Obergefell* unconstitutional and then said that the judges did not have to follow it, putting Circuit Court judges in the position of either not following the chief judge of their state or not following the U.S. Supreme Court. He was later brought up on judicial misconduct charges, but his behavior should surprise no one considering that he had done something similar with a display of the Ten Commandments in a state building 10 years earlier. Moore was later suspended in 2016.

In other states, clerks individually refused to issue same-sex marriage licenses, claiming that their religious freedom allowed them to do this. Perhaps the most famous of these was Kim Davis, clerk of Rowan County, Kentucky. She claimed that because state law required that each license have the signature of the county clerk on them the licenses meant that she was participating in the ceremony or endorsing it. She refused and was jailed for contempt of court. When she returned, her deputy clerks issued licenses. This played a role in the 2015 Kentucky governor's race as the successful candidate, Republican Matt Bevin, announced his support for Davis. After the jailing, Davis largely dropped out of the limelight. Bevin, after becoming governor, announced plans to remove judges' names from marriage licenses.

If one supports RFRA, would 2010 (or 2004) be the year to return to? Probably not, as the nation was moving toward the U.S. Supreme Court decisions that granted equal treatment to all marriages. However, 2010 is pretty recent, which eliminates difficulties that occurred in past times of having differences in how we view things today versus how they were viewed in the year religious freedom is "restored" to. The year 2015 would probably not be the year, as marriage equality had been given constitutional protection by then. Thus, even if RFRA is correct to be used, the question remains of what year to use as the benchmark to restore religious freedom to.

These two developments (the removal of judges' names in some states and the general cessation of marriage licenses by some judges) seem to have largely ended the issue of the right to marry as far as states are concerned, or at least ended it for the moment. One thing that seems to happen with this controversy is that many of the same issues (and sometimes even the same people) keep popping up when least expected. The controversy then turned to ancillary rights of marriage, including the marriage ceremony and family rights. One of the marriage ceremony issues focused on when industries were allowed to discriminate. The focus was usually on bakeries and florists, who typically were involved in weddings. Many bakeries refused to sell wedding cakes to same-sex couples on religious grounds, claiming that their religion did not allow same-sex marriage and that by selling a cake they were endorsing the practice. Although not usually associated with weddings, a pizzeria or two also moved into the controversy. It should be noted that one of the pizzerias in question had not been called upon to serve a wedding but decided to step forth and assert its right not to serve gay and lesbian weddings. The pizzeria also benefited from the attention as it claimed to have suffered discrimination because of its stance, and an online site helping to raise funds for the pizzeria raised over $800,000.[2] There is some question as to whether the pizza company ever was asked to serve a wedding and ever was threatened by any lawsuits or fines.

Some bakeries, florists, and other businesses tested laws which required equal treatment. It should be noted that none of these businesses claimed a general right to not serve same-sex couples or individuals who were LGBT but just those involved on the day of their same-sex marriage. In Oregon, one bakery ran afoul of the laws. It should be noted that the laws in question here are almost always state laws, as the federal government has not (or has not yet) added sexual orientation as a protected class. The bakery was ordered to pay a fine of over $135,000 and paid it. The bakery then contested it, and was still contesting at the time of writing (early 2017).[3] The bakery received a lot of positive press from conservative sources, and it was represented in the courts by the former White House counsel for George H. W. Bush (C. Boyden Gray) (at no cost to the couple).[4] While a lot of attention has been paid to the bakery, little attention has been paid to the pain of the lesbian couple whose cake was denied.[5] Thus, the issue is not as simple as those who would paint it as businesses being driven out of existence by gays and lesbians, and in many cases those who sued were not seeking publicity. The bakeries and other groups also beg the question as to what other groups they would be allowed to deny service to.

As the debate swirled, people opposed to same-sex marriages cast around for a variety of tactics, and as some were claiming religious freedom as a justification for their actions, perhaps it was just a matter of time before some pushed for stronger versions of RFRA on the state level or a first version (depending on what state one was in). In 2014, the debate was in Arizona. Two of the states with the more public debates in 2015 were Indiana and Arkansas. In 2016, the focus moved to Georgia, North Carolina, and Mississippi.

In Arizona, State Bill 1062 dealt with an expansion of that state's RFRA. The law, before the amendment, covered only individuals suing one another and did not include corporations. The amendment would have included corporations and organizations. While proponents painted it as a general widening of religious freedom, the case which sparked it was a denial of photography for a same-sex wedding, which makes one wonder how general the overall bill was aimed to be. The governor vetoed it. It should be noted that to some extent the bill was largely symbolic, as state law already allowed refusing of service for any reason. Religion though was the reason given for the denial of the photography.

In Indiana, the debate was over Bill 101, which was called the Indiana RFRA and claimed to restore religious freedom in Indiana. Various state officials have stated in the past that discrimination against homosexuals should be allowed and have even stated that it would not be clearly illegal to put up a sign stating, "No gays allowed." The bill in question expanded the term "people" to include corporations, and amendments to ban discrimination were not passed. While the governor, future vice president Mike Pence, claimed that this was solely about protecting religious freedom (with very little discussion about what religious freedoms were in jeopardy), the list of guests invited to the bill's signing suggests otherwise, as some invitees had previously suggested that discrimination against gays and lesbians should be allowed. There was a nationwide backlash, even more so than in Arizona, which suggested that the issue was heating up. A wide variety of people spoke out against the bill, including sports figures (significant as there are teams from the NBA, the WNBA, and the NFL in

Indianapolis and the NCAA is headquartered there) and many business figures, including Tim Cook of Apple and Warren Buffet. Some states and cities cancelled nonessential travel to Indiana.

In early April 2015, after the bill's passage, revisions were put in place to ensure that same-sex marriages and LGBT people in general would not be discriminated against (or that at least was the proclaimed purpose of the revisions), and many of the boycotts were dropped. The idea that this whole debate was over religious freedom in general was put into question by some groups who greatly opposed the revisions, arguing that they destroyed the whole purpose of the bill. If the bill was supposed to just protect religious freedom but not freedom to discriminate, this would not have been the case. After the bill's passage, things quieted down in Indiana. It should be noted that the specific religious freedoms were never definitively discussed.

In Arkansas, in 2015, Governor Asa Hutchinson signed a bill that was, in his opinion, aimed at protecting religious freedom. The bill, in his opinion, balanced religion against diversity. The governor stated, after signing, "I think it's sending the right signal, the way this has been resolved, to the world and the country that Arkansas understands the diversity of our culture and workforce but also the importance of balancing that with our sincerely held religious convictions." Hutchinson tried to have his bill comply with RFRA. Its supporters argued that it was needed to allow people to deny services to "messages" (and those carrying those messages) they disagreed with. Chief among those messages was marriage equality. No other reason was cited, even though the supporters claimed it was focused broadly and was not just about marriage equality. The people in favor of the bill claimed it was not discrimination but protection of religious freedom.[6] In an interesting twist, Fayetteville, Arkansas, in 2016, passed an antidiscrimination ordinance which was then challenged under Arkansas's statewide ban.[7] Many who argue against the federal government setting a nationwide standard for discrimination have no trouble with each state setting a statewide standard for discrimination laws.

It should be noted that while only a few states are discussed here, the issue has broken out nearly nationwide. It has been estimated that more than 200 different bills have been introduced dealing with the issue of religious freedom as it interacts with protections for gays and lesbians. Most of these have been in the area of same-sex marriages. Others have been in the general treatment of LGBT people, with some suggesting that religious freedom should allow discrimination against people who are LGBT.

Georgia and North Carolina were also battlegrounds over this issue in 2016. Both of these states have straddled the line between conservative and liberal positions socially and politically. Both states have tried to position themselves as progressive in order to gain business but have also had their conservative moments. For instance, Atlanta's motto for years, unofficially, was "the city too busy to hate." Of course, this was also the city that the 1985 case of *Bowers v. Hardwick*, upholding antigay laws, started in. In 2016, Georgia saw a bill that combined protections for pastors who refused to perform marriages being combined with another bill on a separate issue and then being passed. In its final form, the legislation gave pastors the right to not perform religious ceremonies and gave people the right to not attend ceremonies. This last part seems aimed at the photographers and bakers who did not want to serve same-sex marriages. The act also broadened somewhat the definition of a church and held that faith-based organizations (as broadly defined now) did not have to rent space or offer services to same-sex couples or anyone else they found objectionable. Hiring protections were also affected. In all of these, there was no balancing of a religious person's rights versus any other person's rights. The final part balanced off the government's right to advance its goals versus the church's right to have religious freedom, but this was the only part of the bill that had any such balancing. It should also be noted that the supporter of the original bill opposed a suggested change that would have left local nondiscrimination ordinances in place.

Governor Nathan Deal of Georgia, however, vetoed the bill. Deal used his own religion as a justification for the veto, suggesting in comments that his religion, Baptist, did not call for discrimination but instead called for working with those who one saw as being in sin. There were also economic considerations. The National Football League had suggested relocating the Super Bowl that was scheduled to be in Atlanta in a future year. (The exact year had not been set yet.) Coca Cola, one of the world's largest corporations, and one headquartered in Atlanta, also protested. Besides the Super Bowl, other things were also considered for relocation. For instance, Disney announced that it would not film any more in Georgia if the law was adopted. Thus, there would have been a significant economic impact had it been adopted. Deal did not publicly reference this aspect as much as his personal reaction, but it is hard to believe that it did not play at least some part of a role.

North Carolina in 2016 also had a controversial bill on the topic, but in the case of North Carolina it was signed. Unlike Georgia, the bill resulted from a specific city's desire to increase protections rather than a generic debate. In the case of North Carolina, Charlotte had banned discrimination based on sexual orientation or gender identity. This was dubbed the "bath-room bill," as transgender individuals could choose which bathroom to use under Charlotte's ordinance. The countering North Carolina law required them to use the bathroom corresponding to the gender on their birth cer-tificates. The state in turn banned all local ordinances preventing discrimi-nation based on gender identity and for gays and lesbians. There was a wide-scale backlash in North Carolina. The National Basketball Associa-tion (NBA) moved its All-Star game, quite a few collegiate sporting events moved, and there were notes by some trade groups that conventions would not do as well, even if they were still held. The NBA, though, also dangled a carrot of sorts in front of North Carolina, suggesting that it would try to reschedule the game for 2019 (with the implication that the law would have to be changed by then). The government of North Carolina was not mono-lithic either, as the attorney general of North Carolina refused to defend a bill that he considered unconstitutional.

While the motives of the attorney general are unknown, beyond his statements that the law was unconstitutional, a similar official would con-sider several things before thinking the issue settled. First, of course, are the personal issues, which we see as motivating the governor in Georgia publically, and tied in with this are what the person believes is right and wrong. Second are the issues legally, which are important obviously for an attorney general and should be important for a governor (although not always). Third are the political issues—many public figures have an eye on the future. The attorney general in North Carolina just won (in 2016) the governorship. If political figures decide that a law they support or defend will come back to haunt them politically in the future, they may have this consideration trump the other two, if in conflict. For instance, a public official with an eye on becoming a congressman may have his actions dictated by what he thinks his future constituents in that district will think rather than any other concern. Or, a public official may gamble that public sentiment five years from now will be different than it is now. While one might think that farfetched, do remember that the issue here is same-sex marriage, which saw a sea change in only 20 years, a far shorter period than some political careers.

Political issues are not now as simple, especially on this one, as "the public wants it, so you need to do it" seems to justify many moves. This is something that is often not considered by many on both sides in the issue. Those opposing same-sex marriage seem to be winning now on the local level, but nationwide the other side seems to be winning, and the role of the issue in national elections is still unclear. Political considerations also may have played a role in this case, as North Carolina governor Pat

McRory, a conservative Republican who signed the bill into law, was up for reelection in 2016 and lost (due in part to negative reaction to House Bill 2). He may have signed the bill thinking that it would help him politically (and may have been wrong). The governor has signed an executive order restoring protections for state employees, but this protects only those employed by the state government, obviously. It should also be noted that these laws, claiming to defend individual liberty, in some ways work exactly against that, as they deny the rights of municipalities to set their own policy. In fact, it was a measure in Charlotte, as noted before, that triggered House Bill 2. Some argue that you need a statewide standard, but obviously before this, municipalities had for some time been allowed to set their own policies on these issues, which argues against a standard. Most municipalities are also allowed to set their own standards on other issues, in many states, such as on the age to buy tobacco or minimum wage laws.

The federal government next stepped into the issue, arguing that the North Carolina act violated constitutional protections and threatened to sue North Carolina. North Carolina's governor tried to defend the bill using a variety of justifications. He argued that it created equality, although how this bill created equality for transgendered individuals was very unclear.

It was not just states that were caught up in the controversy, as some retailers did as well. Retailer Target amended its corporate policy to allow people to use the restroom of their chosen identity rather than their birth gender identity. This caused a large amount of controversy, with some people claiming that they would boycott Target. Other groups called for Target to create single-stall restrooms that anyone could use (with the implication being that transgendered people should be shunted off to there). Target mostly did not address the controversy, other than to note that it already had those restrooms in most, if not all, stores and so the suggestion was pointless. This points out the complex web that businesses must weave if they are to solely listen to their customers—very often, national opinion varies from local, and national opinion may not line up with what the most powerful lobbying group in each area wants.

Mississippi also passed similar legislation, although Mississippi's was aimed more squarely at religious liberty and denial of services rather than at the issue of bathrooms. In both cases, a wide variety of protests were noted and some entertainers cancelled concerts, including one by rock superstar Bruce Springsteen. The success of past political protests has varied, with protests against Indiana's law resulting in changes, while protests against Arkansas's law resulting in no substantive changes. This may be because Indiana has positioned itself more as a national leader for business and industry and sports, while Arkansas has not and has no professional sports teams. (Indiana has three: the NFL, NBA, and WNBA.) Similarly, Mississippi has no professional sports teams, and North Carolina has two: the NBA and NFL. North Carolina in many ways shows the diverse demands of a modern state caught between groups aiming for traditionalism and change. There are the professional sports teams in North Carolina, but North Carolina is also known for its connection with NASCAR, long noted as the most conservative of any major professional sports circuit. North Carolina has been caught in the mix as the NBA has moved its All-Star game, and the Atlantic Coast Conference (the main Division I college sports conference of the area) moved all of its championship games out of the state.

It should be noted that there are other factors at play. Oddly enough, there is no stated penalty for going into the bathroom of the opposite sex under the bill. It should also be noted that there are other parts of the bill removing protections and prohibiting lawsuits in areas far removed from bathrooms. One must question then what effect it would have and whether there were other motivations also existing.[8] One might argue that the bill would, for someone who was in the bathroom of the other gender and then attacked someone, remove the defense that person was not in the wrong bathroom, but I doubt that has been used successfully as a defense against assault and battery or any other offense. There are also questions about how it would be enforced.

Throughout, there was a lot more discussion of opinions rather than facts. Few studies were advanced, if any, that showed any attacks occurring in bathrooms because of similar policies in other states or municipalities. Some tried to have it both ways, first arguing that there had been attacks and then retreating behind the idea of protection once the request for studies was made. The argument was that it was better to be protected than to have regrets. Many states, though, allow transgendered people to choose their bathroom, but no assaults have been reported. One must also ask if there are other places where sexual assaults have occurred and if those locations have been shut down. This, of course, is the public policy aspect of those laws not the legal aspect. As noted before as well, this is not really a religious freedom issue, as few religious texts have anything to say about whom you share the bathroom with. Some, however, have tried to connect this to religious freedom, mostly in the muted sense of one's religion not being willing to admit that anyone would prefer to be of the opposite gender from what one is born into. Religious leaders have also opposed these accommodations as some religions opposed most

change and what they see as a "liberal" agenda. (Of course, those supporting the change see it as more an issue of equality than as being part of a
liberal agenda, whether liberals believe more in equality, and exactly what
liberalism is—that's an issue for another time and place.) The exact connection between religion and the bill thus was never directly and clearly
proven, other than that some religions want to deny the right of people to
identify themselves as transgendered.

Bathroom bills and the bathroom issue fail to consider issues of equality. This book would suggest that a balancing approach should be used.
That approach would require that equality be first considered. That equality would allow individuals to use the bathroom of their choice unless
those opposed could demonstrate a clear danger. For instance, have men
dressed up as women (and, despite all the talk about bathrooms in general, the fact is that the fear is of transgendered men who identify
as women attacking women—or men posing as women attacking
women—not transgendered women who now identify as men attacking
men) attacked women in the past? If not, why would the bill change anything? Also, have transgendered individuals been involved in these
attacks? Most studies suggest that far more transgendered people are
attacked than attack. Balancing would force a consideration of the facts.
The balancing approach would also require that if religious liberty be
involved the danger to religious liberty be proven. How does allowing
transgendered people to use the bathroom of their choice threaten
religion?

This issue has been more discussed in North Carolina, as it is probably
more affected by business issues than Mississippi for a variety of reasons.
Among those are the fact that North Carolina has tried to move itself,
somewhat, in recent years into a business hub in terms of banking and
commerce. Mississippi has not, other than casinos, even though efforts
have been made to attract manufacturing.

It should be noted that the new modern economy has played a role
here, as previous discrimination was in the South usually and very few
businesses did direct business down there, or at least those businesses
which did were not subject to social considerations. Businesses now are
more likely to take a stand on such issues. The 1960s did not see many
businesses moving factories to push the South to change, but the 2010s
do see this.

Given the level of tension and hostility exhibited over religions in the
past, I am not sure that allowing people of certain belief systems, which
the courts may call a religion at one time, to have the right to avoid generally applicable restrictions on their actions while not allowing other

groups who believe in things which are not considered religions at the time to do the same is wise. The battle would just shift to what makes up a religion and perhaps even further increase tension. However, I think the battle does not need to even get that far. There should to be a test to determine when a belief is religiously based and when a belief is bigotry hiding in religion or to at least determine that as best we can. The questions here are two: proximity and sanction. The proximity test is a simple one: would most people call the act a religious one? Very few people sell pizzas because they think God, Allah, or Buddha, and so forth tells them to. Actions in areas not religiously motivated deserve less protection because religion is both faith and worship. There is also the reason of expectations on the part of customers. Very few people order pizza expecting a religious element. People do run social service organizations for religious reasons. Similarly, those going to a church food bank sort of expect that a church is behind it (or should). Finally, those going to a religious institution expect religion. I doubt that the Founding Fathers would have expected religious liberty to cover all actions taken, even by religious people.

There is also the question of religious sanction. This way, religious actions are protected while pure bigotry is not. As religion is a system of faith and worship, the first test should be to examine the tenets of the faith one belongs to. If the contested action (only not serving LGBT people during wedding ceremonies and no other times) is not specifically sanctioned, then it should not be automatically protected. Not all actions that reference religion are protected. If one wants to be religious, there are plenty of religious acts to pick from before acting on ones only related to ideas that religious texts might mention. If the contested action is specifically sanctioned, then the question becomes one of the underlying motivation for that action. Is the motivation for the action (not the discrimination) religious? These two tests do not ban bigotry, unfortunately. Plenty of churches in the 1960s were religiously segregationist, even during services. It would, however, lessen bigotry that hides behind the First Amendment. The question then becomes whether or not to allow the discrimination under the two competing parts of the Fourteenth Amendment—religious liberty and equality.

Besides the issue of the most recent RFRAs, the overall area of discussion should be specified. Few (if any) of those favoring legalization of same-sex marriage (or those who have supported the legalization of same-sex marriage since it has happened) have argued for churches or any other religious organization being forced to marry same-sex couples if that would violate their religious ideas. Yoshino wrote, "No mainstream advocate of same-sex marriage has ever argued, to my [Yoshino's] knowledge, that the government can tell a sect how to conduct religious marriages—and with good reason, as he or she would slam up against insuperable objections based on the First Amendment."[9] This author has also been unable to find any cases where churches were ordered to be forced to marry same-sex couples in violation of their religious ideas. One might also be tempted to hold that the Fourteenth Amendment applied only to race or that the Fourteenth Amendment should be frozen in time with the ideas of the late nineteenth century. However, as Yoshino notes, "the framers of the clause [the equal protection clause in the Fourteenth Amendment] made no mention of race, even though they did in the roughly contemporaneous Fifteenth Amendment. . . . By speaking of 'equal protection of the laws' in general terms, the clause left the meaning of equality to the intelligence of later generations."[10] This will also be more discussed in the concluding chapter.

Finally, one might be tempted to think that the "equal protection of the laws" referred only to governmental treatment. However, there are two problems with that idea. First, the government has already held that same-sex marriages were to be treated equally by the state as opposite-sex marriages. It would be odd to require the government to give more equality than the average person. It also would be odd to grant equality at the courthouse but not require it elsewhere. The second is that this view does not hold in other areas. Racial equality, for instance, is mandated in federal law, at least in terms of public accommodations. The state would thus be saying that, even though the Fourteenth Amendment does not specify what types of equality are covered, and even though the courts have said that same-sex marriages are the same as opposite-sex marriages in the eyes of the law, we do not expect individuals to treat the couples the same way.

Gendered laws also relate to this case, as codified gender relations tend to create discrimination. Historian J. R. Pole writes, "The concept of gender has had a historical tendency to reflect ultimate inequalities of power."[11] Removing the issue of bathrooms from gender would lessen that discrimination.

Religious freedom works both ways, and the exact parameters of the interaction between people's religious freedom have not yet been worked out. One case before *Obergefell v. Hodges* bears consideration. In 2014, North Carolina had banned same-sex marriages. Several churches sued, claiming that this was a violation of their religious freedom to marry whomever they choose in their ceremonies. The federal courts agreed in *The General Synod of the United Church of Christ v. Cooper*, holding that marriage equality was actually a protected religious freedom. Exactly how much one party can impose one's marriage beliefs on another is still out, as this was a case of an individual (or a church, which the courts generally consider to be equal to a person, like some corporations) versus a governmental law. Can one favoring marriage equality use religious freedom to sue those opposed to it? Religious freedom laws do not seem to consider that circumstance, as they look more at when government can penalize people and are used more in the area of those opposed to marriage equality. While some aspects of marriage equality has been put into law, it has not been all, and so lawsuits from the other side of the marriage equality debate are possible as well. Many nuances to the issue have yet been considered. In the parallel area of religious issues in education, some groups seem to favor government support of religion, as long it is its religion, rather than taking a general stance of allowing any religion in or keeping all religions out, and one might suspect that most groups, regardless of public stance, take a similar view here. The law's treatment, though, is still developing.

It should also be noted that some have argued that few new state-level religious freedom restoration acts will be passed and that current ones will have to be relied on. This is not settling for at least three reasons. First, many states currently have state versions of the federal RFRA (and, of course, if a constitutional claim is only rare, in terms of how many states it can be raised in, that does not make it any less valid). Second, this argument misreads the political climate in at least some states. While Georgia did back off its RFRA-type law and Indiana modified it, Indiana did not repeal its law and North Carolina is still defending its RFRA-type laws (and Mississippi and Arkansas passed their own RFRA-type laws). While some states (and some businesses) favor being for LGBT rights for business and personal reasons, other states (and other businesses) find the other side more politically and economically appealing. All politics is local, it has been often said, and on this issue that might be even more the case. One might argue that it would be silly for politicians to challenge long-settled legal questions but that ignores two things—first, politicians are often motivated by votes and not legal logic, and, second, politicians are still trying to overturn (or at least be seen as symbolically fighting against) the Supreme Court decisions banning school prayer nearly 60 years after that decision. Finally, one's constitutional rights, nationwide, are supposed to be guaranteed across the country. If it truly is just a state constitutional issue, then it should not be in front of the U.S. Supreme Court.

One should also not assume that the failure or non-enactment of RFRA-type laws on the state level will cause an end to efforts to restrict rights. Another way to accomplish the same goals is a ballot initiative in some areas. On the negative side for those wanting the restriction is that not all states allow ballot initiatives, and some make them very difficult to conduct. On the other side, ballot initiatives do not allow as much scrutiny as to motive. Regarding California's Proposition 8, which banned same-sex marriages, author Kenji Yoshino wrote, "The desire to cloak religious intent may explain why faith-based opposition to same-sex marriage has turned to ballot initiatives."[12] Yoshino added,

> In debating legislation, such opponents risk leaving a paper trail about the religious basis for their vote, and courts or voters may call them to account. For an ecclesiastical majority with lawmaking ambitions, a ballot initiative is the friendliest forum. Shielded, often literally, by a curtain, voters may cast their ballots on whatever grounds they wish, even religious ones. If the law is challenged in court, it will be much harder to discern whether it was passed with the requisite secular purpose because it will be harder to discern purpose of any kind. As gay people have emerged from the closet, some religious opponents of gay rights have retreated into the "closet" of the voting booth to express their views.[13]

This suggests that such initiatives will continue to be used to oppose equal rights for LGBT people, particularly in marriage. Thus, one cannot (and should not) assume that this issue will end if things like RFRAs do not continue to be based on the state level. It will just make it more difficult for such ordinances to be passed, as some states do not allow initiatives and referendums, and it will then just slow. One might wonder if the issue will ever end, but it is always difficult to predict the future.

Finally, the free exercise clause popped up in other areas in the 2010s, although they were phrased more in the area of free exercise than in the area of a religious exemption to laws, although both might apply. In 2012, the U.S. Supreme Court considered the case of *Hosanna-Tabor Evangelical Lutheran Church and School v. Equal Employment Opportunity Commission*. That case centered on a teacher and minister who had narcolepsy who had been dismissed and who had argued that the ADA (Americans with Disabilities Act) prevented her from being dismissed, as she should be accommodated. The church held that the threat of legal action, along with insubordination, resulted in her dismissal. The church's own policy banned such lawsuits and wanted church disputes to be handled internally (which would, of course, always wind up with the church winning). The church invoked a "ministerial exception," meaning that churches should be able to control their own ministers. The Supreme Court sided with the church. The Court looked at a number of different issues, including whether or not this person was a minister. As she had presented herself as such (and because a formal request, or call, from the congregation was needed), she clearly was a minister. It should be noted that the Supreme Court considered this a more open-and-shut case than many, as the district court had found for the church on a motion for summary judgment. In layman's terms, summary judgment for the defendant means that even if all the facts in question go the way of the plaintiff, the defendant (or whoever is filing for summary judgment) still wins the case, as the law is so clearly on the defendant's side. The Court recapped history, holding that control of property and control of the clergy rested solely in the church. The Court even held that the Supreme Court generally should not ask if the church followed its own procedures. The court allowed for a ministerial exception and held that this case did not contradict *Smith*, the peyote case, as the peyote case covered a physical act while this case covered a church's own internal mission. The concurrence filed argued that one did not need to be an ordained minister, as many other religions did not have ordinations or something similar to it. The concurrence would have looked more at the activities undertaken rather than the formal nature of what qualified the person to hold that position.

Another case was *Christian Legal Society v. Martinez*, decided by the U.S. Supreme Court in 2010. That case concerned the University of California's Hastings College of the Law. That body had developed a nondiscrimination policy which required all student groups to admit all students regardless of belief. The Christian Legal Society (CLS) wanted to exclude those who would not swear to support a statement of beliefs and also to exclude those who supported anyone whose behavior violated those beliefs. The group at question here were LGBT students. (While this was treated as a freedom of association and speech case, the beliefs here emanated from religion and so are being discussed here, as one could have claimed an exemption to the policy based on the freedom of religion.) The Supreme Court held that the CLS could be banned from being recognized as an official group. First noted was that the school had clearly set up a limited public forum. Justice Ruth Bader Ginsburg, who wrote the majority opinion, held that an option suggested by the society would not work. The society wanted the school to allow bans on conduct, but not status, and the Court held that this was unworkable. The Court then held that the society's proposed distinction between belief and conduct would not work in the area of LGBT students (the society had wanted to ban those who engaged in homosexual conduct but claimed to allow those who were LGBT), as there really was no distinction here.

Two justices wrote concurrences. First, John Paul Stevens held that the proposed ban on LGBT members could be used to exclude minorities or exclude those who did not hold the same dislike for minorities as a larger group. Second, Justice Kennedy wrote to note that the freedom of association was being restricted here but that the benefits of the policy promoting all being welcome outweighed the harm.

The dissent held that this was more of a "nondiscrimination" policy than an "all comers" policy. While the difference might seem small, according to past cases, if the policy was one of nondiscrimination, then the freedom of association came into play, as the burden on the message of the group should be considered. If the group's message was burdened by this nondiscrimination policy (and, of course, if it was a policy of nondiscrimination), then the policy could be struck down. In a previous case, the right of the Boy Scouts to exclude homosexuals had been upheld as forcing them to accept homosexuals had been held to burden their message. It is interesting, in light of *Burwell* only four years later, that the issue of religion and the right of an organization to religious freedom was not a major focus. This makes *Burwell* seem even more like an outlier. Many in the media noted at the time, correctly, that this did not conclude the issue and that more litigation would occur, particularly with a 5–4 split on the Court and the two concurrences.

One other case from this time period had religious implications but was not a straightforward religious freedom case (or dealt with mostly as a religious case at all). This was the case of *Snyder v. Phelps* (2011), which dealt with the Westboro Baptist Church and their picketing of funerals. The Church had, for several years, protested at a variety of funerals, including some military ones. Their protests aimed to convince people that God hated the U.S. military as it allowed homosexuals to serve. Thus, any death of a U.S. military member was pleasing to God in the eyes of Westboro Baptist. This was, obviously, both quite controversial and upsetting to many in the military and their families. Various places tried to shut off the protests, with only limited success. This lawsuit was another such attempt. In this case, the Church was sued for a tort of emotional distress, as the father of the victim stated that he had been put through emotional distress due to the protests at his son's funeral. The trial court awarded him damages of $10 million, which were reduced and then the Circuit Court of Appeals reversed it, holding that speech in a public area was protected.

The Supreme Court ruled that even outrageous speech deserved protection. It should be noted that the Supreme Court and appeals court both noted that there was no clear evidence that the funeral had been disrupted, and this suggests that the rulings might have been different (or at least closer) had the funeral been disrupted. However, this was looked at as mostly a freedom of speech and expression case, not a freedom of religion case. No religious exemption from the tort was suggested but more one of whether the expression could be allowed in a public area. Of course, it should be also noted that the Westboro Baptist Church could claim a religious exemption as it is clearly (at least in terms of the law) a church and so fits clearly under the First Amendment's freedom of religion. At the very least, it is more of a church and closer to the core of the First Amendment than the Hobby Lobby corporation. Thus, if Hobby Lobby gets a pass on the law, does Westboro Baptist? It is a fair question to ask of those who would support Hobby Lobby. One might be inclined to say no, based on Westboro Baptist being viewed very negatively but one's public opinion ratings are not supposed to affect constitutional law.

As of the first printing, the U.S. Supreme Court has agreed to hear a Colorado case balancing freedom of religion, marriage, business, and prejudice. In 2012, a baker refused to bake a cake for a gay couple who were getting married in Massachusetts (Colorado did not allow same-sex marriages at the time), and the baker had been charged under Colorado's anti-discrimination ordinance. The baker claimed religious freedom as a defense. After losing in the Colorado Supreme Court, the baker appealed to the U.S. Supreme Court. This is not fully parallel to a case under an RFRA-type law, as Colorado has an anti-discrimination ordinance (and does not have an RFRA-type law). The case is Masterpiece Cakeshop v. Colorado Civil Rights Commission. It should be heard sometime in the 2017–2018 term.

Conclusion: A Necessary Balance

This text has examined the intersection between different constitutional civil liberties, both historically and in the modern era. In the past, this has meant the intersection between civil liberties and government, but in the present, this collision is largely between the civil liberties of individuals. It is important to remember that the terms are not reserved for minority groups, particularly in reference to constitutional protections of broader liberties. The phrase "civil rights and liberties" can be substituted for "civil liberties" without changing this, even though some definitions reserve "civil liberties" for those cases relating to the First Amendment while using "civil rights" with regard to other broader liberties or in reference to racial minorities.

One such broader liberty is the freedom to assemble protected by the First Amendment. Marriage is, in many ways, the most important assembly in which one can participate. Thus, cases relating to marriage equality may well pit two First Amendment rights against each other. Even if equality is considered solely based on the Fourteenth Amendment, the conflict between constitutional rights and liberties remains. On the one hand, civil rights activists have successfully argued that marriage equality is a liberty granted to couples regardless of gender. On the other, some conservative Christian groups, particularly fundamentalist Christians, believe that the religious liberty granted under the First Amendment includes the freedom to discriminate even in functions unrelated to religion.

Let us be clear here—this book is neither proposing to force opposed religious organizations to perform same-sex marriages nor suggesting direct regulation of religious organizations as a whole. There is some, but not much, discussion of setting parameters for directly affiliated religious entities, such as schools or hospitals. The First Amendment has always differentiated between the religious activities of a church and activities outside of a church (when the broader definition of a church, as a religious organization as a whole, is considered). This necessitates an evaluation of the line between religious and secular activities, lest all activities fall under the umbrella of religious freedom, which seems an unreasonable stretch of the First Amendment. Finally, it requires an analysis of when the activities of someone with deep religious feelings can be regulated. If religious people are exempt from regulation, while secular individuals are not, the issue simply shifts to ask what a religion is. While these questions are sticky ones, they must be answered in order to determine the boundaries of religious freedom outside of a church.

Given the level of tension and hostility religions can inspire, it does not seem reasonable to simply exempt those who follow named religious systems from generally applicable restrictions on their actions while not granting the same exemptions to groups that believe in things which are not considered religions at the time. The battle would just shift to what makes up a religion and perhaps even further increase tension. However, the battle does not need to even get that far.

The key interaction, at least in the press, has asked at what point a state can require one individual to treat another fairly. It is not sufficient to paint the issue solely in terms of religious freedom, as doing so effectively strips all limits from religious freedom. After all, religion has been used to justify both human sacrifice and slavery over the course of human history. There is no question that such extremes would not be protected by the First Amendment today. In addition to being human rights, those rights are also enshrined in the Constitution, which means that the religious freedoms of one person *are* limited by the personal rights of another.

Some political positions, such as libertarianism, argue that the state should never be allowed to limit any constitutionally enshrined liberties. However, even outside of extreme cases, even a brief study of U.S. history with regard to the evils suffered by African Americans and other minorities would caution one against taking a simplistic view that allowed for those with the loudest voices and greatest numbers automatic victory in cases of conflict. Another view states that only governmental actions are affected by the Bill of Rights. Once again, the late nineteenth century cautions against this. Most constitutional liberties erode if the only protection is against the government's direct action.

Finally, some believe that only certain groups, as defined by a government, should be protected. Two items there suggest pause. First, note that this does not solve the issue but merely transfers it, in an adult version of hot potato. Politicians would still need to define what groups would be protected. This would activate the political arena, which would not necessarily be pleasing to those on the libertarian side of the issue, who want the government out of it, nor to the other sides who rightly note that the political system did not solve the issue in the first place and are skeptical of its ability to do so now. Second, the legal system itself resists such definitions. In 1938, the Supreme Court held in *Carolene Products* that legislation which targeted "discrete and insular minorities" was particularly suspect. The phrase would seem to apply here. Those opposing equal treatment of same-sex marriages might argue that gays and lesbians are not discrete and insular minorities, but if a group has been the only one discriminated against in a particular fashion (in the area of marriage) for the last 50 years (since the end of bans on interracial marriage) the vocabulary seems apt indeed.

In fact, most scholarly discourse on the issue focuses on the use of that term rather than whether gays and lesbians fit the definition. In some ways, the argument is circular. The success of those favoring discrimination against gays and lesbians emphasizes the nature of this minority group, which in turn allows (or perhaps requires) the government to pursue actions promoting equal treatment.

Some who argue that race should be protected from discrimination while sexual orientation should not claim that the former is a born trait while the latter is a chosen behavior. Two issues, at least, argue against this perspective. First, there is a good deal of evidence holding that sexuality is *not* chosen, or at least not in all cases. Thus to allow discrimination would be to allow prejudice against an innate characteristic. Second, courts typically hold against laws targeting minorities. It would then seem the government should be motivated to avoid prejudice against gays and lesbians.

However, neither all states nor the federal government has moved to protect against discrimination on the basis of sexual orientation. It would be impossible to allow discrimination (either individually or governmentally) based on chosen sexuality while banning it because of innate sexuality. One can easily imagine the sticky wicket of questions. "Before I sell you a wedding cake, I need to know if your sexual orientation is chosen or innate?" "How sure are you that it is innate?" "Have you taken a test to see if it is innate?" (And surely someone would develop one, regardless of its effectiveness. More likely five or six tests would be developed, one representing every political perspective and a special mobile app.) In other words, trying to make such a determination would be stupid, irrelevant, and pointless, and, more to the legal point, would not solve the issue.

Perhaps the issue of whether discrimination should be allowed will return to the political arena. At first blush, this seems favorable to those in favor of discrimination. However, growing support for minority rights in the last 20 years suggests that politicians might not be as opposed to LGBT rights in general as they have been in the past.

Opponents of marriage equality still hold to the argument that sexual orientation is a choice and insist that discrimination based on choices is permitted. And indeed, the legal system discriminates routinely based on choices. The real issue is what choices can be the focus of discrimination. In fact, many of the things humans hold most dear are choices. After all, half of this debate about the allowed interaction between religion and sexual orientation is. Religion is, unquestionably, a choice. If discrimination solely on the basis of choice is allowed, then should not discrimination on the basis of religion be allowed? Freedom of religion is protected by the First Amendment, but the Supreme Court has distinguished between religious belief and religious action, ultimately concluding that actions can be the focus of regulation while beliefs cannot. Allowing discrimination against those who choose to be LGBT would toss the issue back into the legislative realm, and drafting an amendment to protect the choice of sexual orientation is again fraught with difficulty, not only because scientific studies have repeatedly determined that sexual orientation is not a choice.

Ultimately, the debate returns to the question of what religious actions are protected. Does religion allow a believer to practice discrimination against anyone solely because of sexual orientation? Before that question can be addressed, the shrewd analyst must also ask whether sexuality in general is already protected. If the Constitution allows the choice of dress to the point of wearing obscenities, does it allow the symbolic speech of sexual choice or the symbolic statement of one's sexual orientation, chosen or otherwise? Many areas remain to be litigated. Thus, though opponents of marriage equality may call sexual orientation a choice, this determination does not create an arena where discrimination is permissible. Finally, marriage in general is a choice, and discrimination against married people in general is usually viewed with disfavor.

Historically, federal courts have only had to evaluate the ways in which the First Amendment applies to the government practices, not individual ones. Indeed, some argue that the First Amendment (and others) only prevents government discrimination but that avenue is not necessarily determinative either. If that is the correct view, then racial and gender discrimination would also become permissible. While the Fourteenth

Amendment is generally aimed at banning racial discrimination, it was worded much more broadly and addresses more than that one issue.

Indeed, history points out that merely banning government action does not create true equality. In the late nineteenth and early twentieth centuries, much of the discrimination against African Americans, particularly in the South, did not come from the government; it came from individuals. The government allowed hotels and restaurants to turn away African Americans, though it rarely legally mandated such. African Americans were not hired at the same rate as whites, even though few government regulations directly controlled employment. Thus, if the Fourteenth Amendment is to create equality, individual discrimination must be considered in addition to government discrimination.

All of these factors seem to point to the issue returning to the political arena. But those who favor discrimination practiced under the umbrella of religious freedom might do well to read those polls again. That is not to say that the issue has been decided forever in favor of marriage equality. Its supporters cannot rest easy, as the last 25 years have been a hard struggle.

Is this constant jockeying the best solution? Though the question steps very much into political science grounds and future casting, history does offer some parallels. Many states had bans on interracial marriage in the early twentieth century, and all of those had ended by 1970 (following the *Loving v. Virginia* case in 1967). However, the debate about interracial marriage prior to the 1960s more closely resembles the debate about marriage equality in the early 2000s. By the time of the *Loving* decision, the number of states with interracial marriage bans had dropped dramatically. In contrast, 30 states had interracial marriage bans in the early- to mid-1950s. The power shifts between the 1950s and the *Loving* decision closely resemble those taking place now in the marriage equality debate.

Several things can be learned from that comparison. One is that courts have not forced churches and other religious institutions to add the *Loving* decision to their doctrine. No unwilling church has been ordered to marry an interracial couple. Though few churches had bans on interracial marriage at the time of *Loving*, Dr. Martin Luther King Jr. noted that Sunday morning was the most segregated hour in America. Some Southern white churches also actively promoted segregation in all things, surely including interracial marriage. Jonathan Daniels, one of the civil rights martyrs, noted that he, as an Episcopal seminary student, was not allowed to bring African Americans into a white church in Selma in 1965, just two years before *Loving*.[1] Attitudes in the South had not shifted dramatically by 1967, so it is certain that churches did not scramble to embrace the *Loving* decision, and the court system did not require them to do so.

Those who favor religion-based discrimination due to sexual orientation would do well to pay attention to those examples. History demonstrates what is *not* at stake—religions are not being forced to change their own policies, and no state has established what a religion can and cannot do. Beyond that, the *Loving* decision, by extension, asks whether or not general discrimination against interracial couples is legal. Today's parallel to this question lies in claims that businesses should be able to deny business services to same-sex couples. Courts have consistently opposed racial discrimination in business, on any grounds. It seems difficult to argue that religious freedom permits business discrimination, if for no other reason than that it turns gray areas into murky morasses. How should the legal system determine what kinds of discrimination are allowed and under what circumstances they may be practiced? At what point would allowing such discrimination, in order to support the freedom of religion, violate the Fourteenth Amendment's guarantees of equality?

The rhetoric and rationale of those who opposed interracial marriage on religious grounds in the 1950s and 1960s roughly parallels the rhetoric used by marriage equality's opponents in the 2010s. Those who favor state versions of the RFRAs, at least recently, have claimed that their support is not *only* about same-sex marriage and LGBT rights but about all religions and all circumstances. However, this definition is far too broad, and the actual motivation for writing the RFRAs along with the ways in which they are applied nearly always relate to LGBT issues. Marriage equality's opponents are attempting to gain allies and hide their motives by suggesting all religions and all religious choices are at risk from government intervention.

Only a few years have passed since the *Obergefell v. Hodges* decision proclaimed that the federal Constitution requires marriage equality. This is not enough time to determine the decision's long-term effects on religion. But a look at the 50 years since the *Loving* decision suggests that, while many religions have voluntarily changed racist rhetoric, no court has mandated such an adjustment.

Broadening the debate, though, when faced honestly, creates its own set of issues. Nearly *all* federal laws against discrimination could probably be interpreted to violate one religion or another. The Supreme Court found that Hobby Lobby craft stores did not have to pay for insurance that would fund certain types of birth control that violated the tenants of the company's owners' religion. Whereas an historical examination of the

Loving decision shows a generally positive social trend when legal decisions favor equality, an examination of historical parallels to the *Hobby Lobby* decision reveals quite the opposite.

Religious groups hoping to use the First Amendment to evade all generally applicable laws closely resemble those nineteenth-century corporations that manipulated the Constitution to force federal decisions that were unfavorable to workers. Indeed, corporations held nearly all power against the individual and against the government. While "closely held corporations" are now needed to gain constitutional protections such as those enjoyed by large companies in the past, broadening the *Hobby Lobby* decision, or even applying it widely, would provide incentives for companies to reorganize for financial gain and other benefits. After all, corporations that did not have to pay minimum wage or overtime could save a lot of money.

To be fair to those favoring the *Hobby Lobby* decision, nothing so drastic has yet been argued in federal court. However, because of the broad nature of some state bills, issues relating to discrimination based on the freedom of religion have far more potential to reach state courts. House Bill 2 in North Carolina, for instance, cancelled some antidiscrimination lawsuits outright. Those favoring religious accommodation must consider the point at which public and legislative favor will swing against laws striking down all protective laws.

It could be argued that laws like North Carolina's House Bill 2 only allow religious-based discrimination against certain things, such as same-sex marriage and certain birth control items. However, the problems with that perspective are several as well. First, the First Amendment is very general and does *not* limit itself to specific items. First Amendment claims should be general in nature in order for any related decision to legally be effective. Second, and possibly of greater importance, the word "discrimination" bears scrutiny. The denial of services, for whatever reason, is a form of discrimination, and when a law allows religion-based discrimination, it effectively favors the freedom of religion over the right to equality. Indeed, it assumes that it is, in fact, a violation of the First Amendment to require a business to serve all equally or allow its employees access to privately choose their form of birth control. Finally, it is also more difficult to cloak oneself in the guise of religion while targeting only certain things. Thus, the political stance favoring the denial of services to same-sex couples and disallowing individual control of contraceptive choices is not as simple or solid as it might seem at a glance.

As the *Obergefell* decision will probably not be overturned (and is supported by most), those opposing marriage equality have had to face a concept that was not previously socially acceptable. Rather than dealing with it, some are attempting to weaken the right to an equal marriage by denying services to same-sex couples. This attitude, in addition to drawing support from many fundamentalist Christian churches, also serves to rally votes for some politicians.

How much of this most recent tussle is about change and being forced to accept change and deal with differences? In addition to the *Hobby Lobby* and *Obergefell* decisions, one favoring discrimination and the other equality, the legal system has had to balance the rights of transgender individuals against social objections. Just as an increasing body of scientific evidence demonstrates that sexual orientation is innate, numerous scientific studies argue that gender identity is about far more than genitalia. There have always been transgendered people, plenty of whom doubtless have used the bathroom corresponding to the gender they identify with rather than their assigned sex. However, until recently, the rest of the population has not been forced to deal with the idea. Now that the issue is public, there is a great hue and cry, largely from the same groups opposed to marriage equality, tossing out unproven claims of child endangerment to garner social support from other groups. The country has seen a bevy of state-level "bathroom bills" requiring (or allowing), on the one hand, businesses to allow visitors to choose which bathroom to use and, on the other, mandating that transgender people use only the bathroom of the gender on their birth certificates. Though the federal courts have yet to take a stance, and attempts to pass a federal bathroom bill have failed, this issue will doubtless be one of the next put before the Supreme Court.

One might object that all of the opprobrium is pointed toward those wanting to claim their First Amendment rights to religious freedom. But it is impossible to deny that these groups effectively want religious freedom to trump equality, thereby allowing discrimination against same-sex couples, transgendered individuals, and others. However, legal decisions favoring equality have created greater social good than those *denying* equality, whatever the reason for the discrimination.

When seeking balance, however, both parties' needs must be considered, though. When equality is favored, the Fourteenth Amendment is placed above the First Amendment in certain instances. This is problematic because *all* of the amendments to the Constitution are supposed to be equal. The Bill of Rights' framers did not put the amendments in any order of importance before sending them out to the states, as best can be told. (The First Amendment was originally the Third when the Bill of Rights was sent out to the states. It became the First Amendment when the first two *proposed* amendments were not ratified.)

It could be argued that those decisions closest to the present have the most bearing on current affairs. By this logic, the Fourteenth Amendment was written later, and its understanding of equality's importance should have greater legal standing than First Amendment claims to the freedom of religion. While this might be true, the problem is not the order of the First and Fourteenth Amendments. The problem is that the Fourteenth Amendment also protects liberty, including religious liberty. Thus, in some ways, the courts are balancing one element of the Fourteenth Amendment against another, without fully examining the idea that businesses should only be exempt from generally applicable laws in strict and narrow circumstances.

A final argument might be that religious liberty never trumps equality, which is even more fundamentally important to life. This seems less compelling than others and bears too much resemblance to the argument that religious liberty should always trump because *it* is more fundamental. Indeed, this view would allow the forces of equality to dictate religion. Those wanting gender equality could require a church that did not allow women or minorities to be religious leaders to violate their own deeply held principles to hire them anyway. Instead of merely privileging equality over religion, it could destroy religion (or at least some religions). This seems to go directly against the principles underlying both the freedom of religion *and* equality.

Thus, it seems the Court *must* determine boundaries for when religious liberty should be more important than equality (and vice-versa). One key question to be answered is what groups are protected by the freedom of religion and whether a corporation can claim the same rights to religious liberty as an individual. For the present, according to the *Hobby Lobby* decision, the courts have said yes. However, history suggests a general decrease in the legal power granted to corporations, even as those entities grow larger in size. Moreover, history shows that corporations overstretching their power ultimately cause social harm, rather than good, and suggests that the court system will eventually take notice.

Thus, it seems clear that churches should receive more protections than corporations or individuals. The principle of freedom of religion *must* decrease once someone steps out of the wholly religious realm, or else it would be unlimited. Those presenting the Founding Fathers as demigods frequently point out how religious they were. These claims seem to overlook Thomas Jefferson's demand for a total wall between church and state. It also is problematic, as pointed out earlier in the book, as not all of the Founding Fathers who wanted religion to have an impact agreed on what religion meant or what that impact should be. Moreover, if religious concerns cloaked all activity, then at some point, the freedom *of* religion would come into conflict with the freedom *from* religion guaranteed in the First Amendment. Moreover, the Founding Fathers clearly distinguished between personal religion and the exercise of government. If religions all agreed with one another and if religion checked all laws, then federal and state governments would soon become unnecessary.

In the end, the question remains the same. When should one person's constitutional claim to religious liberty outweigh another person's claim to constitutional equality? Religious liberty is defined more vaguely than other liberties, making the question far more complex than it might seem. Freedom of speech and the press are also vague ideas, but both can be more easily discussed in terms of limits than can be freedom of religion. Moreover, these other liberties have been assigned liberties and categories. They are neither universal nor all encompassing. Libel and slander, for example, are not protected by the freedoms of press and speech, and they are strictly defined concepts that protect people from suffering when others spread lies.

Similarly, the Fourth, Fifth, and Ninth Amendments are typically raised in conversations about the right to privacy, the right to being invaded by the Hobby Lobby corporation when it chooses what forms of contraception it will allow its employees to access in an insurance plan. Do all individuals have the same rights to privacy or are there different classes?

Religion resists simply defined classes, and perhaps it should. There are a huge number of religions, each with its own set of beliefs. Religion, more than other matters, is a highly individual practice, which is not the case with other freedoms. Thus, any limits placed on the freedom of religion must acknowledge this complexity. Nonetheless, its importance must be weighed against the right to equal treatment under the law.

Previously, the Supreme Court has considered religion to be a communal activity. In reference to Justice Jackson's opinion in the *Barnette* flag salute case of 1943, William Miller writes:

> Justice Jackson broadened the issue to a general freedom of the mind and spirit and opinion, which government here [in the United States] does not control, about which no official can "proscribe," which is sound enough for the broader understanding of the moral foundations of the United States—but for our purpose we would discriminate the distinct realm of religion, as something more (and often something less as well) than a cluster of ideas or opinions held in an individual's mind. Religion includes practices as well as "opinions," and practices and beliefs that are engaged in and affirmed communally and not primarily by solitary individuals.[2]

Considering only the word "communal," companies might seem to be communities. But remember that the *Hobby Lobby* case rested on the assumption that some corporations could claim legal personhood. Moreover, corporations are built around mutually shared economic, rather than psychological, personal, or supernatural, concerns.

Religion is and should be a communal way to share those indefinable concerns, but it is quite different to say religious practices should enjoy the same protections as religious beliefs and another thing still to argue that business practices based in religious beliefs should enjoy the same protections as religious practices based in that same system. Without drawing a line between these factors, the courts effectively make the freedom of religion limitless.

Thus, one compromise position for those who believe some religious individuals and businesses should be exempt from generally applicable laws, like the Affordable Care Act, would be to propose limits to the proposed exemption. This is not to say that one should be forced to prove sincerely held beliefs.

There are other concerns as well. Legal scholars Christopher Eisgruber and Lawrence Sager write, "There are good reasons to be wary of the claim that the Free Exercise Clause should be read to give religiously motivated persons a presumptive right to disobey the law. Prominent among these is that it seems at war with the very idea of religious freedom . . . [such an exemption for a religious organization] in that it imposes a test of religious orthodoxy as a condition of constitutional entitlement."[3] Their argument is that once the rights on spirituality have been made conditional, the law would then need to determine how spiritual a claim was. A better test would be to consider how clearly the religion's doctrines specifically require or promote the action in question.

When one individual's sincerely held beliefs interfere with another's equality, the burden of proving that a religious infringement has actually occurred should be higher. For example, a religion's doctrines should be examined for evidence that the religion does indeed require the suggested discrimination specifically. This is not a complete solution, nor should it be the only balancing factor, but it is a unique proposition that the Court has never considered.

If religion is somewhat communal, communal doctrines should at least attempt to dictate follower behaviors. Freedom of religion should not allow one person to run roughshod over another. If a religion's doctrines don't require or even sanction the discrimination, then it seems unreasonable that the freedom of religion protects the practice. Doctrinal beliefs should not be the only balancing factors here, or else religion would have the opportunity overwhelm all other constitutional guarantees. Individual religions could simply modify their doctrines to prohibit anything inconvenient and then hide behind the First Amendment. However, it seems unreasonable for a person to be able to claim religious freedom without expanding upon the claim and justifying it in some way. Stated doctrine is the most obvious justification, and courts should consider this in their decisions.

For instance, if a religious group refuses to hire a woman in a position of leadership and if that claim is substantiated by doctrine, then the courts should factor this into their decision. Other factors, however, would be relevant, such as the degree to which the organization in question was actually connected to religious practice. Current labor law addresses this concern, in allowing the ministerial exemption from equal employment for religious organizations. However, when a religion merely says "hate the sin, love the sinner; being homosexual is a sin," then there is no specific proscription in the doctrine against same-sex marriage, merely a vague statement relating to homosexuality and love. Again, doctrine should not be the only concern, as even a doctrine against homosexuality or same-sex marriage is not a doctrine inviting adherents to discriminate against gay men and lesbians. Nor is it a requirement that one should discriminate against same-sex couples, and only on their wedding day.

Eisgruber and Sager argue for an equal liberty, where the freedom of religion is treated the same as other liberties, not privileged above them. It seems reasonable that equality and the liberty to marry (or the right to privacy, which includes the right to marriage and choose one's own contraceptives) should therefore be factored equally with the freedom of religion. They write, "Equal Liberty depends on the proposition that religiously motivated conduct [deserves] meaningful constitutional protection, and it provides an equality-based test to effectuate that protection. The idea, in brief, is that minority religious practices, needs and interests, must be as well and as favorably accommodated by government as are more familiar and mainstream interests."[4]

Three things bear note here (at least). First, the second sentence of the aforementioned quote clarifies that this measure is intended to give minority interests fair treatment. Most recent claims have come from majority, mainstream interests that are familiar (and sometimes trumpet that familiarity) but the primary focus of the Bill of Rights is to protect minorities. Certainly, the mainstream interests enjoy its protections, but they are generally already insulated by virtue of their popularity. Second, note that Eisgruber and Sager do allow for legal consideration of religious liberty, but only consideration and only in terms of balancing the scales. Third, the interests and practices of minority religions are supposed to be accommodated. Whether the religion in question is a majority or minority, *accommodated* and *excused* are two totally different ideas. To be granted total exemption from a generally applicable law, as is more common today, it seems a religion should bear a heavier burden of proving it is experiencing an infringement.

Eisgruber and Sager on the whole argue for equal liberty. They write:

> The model, which we call "Equal Liberty," [capitalization in original] has three distinct components. First, it insists in the name of equality that no members of our political community out to be devalued on the spiritual foundation of their important commitments and projects. Religious faith receives special constitutional solicitude in this respect, but only because of its vulnerability to hostility and neglect. Second, and again in the name of equality, Equal Liberty insists that aside from this deep and important concern with discrimination, we have no constitutional reason to treat religion as deserving special benefits or as subject to special disabilities. Finally, Equal Liberty insists on a broad understanding of constitutional liberty generally. It demands that all persons—whether engaged in religiously inspired enterprises or not—enjoy the rights of free speech, personal autonomy, associative freedom and private property that, while neither uniquely relevant to religion nor defined in terms of religion, will allow religious practice to flourish.[5]

Their explanation is helpful as a starting point, though it does not answer all of the questions. For instance, what happens when one person's personal autonomy and associative freedom conflicts with another person's right to private property (including a business)? That is basically what is occurring with the examples of the bakery, the florist, and the pizzeria that are being (or could be) sued for discriminating against same-sex couples. Those who favor religious exemptions that allow discrimination argue that by being forced to serve those whose practices are at moral odds with their own beliefs, the business owners' religious beliefs are being violated.

Rights are in conflict here. Equal liberty is fine for a starting point, but how does a court decide how to balance the law when such conflicts arise? Once again, the equal liberty model looks at a battle between government and the people or between the government's treatment of two different groups (a religious soup kitchen and a non-religious one was one of Eisgruber and Sager's examples). However, a different kind of balancing act is required when two different individuals' rights conflict.

The legal system needs another paradigm. When the government has an overarching goal for the good of the overall society and individual rights (or the organizational) come into conflict, then the test of equal liberty can be applied. Here, though, more specificity is needed. Nebulous equality is less useful when one group or individual must win in a conflict. The courts need a method to apply boundaries. One might say that religious liberty cannot be bounded, but then religious liberty becomes the only consideration and the individual becomes unbounded.

The First Amendment's goal is to give liberty to an individual, not to give an individual free reign to do whatever his or her religion says, especially when those religious commands directly impact another person. (Whether the First Amendment gives free reign when another person is not impacted is a different issue and one that moves back into the balancing issue between the individual and government.) The RFRA can control when no one else's liberty is impacted, but it should only be one factor when another liberty, particularly the liberty of equality, is at issue.

It should also be noted that privileging religion, if that approach is adopted, does not move religion out of the political arena, as privileging religion to get one out of generally applicable laws just changes the question. Originally, the question was if the laws were justified (a version of the generally applicable laws doctrine growing out of *Carolene Products* and *Reynolds*), but now some argue that religion exempts people. The question then is, What is religion? The answer privileges some conduct as religious and other conduct as not, and if all conduct is religious (one way to get out of figuring out what a religion is), then nothing can be banned.

Eisgruber and Sager point out that, as of the time of their writing, in 2007, thus not that long ago, no one was talking about wholly unburdened religion. "The Free Exercise Clause, for example, refers to laws that prohibit the 'free exercise' of religion. Free from what? From all burden whatsoever? Nobody takes that position—nobody supposes, for example, that government is obliged to subsidize religion so as to render it costless. From all legally imposed burdens? Nobody takes that position, either—government can criminalize murder even if it thereby interferes with religions that endorse human sacrifice."[6] One might hold that murder is conduct that all object to, but discrimination is allowed by some, or that not associating with certain people is not allowed by some, and this seems to rest constitutional exemptions from general laws on majority rule, which is seemingly the opposite of why the Bill of Rights was established (and also runs contrary to the evidence, which is that a sufficient amount of people thought the conduct was not acceptable or else they would not have banned it, in the cases where people are claiming constitutional exemptions from specific current laws).

The cases under consideration for personal exemptions are now more in the area of where one person's rights are always being balanced off against another's, rather than against society's or the government's. The *Smith* case of 1990, dealing with peyote, presented individual rights being balanced off perhaps against society's and perhaps against the government's. With the current personal exemptions debated, there is always another person involved. Public opinion frequently favors individual liberty unless there is a compelling governmental objective in such cases. One might object that there are two individuals here, or at least an individual and a corporation, and that is true. However, the complainant for religious freedom in the *Smith* case sought constitutional protection for practices doctrinally condoned by his minority religion. The *Hobby Lobby* case presents the exact opposite situation. Smith wanted his religious practices to be accommodated. Businesses wishing not to serve same-sex couples ask the law to condone discrimination.

A different, more protective, test in these cases is needed than in *Smith*, in order to privilege the individual. The individual should count more than society and so should weigh more heavily. An example will help here. If any individual has a religious practice, like Smith's (in the peyote case), that is banned, but no individual is directly harmed, then most of society apparently believes that RFRA should apply and there should be a compelling governmental interest to restrict the behavior. However, if Smith's use of peyote would directly impact another person's liberty, a lower standard should be required to justify regulation of the practice by government. The liberties should be weighed off against one another, rather than the religious liberty being automatically preferred.

Religious liberty should be weighed no more than any other constitutionally protected liberty. If all religious liberties are equal, then perhaps sex-couples would be preferred; after all, they are having both their equality and their right to associate infringed upon (in addition to their privacy), where only a single right, the individual freedom of religion, is in question on the other side. At the very least, the right to an equal marriage must be weighed equally with the claim of religious liberty.

So, what test is being proposed here, and should it be different for a business owner?

The second answer seems to be yes, because an answer of no means that whatever cannot be regulated in a church would not be regulated in a business. One might answer that the only types of businesses affected are closely held ones, but it does not take a genius to realize that soon almost every business would be one of the closely held if at all possible. Examples in race and gender discrimination, as well as less constitutionally suspect categories like pay jump, quickly to mind. The 1964 Civil Rights Act bans discrimination based on race in hiring. If all businesses, or all closely held businesses, need to be treated like churches, then racial discrimination could not be banned, as some religions still discriminate on the basis of race. The same is true with gender discrimination. Businesses could also start hiring employees who worked for poverty level wages, claiming their religion mandated their workers should be poor, as poverty is blessed, and the business could compare its workers to the priests of the Catholic Church, who generally take a vow of poverty.

Limitations should differentiate between the church itself as a physical entity, and more importantly as a type of entity, and a business. Businesses exist to make money while churches do not. Religious entities are usually non-profit. Businesses are for-profit. If a business does not seek profit, it should only pay employees, not stockholders and owners. For most businesses, including most closely held ones, that is not the case. Different entities deserve different treatment—if that was not the case, why do law schools offer multiple courses in business law?

A larger issue also needs to be considered here, and that is purpose. A religion exists usually to discuss a Supreme Being, to offer a code for living, and often to discuss afterlife. Thus, religion is aimed at creating right conduct for a higher purpose, not just because it is right. "Live right for the afterlife," not "live right for now," many religious entities say. For that reason, they are different from businesses. Businesses act in the here and now to survive until tomorrow or next year, not because they think their current conduct will result in the business being ushered into the afterlife. Corporations, after all, being effectively immortal, cannot enter the afterlife. If religion means anything, a business is *not* religion.

Finally, even if an individual does claim that religion mandates an action, there should be standards on that claim. Basing something solely on an individual's own interpretation allows far too much leeway. Anything could be defended on that basis. If the individual is part of any kind of organized religion, that religion's doctrines should be scrutinized in relationship to the individual's claim, and experts both within and outside of the religious organization in question should be consulted as to the appropriate interpretation of that doctrine. After all, most of the major constitutional claims litigated to the Supreme Court have dealt with conduct specifically regulated by one's own church standards.

To put the issue on point with the bakeries that want to discriminate against same-sex couples only on their wedding day (but no other day), the courts should ask whether the person's own church justified that level of conduct. This would still allow discrimination in some instances. But since religion includes practices, religious freedom must also allow some level of protected practices. One might also argue that there are few religions which allow some of the practices discussed earlier, like racial discrimination. However, how common a practice is should not factor into constitutional law.

This increases conflict between individuals in that it forces individuals to state their religions and expose them. However, claimants of a religious infringement cannot have it both ways. Individuals cannot claim that, in some instances, they live a religious life which justifies exemptions from the law and, in other cases, object to having to publicly state and follow their own religion.

This is not the same thing as mandating that anyone name his or her religion. The situation applies only if religious liberty and infringement upon it is being invoked. Of the various ideas advanced here, this is probably the least controversial. A wide variety of businesses already state their policies on religion in their advertising. Many symbols are used to either state the religion of the person who runs the business or state what charities the group supports. Very often, those charities and causes announce a religious affiliation. It is not discriminatory or limiting to ask a claimant to the protections of religious freedom to name the religion being threatened and to publicly point to the doctrine defending that practice.

Such a practice might touch off a public debate. But public debate is hardly anything new and is, in fact, part of the healthy discourse of a democracy. Other public debates already exist, with Kim Davis and the various Supreme Court decisions dominating the headlines. The last 20 years of public debate have, in fact, been needed to promote the trend toward equality. Furthermore, absent public debate, two possibilities arise, both of which run contrary to the American beliefs in equality and the freedom of religion. Perhaps the conversation could be swept under the rug, returning the nation to the 1940s, when LGBT people lived closeted lives, constantly fearing exposure. Or perhaps religion could suddenly lose relevancy, with the nation becoming wholly secular in practice. Both of these seem highly unlikely, but it is the existence of public debate that helps ensure the survival of both equality for minority rights and the freedom of religion. Thus, the question is not "should we debate?" but "what should we debate?" and "what shall we balance?"

Most of all, that debate cannot take place unless the press and the courts show respect for differing views. Respect means that one side should not be able to accuse the other of bigotry without fully defending its claim, nor should the other condemn the first to hell without an equally thorough defense. Walking away when the debate has stopped producing any results is a good thing, but without thoughtful engagement, little positive is likely to happen. If both sides just throw invectives, neither will gain. In order to move America forward on the issue, honest dialogue is needed. "Think about this" is something that both sides need to tell the other. Both sides need to also consider what protections they will allow for the other. What level of religion should we protect and what level of equality?

Views are also not monolithic. Both sides need to avoid using the word "The," with capital letters, as in "The LGBT view" or "The Baptist view." There are many different views on all sides of the issue, all of them deserving of consideration.

All of these points, though, relate only to public debate. The actual balancing must go on in the courts. It should be a balancing, and a public, one, because otherwise religious views are given free rein to accomplish their goals, up to some invisible barrier (and the only one suggested by the *Hobby Lobby* decision is racial equality). This also is important for religion, as most religious groups probably do not want to be tarred with the brush of allowing crimes and discrimination to occur and then be excused (by requesting exceptions) under the banner of religious liberty.

What is being placed on each side of the scales of justice is clear. What the courts must do is figure out a place to put the fulcrum for the best balance. Examining each claim carefully, along with requiring clarity and specificity, is the first necessary step. Then, when both claims are proven, are constitutional, and are in conflict, the court must then decide which constitutional right is slighted. Justice sometimes should be blind but in this case must look carefully into the merits of both sides. This is new ground, as previous claims have usually been the individual against government, but in this case it is individual versus individual often. History provides a guide, but as these claims are different from those of the past, history should not be blindly followed by justice either. Let the balancing begin.

Notes

Introduction

1. The Declaration of Independence, para. 2 (U.S. 1776).
2. https://www.archives.gov/founding-docs/bill-of-rights-transcript
3. https://www.ourdocuments.gov/doc.php?flash=true&doc=43&page=transcript
4. J. R. Pole, *The Pursuit of Equality in American History*, Rev. ed. (Berkeley: University of California Press, 1993), 35.
5. Ibid., xi.
6. Ibid., 4.
7. Ibid., 37.
8. Ibid., 181.
9. Louis Brandeis and Samuel Warrein, "The Right to Privacy," *Harvard Law Review* 4 (1890): 193–220.
10. Bette Novit Evans, *Interpreting the Free Exercise of Religion: The Constitution and American Pluralism* (Chapel Hill: University of North Carolina Press, 1997), 23.
11. James Henry Hammond, "The 'Mudsill' Theory," http://www.pbs.org/wgbh/aia/part4/4h3439t.html and *Loving v. Virginia*, 388 US 1 3 (quoting the district court).
12. Evans, 119.
13. Christopher L. Eisgruber and Lawrence G. Sager, *Religious Freedom and the Constitution* (Cambridge, MA: Harvard University Press, 2007), 101.
14. J. E. Barnhart quoted in Evans, 47.
15. Evans, 51.
16. Ibid., 53.
17. Brian A. Garner, *Black's Law Dictionary*, 10th ed. (St. Paul, MN : Thomson Reuters, 2014), 1482.
18. Ibid., 415.
19. Pole, 90.
20. Peter Irons, *The Courage of Their Convictions* (New York: Free Press, 1988).

21. Carolyn N. Long, *Religious Freedom and Indian Rights: The Case of Oregon v. Smith* (Lawrence: University Press of Kansas, 2000), 51.

22. John Witte and Joel A. Nichols, *Religion and the American Constitutional Experiment*, 3rd ed. (Boulder, CO: Westview Press, 2016), 306–338, especially 329.

Chapter 1. The Founding Generation

1. Nearly all of the amendments have been analyzed time and again, but religious freedom is the focus here. This comment is not meant to imply that any clause in the Bill of Rights has been without hot debate.

2. William Lee Miller, *The First Liberty: America's Foundation in Religious Freedom* (Washington, D.C.: Georgetown University Press, 2003), 147.

3. Ibid.

4. Ibid., 171.

5. Richard Labunski, *James Madison and the Struggle for the Bill of Rights* (New York: Oxford, 2006), 20.

6. Jack N. Rakove, *Original Meanings: Politics and Ideas in the Making of the Constitution* (New York: A.A. Knopf, 1996), 317.

7. Ibid., 316.

8. Miller, 103.

9. Ibid., 103.

10. Donald L. Drakeman, *Church, State and Original Intent* (Cambridge, UK: Cambridge University Press, 2010), 197.

11. Labunski, 215.

12. Rakove, 291.

13. Miller, 195.

14. Ibid., 196.

15. Christopher L. Eisgruber and Lawrence G. Sager, *Religious Freedom and the Constitution* (Cambridge, MA: Harvard University Press, 2007), 72.

16. J. R. Pole, *The Pursuit of Equality in American History*, Rev. ed. (Berkeley: University of California Press, 1993), 99.

17. Gregg Frazer, *The Religious Beliefs of America's Founders: Reason, Revelation and Revolution* (Lawrence: University Press of Kansas, 2014), 1.

18. Ibid., 51.

19. Ibid., 81.

20. Ibid., 46.

21. *The Founders' Constitution*, Vol. 5, Bill of Rights, Document 2, http://press-pubs.uchicago.edu/founders/documents/bill_of_rightss2.html

22. Miller, 54.

23. Frazier, 37–38.

24. Ibid., 38.

25. Ibid., 27.

26. Miller, 55.

27. Quoted in Eisgruber and Sager, 23.

28. Miller, 92.

29. James H. Hutson, *Forgotten Features of the Founding: The Recovery of Religious Themes in the Early American Republic* (Lanham, MD: Lexington Books, 2003), 146.

30. Miller, 103.

31. James Madison, "Detached Memoranda," http://press-pubs.uchicago.edu/founders/documents/amendI_religions64.html

32. Ibid.

33. Rakove, 312.

34. Miller, 119.

35. Frazier, 27.

36. Miller, 123.

Chapter 2. Freedom from Religion

1. *Barron v. Baltimore*, 32 U.S. 243, 251 (1833).

2. Thomas Jefferson to Major John Cartwright Monticello (June 5, 1824). http://www.let.rug.nl/usa/presidents/thomas-jefferson/letters-of-thomas-jefferson/jefl278.php

3. *Vidal v. Girard's Executors*, 43 U.S. 127, 198.

4. "The Universal Law of Slavery," by George Fitzhugh, http://www.pbs.org/wgbh/aia/part4/4h3141t.html

5. Pole, 144.

6. See generally Don E. Fehrenbacher, *The Dred Scott Case: Its Significance in American Law and Politics* (New York: Oxford University Press, 2001).

7. Miller, 99.

8. National Archives, Amendments 11 to 27, http://www.archives.gov/exhibits/charters/constitution_amendments_11-27.html

9. David A. Skeel, *Debt's Dominion: A History of Bankruptcy Law in America* (Princeton, NJ: Princeton University Press, 2001).

10. The 1894 New York Constitution at https://www.nycourts.gov/history/legal-history-new-york/documents/Publications_1894-NY-Constitution.pdf

11. Matthew Burton Bowman, *The Mormon People: The Making of an American Faith* (New York: Random House, 2012), 128.

12. Ibid., 128–129.

13. Ibid., 141.

14. *Reynolds v. United States*, 98 U.S. 145, 166 (1878).

15. Ibid., 166–167 (1878).

16. Bowman, 145.

Chapter 3. Religious Exemptions from the Gilded Age through the 1920s

1. Clifford Putney, *Muscular Christianity: Manhood and Sports in Protestant America, 1880–1920* (Cambridge, MA: Harvard University Press, 2001), 1.

2. Oliver Wendell Holmes Jr., *The Common Law* (Boston: Little, Brown and Company, 1881), 1.

3. *Schenck v. United States*, 249 U.S. 47, 52 (1919).

4. *Abrams v. United States*, 250 U.S. 616, 628 (1919).

5. *Abrams v. United States*, dissent, 250 U.S. 616, 630 (1919). See also, generally, Richard Polenberg, *Fighting Faiths: The Abrams Case, The Supreme Court, and Free Speech* (Ithaca, NY: Cornell University Press, 1987).

6. *Gitlow v. People of New York*, 268 U.S. 652, 666 (1925).

Chapter 4. *Sherbert* and *Yoder*

1. *United States v. Carolene Products Co.*, quoted in Kermit Hall, Paul Finkelman, and James Ely, *American Legal History: Cases and Materials,* 4th ed. (New York: Oxford University Press, 2011), 495.

2. *United States v. Carolene Products Co.*, quoted in Hall, Finkelman, and Ely, 496.

3. John Witte, *Religion and the American Constitutional Experiment,* 2nd ed. (Boulder, CO: Westview Press, 2005), 124.

4. Peter Irons, *Courage of their Convictions* (New York: Free Press, 1988), 15–24, especially 17.

5. Ibid., 21.

6. *West Virginia v. Barnette*, 319 US 624, 636 (1943).

7. Ibid., 636.

8. Ibid., 638.

9. Ibid., 641.

10. Ibid., 642.

11. Ibid., dissent, 646–647.

12. Ibid., 653.

13. Merlin Owen Newton, *Armed with the Constitution: Jehovah's Witnesses in Alabama and the U.S. Supreme Court, 1939–1946* (Tuscaloosa: University of Alabama Press, 1995), quoting the Supreme Court, 131.

14. J. R. Pole, *The Pursuit of Equality in American History.* Rev. ed. (Berkeley: University of California Press, 1993), 330.

15. Jim Newton, *Justice for All: Earl Warren and the Nation He Made* (New York: Riverhead Books, 2006), 395.

16. Dan Seeger, quoted in Irons, 155.

17. Ibid., 156.

18. Ibid., 163.

19. Shawn Francis Peters, *The Yoder Case: Religious Freedom, Education and Parental Rights* (Lawrence: University Press of Kansas, 2003).

20. Ibid., 109.

21. Ibid., 115.

22. William Lee Miller, *The First Liberty: America's Foundation in Religious Freedom* (Washington, D.C.: Georgetown University Press, 2003), 217.

23. Bette Novit Evans, *Interpreting the Free Exercise of Religion: The Constitution and American Pluralism* (Chapel Hill: University of North Carolina Press, 1997), 133.

Chapter 5. *Smith*, RFRA, and Its Limitations (1980–1995)

1. *United States v. Lee* 455 U.S. 252, 257 (1982).
2. Mark A. Weitz, *Clergy Malpractice in America: Nally v. Grace Community Church of the Valley* (Lawrence: University Press of Kansas, 2001), 92.
3. Ibid., 95.
4. Ibid.
5. Ibid., 123.
6. See generally, Carolyn N. Long, *Religious Freedom and Indian Rights: The Case of Oregon v. Smith* (Lawrence: University Press of Kansas, 2000).
7. Ibid., 186.
8. Ibid., 188.
9. Ibid., 189.
10. Ibid., 191.
11. Barry W. Lynn et al., *The Right to Religious Liberty: The Basic ACLU Guide To Religious Rights* (Carbondale: Southern Illinois University Press, 1995). eBook collection, EBSCOhost (November 17, 2016). http://web.b.ebscohost .com.libproxy.troy.edu/ehost/detail/detail?sid=0cdfc722-ac05-4761-83b5-ee3 8aa5fda9b%40sessionmgr120&vid=0&hid=123&bdata=JnNpdGU9ZWhvc3 QtbGl2ZQ%3d%3d#AN=2310&db=nlebk
12. Christopher L. Eisgruber and Lawrence G. Sager, *Religious Freedom and the Constitution* (Cambridge, MA: Harvard University Press, 2007), 46.

Chapter 6. From RFRA to *Hobby Lobby*

1. J. R. Pole, *The Pursuit of Equality in American History*, Rev. ed. (Berkeley: University of California Press, 1993), 122.
2. Ibid., 457.
3. Ibid.
4. Michael Harrington, *The Other America: Poverty in the United States* (New York: Macmillan, 1962).
5. http://www.politifact.com/punditfact/statements/2014/jul/01/sally-kohn/ did-hobby-lobby-once-provide-birth-control-coverag/
6. Martin S. Lederman, "Reconstructing RFRA: The Contested Legacy of Religious Freedom Restoration," 125 *Yale Law Journal Forum* 416 (2016), http:// www.yalelawjournal.org/forum/reconstructing-rfra-the-contested-legacy-of-religious- freedom-restoration
7. Ibid.
8. Douglas NeJaime and Reva B. Siegel, "Conscience Wars: Complicity-Based Conscience Claims in Religion and Politics," 124 *Yale Law Journal*, May 2015, 2202–2679.
9. Ibid.

Chapter 7. Marriage Equality and Beyond

1. Kenji Yoshino, *Speak Now Marriage Equality on Trial: The Story of Hollingsworth v. Perry* (New York: Broadway Books, 2016), 100.

2. James Quelly, "$828,000 Raised for Indiana Pizzeria That Said It Won't Cater Gay Weddings," *LA Times* (April 3, 2015). http://www.latimes.com/nation/nationnow/la-na-nn-indiana-pizzeria-gay-rights-20150403-story.html

3. Casey Parks, "Oregon Lawyers: Sweet Cakes by Melissa $135,000 Damage Award Was Justified," *Oregon Live* (August 24, 2016). http://www.oregonlive.com/portland/index.ssf/2016/08/oregon_lawyers_sweet_cakes_by.html

4. Casey Parks, "Sweet Cakes Owners Have a New Lawyer: George H.W. Bush's Counsel," *Oregon Live* (February 23, 2016). http://www.oregonlive.com/business/index.ssf/2016/02/sweet_cakes_owners_have_a_new.html

5. Casey Parks, "The Hate Keeps Coming: Pain Lingers for Lesbian Couple Denied in Sweet Cakes Case," *Oregon Live* (July 2, 2016). http://www.oregonlive.com/pacific-northwest-news/index.ssf/2016/07/sweet_cakes_lesbians.html

6. Eric Bradner, "Arkansas Governor Signs Amended 'Religious Freedom' Measure," CNN (April 2, 2015). http://www.cnn.com/2015/03/31/politics/arkansas-religious-freedom-anti-lgbt-bill/

7. "Arkansas AG Asks for Oral Arguments over LGBT Protections," *Washington Times* (September 28, 2016). http://www.washingtontimes.com/news/2016/sep/16/arkansas-ag-asks-for-oral-arguments-over-lgbt-prot/

8. http://www.ncleg.net/Sessions/2015E2/Bills/House/PDF/H2v4.pdf

9. Yoshino, 103.

10. Yoshino, 119.

11. J. R. Pole, *The Pursuit of Equality in American History*, Rev. ed. (Berkeley: University of California Press, 1993), 352.

12. Yoshino, 58.

13. Ibid.

Conclusion. A Necessary Balance

1. Charles W. Eagles, *Outside Agitator: Jon Daniels and the Civil Rights Movement in Alabama* (Chapel Hill: University of North Carolina Press, 1993), especially 67–71.

2. William Lee Miller, *The First Liberty: America's Foundation in Religious Freedom* (Washington, D.C.: Georgetown University Press, 2003), 227.

3. Christopher L. Eisgruber and Lawrence G. Sager, *Religious Freedom and the Constitution* (Cambridge, MA: Harvard University Press, 2007), 11.

4. Ibid., 13.

5. Ibid., 52–53.

6. Ibid., 68–69.

Select Bibliography

Books

Alschuler, Albert W. *Law without Values: The Life, Work, and Legacy of Justice Holmes*. Chicago: University of Chicago Press, 2000.

Beeman, Richard R. *Plain, Honest Men: The Making of the American Constitution*. New York: Random House, 2009.

Bellamy, Edward. *Looking Backward: 2000–1887*. New York: Oxford University Press, 2009.

Berkin, Carol. *A Brilliant Solution: Inventing the American Constitution*. New York: Harcourt, 2002.

Bilder, Mary Sarah. *Madison's Hand : Revising the Constitutional Convention*. Cambridge, MA: Harvard University Press, 2015.

Bowen, Catherine Drinker. *Miracle at Philadelphia: The Story of the Constitutional Convention, May to September, 1787*. Boston: Little, Brown, 1966.

Bowman, Matthew Burton. *The Mormon People: The Making of an American Faith*. New York: Random House, 2012.

Bradley, Gerard V. *Challenges to Religious Liberty in the Twenty-First Century*. New York: Cambridge University Press, 2012.

Eagles, Charles W. *Outside Agitator: Jon Daniels and the Civil Rights Movement in Alabama*. Chapel Hill: University of North Carolina Press, 1993.

Eastland, Terry, ed. *Religious Liberty in the Supreme Court: The Cases That Define the Debate over Church and State*. Washington, DC: Ethics and Policy Center, 1993.

Eisgruber Christopher L., and Lawrence G. Sager. *Religious Freedom and the Constitution*. Cambridge, MA: Harvard University Press, 2007.

Evans, Bette Novit. *Interpreting the Free Exercise of Religion: The Constitution and American Pluralism*. Chapel Hill: University of North Carolina Press, 1997.

Fehrenbacher, Don E. *The Dred Scott Case: Its Significance in American Law and Politics*. New York: Oxford University Press, 2001.

Frazier, Gregg. *The Religious Beliefs of America's Founders: Reason, Revelation and Revolution.* Lawrence: University Press of Kansas, 2014.

Garner, Brian A. *Black's Law Dictionary*, 10th ed. St. Paul, MN : Thomson Reuters, 2014.

Gill, Anthony James. *The Political Origins of Religious Liberty.* Cambridge Studies in Social Theory, Religion, and Politics. Cambridge, NY: Cambridge University Press, 2008.

Gordon, Robert W. *The Legacy of Oliver Wendell Holmes, Jr. Jurists Profiles in Legal Theory.* Stanford, CA: Stanford University Press, 1992.

Gutzman, Kevin Raeder. *James Madison and the Making of America*, 1st ed. New York: St. Martin's Press, 2012.

Hall, Kermit, Paul Finkelman, and James Ely. *American Legal History: Cases and Materials*, 4th ed. New York: Oxford University Press, 2011.

Harrington, Michael. *The Other America: Poverty in the United States.* New York: Macmillan, 1962.

Holmes, Oliver Wendell, Jr. *The Common Law.* Boston: Little, Brown, 1881.

Hutson, James H. *Forgotten Features of the Founding: The Recovery of Religious Themes in the Early American Republic.* Lanham, MD: Lexington Books, 2003.

Irons, Peter. *Courage of Their Convictions.* New York: Free Press, 1988.

Jefferson, Thomas, and Jerry Holmes. *Thomas Jefferson : A Chronology of His Thoughts.* Lanham, MD: Rowman & Littlefield, 2002.

Labunski, Richard. *James Madison and the Struggle for the Bill of Rights.* New York: Oxford, 2006.

Lederman, Martin S. "Reconstructing RFRA: The Contested Legacy of Religious Freedom Restoration." *Yale Law Journal Forum* 125 (2016), http://www.yalelawjournal.org/pdf/Lederman_PDF_pt9q3ynr.pdf

Levy, Leonard W. *The Establishment Clause : Religion and the First Amendment*, 2nd ed., Rev. ed. Chapel Hill, University of North Carolina Press, 1994.

Levy, Leonard W. *Legacy of Suppression; Freedom of Speech and Press in Early American History.* Cambridge, MA: Belknap Press of Harvard University Press, 1960.

Long, Carolyn N. *Religious Freedom and Indian Rights: The Case of Oregon v. Smith.* Lawrence: University Press of Kansas, 2000.

Merriman, Scott A. *Religion and Law in America: An Encyclopedia of Personal Belief and Public Policy.* Santa Barbara, CA: ABC-CLIO, 2007.

Merriman, Scott A. *Religion and the State: An International Analysis of Roles and Relationships.* Santa Barbara, CA: ABC-CLIO, 2009.

Miller, William Lee. *The First Liberty: America's Foundation in Religious Freedom.* Washington, DC: Georgetown University Press, 2003.

NeJaime, Douglas, and Reva B. Siegel, "Conscience Wars: Complicity-Based Conscience Claims in Religion and Politics." *Yale Law Journal* 124 (2015): 2202–2679, http://www.yalelawjournal.org/article/complicity-based-conscience-claims

Newton, Jim. *Justice for All: Earl Warren and the Nation He Made.* New York: Riverhead Books, 2006.

Newton, Merlin Owen. *Armed with the Constitution: Jehovah's Witnesses in Alabama and the U.S. Supreme Court, 1939–1946.* Tuscaloosa: University of Alabama Press, 1995.

Onuf, Peter S. *The Mind of Thomas Jefferson.* Charlottesville: University of Virginia Press, 2007.

Orwell, George. *1984.* Harlow, UK: Pearson Education, 2008.

Peters, Shawn Francis. *The Yoder Case: Religious Freedom, Education and Parental Rights.* Lawrence: University Press of Kansas, 2003.

Pole, J. R. *The Pursuit of Equality in American History,* Rev. ed. Berkeley: University of California Press, 1993.

Polenberg, Richard. *Fighting Faiths: The Abrams Case, The Supreme Court, and Free Speech.* Ithaca, NY: Cornell University Press, 1987.

Putney, Clifford. *Muscular Christianity: Manhood and Sports in Protestant America, 1880–1920.* Cambridge, MA: Harvard University Press, 2001.

Rakove, Jack N. *Original Meanings: Politics and Ideas in the Making of the Constitution.* New York: A.A. Knopf, 1996.

Rosen, Jeffrey. *Louis D. Brandeis: American Prophet.* New Haven, CT: Yale University Press, 2016.

Sarat, Austin. *Legal Responses to Religious Practices in the United States: Accommodation and Its Limits.* New York: Cambridge University Press, 2012.

Urofsky, Melvin I. *Louis D. Brandeis: A Life,* 1st ed. New York: Pantheon Books, 2009.

Weitz, Mark A. *Clergy Malpractice in America:* Nally v. Grace Community Church of the Valley. Lawrence: University Press of Kansas, 2001.

Witte, John, and Joel A. Nichols. *Religion and the American Constitutional Experiment,* 3rd ed. Boulder, CO: Westview Press, 2016.

Yoshino, Kenji. *Speak Now Marriage Equality on Trial: The Story of* Hollingsworth v. Perry. New York: Broadway Books, 2016.

Documents Contained on the Web

Fitzhugh, George. "The Universal Law of Slavery," http://www.pbs.org/wgbh/aia/part4/4h3141t.html

Hammond, James Henry. "The 'Mudsill' Theory," http://www.pbs.org/wgbh/aia/part4/4h3439t.html

Newspaper Articles

Parks, Casey. "The Hate Keeps Coming: Pain Lingers for Lesbian Couple Denied in Sweet Cakes Case," *Oregon Live,* July 2, 2016. http://www.oregonlive.com/pacific-northwest-news/index.ssf/2016/07/sweet_cakes_lesbians.html

Parks, Casey, "Oregon Lawyers: Sweet Cakes by Melissa $135,000 Damage Award Was Justified," *Oregon Live*, August 24, 2016. http://www.oregonlive.com/portland/index.ssf/2016/08/oregon_lawyers_sweet_cakes_by.html

Parks, Casey, "Sweet Cakes Owners Have a New Lawyer: George H.W. Bush's Counsel, *Oregon Live*, February 23, 2016. http://www.oregonlive.com/business/index.ssf/2016/02/sweet_cakes_owners_have_a_new.html

Quelly, James. "$828,000 Raised for Indiana Pizzeria That Said It Won't Cater Gay Weddings," *LA Times*, April 3, 2015. http://www.latimes.com/nation/nationnow/la-na-nn-indiana-pizzeria-gay-rights-20150403-story.html

Legal Documents

Amendments to the Constitution: http://www.archives.gov/exhibits/charters/constitution_amendments_11-27.html

1894 New York Constitution: https://www.nycourts.gov/history/legal-history-new-york/documents/Publications_1894-NY-Constitution.pdf

Madison, James "Detached Memoranda": http://press-pubs.uchicago.edu/founders/documents/amendI_religions64.html

Cases Quoted from or Specifically Cited

Abrams v. United States, 250 U.S. 616 (1919).
Bob Jones University v. United States, 461 U.S. 574 (1983).
Bowen v. Roy, 476 US 693 (1986).
Braunfeld v. Brown, 366 U.S. 599 (1961).
California v. Grace Brethren Church, 457 U.S. 393 (1982).
Cantwell v. Connecticut, 310 U.S. 296 (1940).
Chaplinsky v. New Hampshire, 315 U.S. 568 (1942).
Christian Legal Society v. Martinez, 561 U.S. (2010).
Church of Lukumi Babalu Aye v. Hialeh, (1993). 508 U.S. 520 (1993).
Church of the Holy Trinity v. United States, 143 U.S. 457 (1892).
City of Boerne v. Flores, 521 U.S. 507 (1997).
Cleveland v United States, 329 U.S. 14 (1946).
Engle v. Vitale, 370 U.S. 421 (1962).
Epperson v. Arkansas, 393 U.S. 97 (1968).
Farrington v. Tokushige, 273 U.S. 284 (1927).
The General Synod of the United Church of Christ v. Cooper, No. 3:2014cv00213—Document 120 (W.D.N.C. 2014).
Gitlow v. People of New York, 268 U.S. 652 (1925).
Gobitis v. Minersville School District, 310 U.S. 586 (1940).
Goldman v. Weinberger, 475 U.S. 503 (1986).
Gonzales v. O Centro Espirita Beneficente Uniao do Vegetal, 546 U.S. 418 (2006).

Gonzalez v. Roman Catholic Archbishop of Manila, 280 U.S. 1 (1929).
Good News Club v. Milford Central School, (2001) 533 U.S. 98 (2001).
Hamilton v. Regents of the University of California, 293 U.S. 245 (1934).
Heffron v. International Society for Krishna Consciousness, 452 U.S. 640 (1981).
Hobby Lobby v. Burwell, 573 U.S. ___ (2014).
Hollingsworth v. Perry, 570 U.S. ___ (2013).
Hosanna-Tabor Evangelical Lutheran Church and School v. Equal Employment Opportunity Commission, 565 U.S. ___ (2012).
In Re Summers, 325 U.S. 561 (1945).
International Society for Krishna Consciousness v. Lee, 505 U.S. 672 (1992).
Jones v. City of Opelika, 316 U.S. 584 (1942).
The Late Corporation of Jesus Christ of Latter Day Saints v. United States, 136 U.S. 1 (1890).
Lee v. International Society for Krishna Consciousness, 505 U.S. 830 (1992).
Locke v. Davey, 540 U.S. 712 (2004).
Lovell v. City of Griffin, 303 U.S. 444 (1938).
Loving v. Virginia, 388 U.S. 1 (1967).
McGowan v. Maryland, 366 U.S. 420 (1961).
McNally v. Grace Community Church of the Valley, 47 Cal. 3d 279 (1988).
Murdock v. Pennsylvania, 319 U.S. 105 (1943).
Murphy v. Ramsey, 114 U.S. 15 (1885).
Obergefell v. Hodges, 576 U.S. (2015).
Petit v. Minnesota, 177 U.S. 164 (1900).
Pierce v. Society of Sisters, 268 U.S. 510 (1925).
Poulous v. New Hampshire, 345 U.S. 395 (1953).
Reynolds v. United States, 98 U.S. 145 (1878).
Schenck v. United States, 249 U.S. 47 (1919).
Schneider v. State of New Jersey, 308 U.S. 147 (1939)
Sherbert v. Verner, 374 U.S. 398 (1963).
Snyder v. Phelps, 562 U.S. (2010).
Soon Hing v. Crowley, 113 U.S. 703(1885).
Speidel v. Henrici, 120 U.S. 377 (1887).
Stone v. Graham, 449 U.S. 39 (1980).
Stromberg v. California, 283 U.S. 359 (1931).
Torasco v. Watkins, 367 U.S. 488 (1961).
United States v. Ballard, 322 U.S. 78 (1944).
United States v. Carolene Products, 304 U.S. 144 (1938).
United States v. Lee, 455 U.S. 252 (1982).
United States v. Schwimmer, 279 U.S. 644 (1929).
United States v. Seeger, 380 U.S. 163 (1965).
Watchtower Bible and Tract Society v. Village of Stratton, 536 U.S. 150 (2002).
West Coast Hotel v. Parrish, 300 U.S. 379 (1937).
West Virginia v. Barnette, 319 U.S. 624 (1943).
Whitney v. California, 274 U.S. 357 (1927).

Widmar v. Vincent, 454 U.S. 263 (1981).
Windsor v. United States, 570 U.S. (2013).
Yates v. United States, in 1957, 354 U.S. 298 (1957).
Zubik v. Burwell, 578 U.S. ___ (2016).

Some Other Relevant Cases and Cases of Interest

Abington School District v. Schempp, 374 U.S. 203 (1963).
Agostini v. Felton, 521 U.S. 203 (1997).
Aguilar v. Felton, 473 U.S. 402 (1985).
Airport Commissioners of Los Angeles v. Jews for Jesus, 482 U.S. 569 (1987).
Ansonia Board of Education v. Philbrook, 479 U.S. 60 (1986).
Archer v. United States (Selective Draft Cases), 245 U.S. 366 (1918).
Arlan's Department Store v. Kentucky, 371 U.S. 218 (1962).
Baker v. Nachtrieb, 60 U.S. 126 (1856).
Bartels v. Iowa, 262 U.S. 412 (1923).
Bassett v. United States, 137 U.S. 496 (1890).
Bender v. Williamsport Area School District, 475 U.S. 534 (1986).
Berea College v. Kentucky, 211 U.S. 45 (1908).
Board of Education of Kiryas Joel Village School District v. Grumer, 512 U.S. 687 (1994).
Board of Education of the Westside Community Schools v. Mergens, 496 U.S. 226 (1990).
Board of Education v. Allen, 392 U.S. 236 (1968).
Bouldin v. Alexander, 82 U.S. 131 (1872).
Bradfield v. Roberts, 175 U.S. 291 (1899).
California v. Grace Brethren Church, 457 U.S. 393 (1982).
Capitol Square Review and Advisory Board v. Pinette, 515 U.S. 753 (1995).
Catholic Bishop of Nesqually v. Gibbon, 158 U.S. 455 (1895).
Chamberlain v. Public Instruction Board, 377 U.S. 402 (1964).
Chatwin v. United States, 326 U.S. 455 (1946).
Christian Legal Society v. Martinez, 561 U.S. 661 (2010).
Church of Scientology of California v. United States, 506 U.S. 9 (1992).
Clawson v. United States, 114 U.S. 477 (1885).
Clay v. United States, 403 U.S. 698 (1971).
Cochran v. Louisiana State Board of Education, 281 U.S. 370 (1930).
Coleman v. City of Griffin, 302 U.S. 636 (1937).
Committee for Public Education and Religious Liberty v. Nyquist, 413 U.S. 756 (1973).
Committee for Public Education and Religious Liberty v. Regan, 444 U.S. 646 (1980).
Cooper v. Aaron, 358 U.S. 1 (1958).
Cooper v. Pate, 378 U.S. 546 (1964).
Corporation of the Presiding Bishop of the Church of Jesus Christ of Latter-Day Saints v. Amos, 483 U.S. 327 (1987).
County of Allegheny v. ACLU, 492 U.S. 573 (1989).

Cox v. New Hampshire, 312 U.S. 569 (1941).

Crane v. Johnson, 242 U.S. 339 (1917).

Cruz v. Beto, 404 U.S. 319 (1972).

Cummings v. Missouri, 71 U.S. 277 (1866).

Cutter v. Wilkinson, 544 U.S. 709 (2005).

Davis v. Beason, 133 U.S. 333 (1890).

Davis v. United States, 495 U.S. 472 (1990).

Dewey v. Reynolds Metals Co., 402 U.S. 689 (1971).

Doremus v. Board of Education, 342 U.S. 429 (1952).

Douglas v. City of Jeannette, 319 U.S. 147 (1943).

Eagles v. Samuels, 329 U.S. 304 (1946).

Edwards v. Aguillard, 482 U.S. 578 (1987).

EEO v. Arabian American Oil Co., 499 U.S. 244 (1991).

Elk Grove Unified School District v. Newdow, 542 U.S. 1 (2004).

Employment Division, Oregon v. Smith (I), 485 U.S. 660 (1988).

Employment Division v. Smith (II), 494 U.S. 872 (1990).

Engel v. Vitale, 370 U.S. 421 (1962).

Epperson v. Arkansas, 393 U.S. 97 (1968).

Estate of Thornton v. Calder, 472 U.S. 703 (1985).

Everson v. Board of Education, 330 U.S. 1 (1947).

Ex Parte Garland, 71 U.S. 397 (1866).

Ex Parte Hans Nielsen, 131 U.S. 176 (1889).

First Unitarian Church v. County of Los Angeles, 357 U.S. 545 (1958).

Flast v. Cohen, 392 U.S. 236 (1968).

Follett v. Town of McCormick, 321 U.S. 573 (1944).

Fowler v. Rhode Island, 345 U.S. 67 (1953).

Frazee v. Illinois Department of Employment Security, 489 U.S. 829 (1989).

Gallagher v. Crown Kosher Super Market of Massachusetts, 366 U.S. 617 (1961).

Gara v. United States, 340 U.S. 857 (1950).

Gibbons v. District of Columbia, 116 U.S. 404 (1886).

Gillette v. United States, 101 U.S. 437 (1971).

Girouard v. United States, 328 U.S. 61 (1946).

Goesele v. Bimeler, 55 U.S. 589 (1852).

Good News Club v. Milford Central School, 533 U.S. 98 (2001).

Gonzales v. United States, 407 (1955).

Grand Rapids School District v. Ball, 473 U.S. 373 (1985).

Harris v. McRae, 448 U.S. 297 (1980).

Hein v. Freedom from Religion Foundation, 551 U.S. 287 (2007).

Hennington v. Georgia, 163 U.S. 299 (1896).

Hernandez v. Commissioner of Internal Revenue, 490 U.S. 680 (1989).

Hernandez v. Veterans Administration, 415 U.S. 391 (1974).

Hobbie v. Unemployment Appeals Commission of Florida 480 U.S. 136 (1987).

Holt v. Hobbs, 574 U.S. ___ (2015).

Hosanna-Tabor Evangelical Lutheran Church and School v. EEOC, 565 U.S. ___ (2012).

Hunt v. McNair, 413 U.S. 734 (1973).

In Re Snow, 120 U.S. 274 (1887).

Jamison v. Texas, 318 U.S. 413 (1943).

Jehovah's Witnesses v. King County Hospital, 390 U.S. 598 (1968).

Jensen v. Quaring, 472 U.S. 478 (1985).

Jimmy Swaggart Ministries v. Board of Equalization of California, 494 U.S. 378 (1990).

Johnson v. Robinson, 413 U.S. 361 (1974).

Jones v. Wolf, 443 U.S. 595 (1979).

Joseph Burstyn v. Wilson, 343 U.S. 495 (1952).

Karcher v. May, 484 U.S. 72 (1987).

Kedroff v. Saint Nicholas Cathedral, 344 U.S. 94 (1952).

Kreshnik v. St. Nicholas Cathedral, 363 U.S. 190 (1960).

Kunz v. New York, 340 U.S. 290 (1951).

Largent v. Texas, 318 U.S. 418 (1943).

Larken v. Grendel's Den, 459 U.S. 116 (1982).

Larson v. Valente, 456 U.S. 228 (1982).

Lee v. Weisman, 505 U.S. 577 (1991).

Lemon v. Kurtzman (I), 403 U.S. 601 (1971).

Lemon v. Kurtzman (II), 411 U.S. 192 (1973).

Levin v. Committee for Public Education and Religious Liberty, 413 U.S. 472 (1973).

Lowrey v. Hawaii (I), 206 U.S. 206 (1907).

Lowrey v. Hawaii (II), 215 U.S. 554 (1910).

Lynch v. Donnelley, 465 U.S. 668 (1984).

Lyng v. Northwest Indian Cemetery Protective Association, 485 U.S. 439 (1988).

Marsh v. Alabama, 326 U.S. 501 (1946).

Marsh v. Chambers, 463 U.S. 783 (1983).

Martin v. Struthers, 319 U.S. 141 (1943).

Maryland and Virginia Churches v. Sharpsburg Church, 396 U.S. 367 (1970).

McCollum v. Board of Education, 333 U.S. 203 (1948).

McCreary County v. ACLU, 545 U.S. 844 (2005).

McDaniel v. Paty, 435 U.S. 618 (1978).

Meek v. Pittenger, 421 U.S. 349 (1975).

Meyer v. Nebraska, 262 U.S. 390 (1923).

Miles v. United States, 103 U.S. 304 (1881).

Mitchell v. Helms, 530 U.S. 793 (2000).

Mueller v. Allen, 463 U.S. 388 (1983).

Mulloy v. United States, 398 U.S. 430 (1970).

Murphy v. Ramsey, 114 U.S. 15 (1885).

Musser v. Utah, 333 U.S. 95 (1948).

National Labor Relations Board v. Catholic Bishop of Chicago, 440 U.S. 490 (1979).

New York v. Cathedral Academy, 433 U.S. 125 (1977).

Niemotko v. State of Maryland, 340 U.S. 268 (1951).

Norwood v. Harrison, 413 U.S. 455 (1973).

Oestereich v. Selective Service System, 393 U.S. 233 (1968).

Ohio Civil Rights Commission v. Dayton Christian Schools, 477 U.S. 619 (1986).

O'Lone v. Estate of Shabazz, 481 U.S. 342 (1987).

Order of St. Benedict v. Steinhauser, 234 U.S. 640 (1914).

Parker Seal Company v. Cummins (I), 429 U.S. 65 (1976).

Parker Seal Company v. Cummins (II), 433 U.S. 903 (1977).

Permoli v. First Municipality of New Orleans, 44 U.S. 589 (1844).

Petit v. Minnesota, 177 U.S. 164 (1900).

Pleasant Grove City v. Summum, 555 U.S. 460 (2009).

Ponce v. Roman Catholic Apostolic Church, 210 U.S. 296 (1908).

Poulous v. New Hampshire, 345 U.S. 395 (1953).

Presbyterian Church in the United States v. Mary Elizabeth Blue Hull Memorial Pres-
byterian Church, 339 U.S. 440 (1969).

Prince v. Massachusetts, 321 U.S. 158 (1944).

Quick Bear v. Leupp, 210 U.S. 50 (1908).

Roemer v. Maryland Public Works Board, 426 U.S. 736 (1976).

Rosenberger v. Rector and Visitors of the University of Virginia, 515 U.S. 819 (1995).

Rusk v. Espinoza, 456 U.S. 951 (1982).

Saia v. New York, 334 U.S. 558 (1948).

Santa Fe Independent School District v. Doe, 530 U.S. 290 (2000).

Schartz v. Duss, 187 U.S. 8 (1902).

Selective Draft Cases (*Archer v. United States*), 245 U.S. 366 (1918).

Serbian Orthodox Diocese v. Milivojevich, 426 U.S. 696 (1976).

Shaare Tefila Congregation v. Cobb, 481 U.S. 615 (1987).

Sicurella v. United States, 348 U.S. 385 (1955).

Simmons v. United States, 348 U.S. 397 (1955).

Slazar v. Buono, 559 U.S. 700 (2010).

Sloan v. Lemon, 413 U.S. 825 (1973).

Smith v. Swormstedt, 57 U.S. 288 (1853).

Soon Hing v. Crowley, 113 U.S. 703 (1885).

Spiedel v. Henrici, 120 U.S. 377 (1887).

Speiser v. Randall, 357 U.S. 513 (1958).

St. Martin Evangelical Lutheran Church v. South Dakota, 451 U.S. 772 (1981).

Stone v. Graham, 449 U.S. 39 (1980).

Taylor v. Mississippi, 319 U.S. 583 (1943).

Terrett v. Taylor, 13 U.S. 43 (1815).

Texas Monthly v. Bullock, 489 U.S. 1 (1989).

Thomas v. Review Board, Indiana Employment Security Division 450 U.S. 707 (1981).

Tilton v. Richardson, 403 U.S. 672 (1971).

Tony and Susan Alamo Foundation v. Secretary of Labor, 471 U.S. 290 (1985).

Town of Greece v. Galloway, 572 U.S. ___ (2014).

Town of Pawlet v. Clark, 13 U.S. 292 (1815).

Trans World Airlines v. Hardison, 432 U.S. 63 (1977).

Treen v. Karen B., 454 U.S. 913 (1982).

Trinity Lutheran Church v. Pauley (pending at time of writing).

Two Guys from Harrison Allentown, Inc. v. McGinley, 366 U.S. 582 (1961).

Tucker v. Texas, 326 U.S. 517 (1946).

United States Catholic Conference v. Abortion Rights Mobilization, 487 U.S. 71 (1988).

United States v. American Friends Service Committee, 419 U.S. 7 (1974).

United States v. Bland, 283 U.S. 636 (1931).

United States v. Macintosh, 283 U.S. 605 (1931).

United States v. Nugent, 346 U.S. 1 (1953).

Valley Forge Christian College v. Americans United For Separation of Church and State, 454 U.S. 464 (1982).

Van Orden v. Perry, 545 U.S. 677 (2005).

Vidal v. Girard's Executors, 43 U.S. 127 (1844).

Village of Scarsdale v. McCreary, 471 U.S. 83 (1985).

Wallace v. Jaffree, 472 U.S. 38 (1985).

Walz v. Tax Commission, 397 U.S. 664 (1970).

Watson v. Jones, 80 U.S. 679 (1871).

Wayte v. United States, 470 U.S. 598 (1984).

Welsh v. United States, 398 U.S. 333 (1970).

Wheeler v. Barrera, 417 U.S. 402 (1974).

Widmar v. Vincent, 454 U.S. 263 (1981).

Witters v. Washington Department of Services for the Blind, 474 U.S. 481 (1986).

Wolman v. Walter, 433 U.S. 229 (1977).

Wooley v. Maynard, 430 U.S. 705 (1977).

Zelman v. Simmons-Harris, 536 U.S. 639 (2002).

Zobrest v. Catalina Foothills School District, 509 U.S. 1 (1993).

Zorach v. Clauson, 343 U.S. 306 (1952).

Index

About the Author

Scott A. Merriman is a lecturer in history at Troy University. He has authored or edited more than a dozen books, including *Religion and the Law in America: An Encyclopedia of Law and Public Policy*, *The History Highway: A 21st Century Guide to Internet Resources*, and *History.edu: Essays on Teaching with Technology*. His most recent article is "Remembering Jonathan Myrick Daniels," published in *Alabama Heritage* (Winter 2014). His first book, *The History Highway*, was selected as a History Book of the Month Club selection. His research interests include the Espionage and Sedition Acts in America and the interaction of religion and the civil rights movement.